# DEMOCRACY AS A WAY OF LIFE IN AMERICA

The United States is a nation whose identity is defined by the idea of democracy. Yet democracy in the United States is often taken for granted, narrowly understood, and rarely critically examined. In *Democracy as a Way of Life in America,* Schneirov and Fernandez show that, much more than a static legacy from the past, democracy is a living process that informs all aspects of American life.

The authors trace the story of American democracy from the American Revolution to the present, showing how democracy has changed over time and the challenges it has faced. They examine themes such as individualism, foreign policy, the economy, and the environment and reveal how democracy has been deeply involved in these throughout the country's history.

*Democracy as a Way of Life in America* demonstrates that democracy is not simply a set of institutions or practices, such as the right to vote or competing political parties, but a complex, multidimensional phenomenon, whose animating spirit can be found in every part of American culture and society. This vital and engaging narrative should be read by students of history, political science, and anyone who wants to understand the nature of American democracy.

**Richard Schneirov** is Professor of History at Indiana State University. He is the author of many books, including *Chicago in the Age of Capital: Class, Politics, and Democracy during the Civil War and Reconstruction* with John B. Jentz.

**Gaston A. Fernandez** is Professor of Political Science at Indiana State University.

# DEMOCRACY AS A WAY OF LIFE IN AMERICA

## A History

*Richard Schneirov and Gaston A. Fernandez*

Routledge
Taylor & Francis Group

NEW YORK AND LONDON

First published 2014
by Routledge
711 Third Avenue, New York, NY 10017

Simultaneously published in the UK
by Routledge
2 Park Square, Milton Park, Abingdon, Oxon OX14 4RN

*Routledge is an imprint of the Taylor & Francis Group,
an informa business*

*Library of Congress Cataloging-in-Publication Data*

Schneirov, Richard.
Democracy as a way of life in America : a history / Richard Schneirov
   and Gaston A. Fernandez.
      pages cm.
   Includes bibliographical references.
   1. Democracy—United States.   2. United States—Politics and
government.   I. Fernandez, Gaston A.   II. Title.
   JK1726.S36  2013
   320.973—dc23
   2013013840

ISBN: 978-0-415-83611-1 (hbk)
ISBN: 978-0-415-83612-8 (pbk)
ISBN: 978-0-203-36197-9 (ebk)

Typeset in Bembo
by Apex CoVantage, LLC

To the Unfinished Task Remaining for Future Generations
of Americans: Democracy

# CONTENTS

# GRAPHS

# DOCUMENT SOURCES AND PERMISSIONS

Every effort has been made to cite the original source material for each work compiled in this collection. In the event that something has been inadvertently used or cited incorrectly, every effort will be made in subsequent editions to rectify the error.

John Dewey, "Creative Democracy: The Task before Us," in *The Essential Dewey*, vol. 1, *Pragmatism, Education, Democracy* (Bloomington: Indiana University Press, 1998), 340–43. Reprinted by permission of the publisher.

Preamble to the US Declaration of Independence (July 4, 1776). National Archives and Records Administration. Accessed at: http://www.archives.gov/exhibits/charters/declaration_transcript.html.

Women's Rights Convention, Seneca Falls, Declaration of Sentiments. (1848). Accessed at: http://www.csus.edu/owl/index/read/sacbee/sen_dec.htm.

Abraham Lincoln, Gettysburg Address, 1863. Accessed at: http://www.abrahamlincolnonline.org/lincoln/speeches/gettysburg.htm.

US Strike Commission, *Report on the Chicago Strike of June–July, 1894* (Washington, D.C.: Government Printing Office, 1894), XLVII–XLVIII.

Franklin Delano Roosevelt, State of the Union Message to Congress, January 11, 1944. Franklin D. Roosevelt Presidential Library and Museum. Accessed at: http://www.fdrlibrary.marist.edu/archives/address_text.html.

Lyndon B. Johnson, "Commencement Address at Howard University, June 4, 1965," in *Public Papers of the Presidents of the United States: Lyndon B. Johnson, 1965*, vol. II, entry 301 (Washington, D.C.: Government Printing Office, 1966), 635–40. Accessed at: http://www.lbjlib.utexas.edu /johnson/archives.hom/speeches.hom/650604.asp.

Stokely Carmichael, "Student Nonviolent Coordinating Committee Position Paper: The Basis of Black Power" (1966) Accessed at: http:// www2.iath.virginia.edu/sixties/HTML_docs/Resources/Primary /Manifestos/SNCC_black_power.html.

Ronald Franklin Inglehart, "Postmaterialism." *Encyclopedia Britannica Online.* Accessed at: http://www.britannica.com/EBchecked/topic/1286234 /postmaterialism. Reprinted by permission.

2012 Republican Platform. Accessed at: http://www.gop.com/2012 -republican-platform_home/.

"Declaration of the Occupation of New York City," Occupy Wall Street, New York City General Assembly, September 29, 2011. Accessed at: http://www.nycga.net/resources/documents/declaration/.

# INTRODUCTION

## Democracy as a Way of Life

*The idea of democracy is a wider and fuller idea than can be exemplified in the state even at its best. To be realized it must affect all modes of human association, the family, the school, industry, religion.*

John Dewey, *The Public and Its Problems* (1927)

Most Americans take democracy as an accomplished fact, an inheritance from the founders that is beyond dispute. It is not something most Americans think about. It is just who we are. Democracy is, in this view, something finished, a static entity. The counterpart of this unexamined attitude is the belief among many of our pundits that democracy is simply the name of our political system, whose central value, rule of the people, is an inconvenient but necessary reality that one must work around. Democracy is merely a means to the end of good policy. Though we hear phrases today of a "crisis in democracy," it almost always means the political system is not producing the outcomes that these political observers or leaders desire.

This book is written as a dissent from both standpoints. Democracy in our view cannot be taken for granted or regarded as something finished. Democracy must be seen as a potential and a trend capable of being stymied and reversed, as well as liberated and accelerated. Moreover, democracy should be viewed as existing in degrees rather than in an all-or-nothing state. The United States is only partially democratic. At all times, democratic and antidemocratic forces have contended with each other, and democracy has waxed and waned in American history. Democracy has always been a question. As the American philosopher John Dewey has put it, it is "the task before us"[1] (see Documents).

We also believe that democracy is not simply a means to some desirable end, whether that is good government, the right kind of market regulation, environmental protection, or international competitiveness. It is an end in itself, an ideal worth striving for, and a faith for guiding future action.

The simplest and best-known definition of democracy is the sovereignty or rule of the people, as opposed to monarchy, aristocracy, oligarchy, or totalitarianism. A more expansive and critical definition that hints at why democracy has been and can remain a high ideal is the one that integrates other ideals: liberty, equality, and community (we use the term *community* to replace the male-centered term *fraternity*). Democracy then is *a self-governing community that values and liberates the different potentialities of its members and harmonizes them with common needs and interests through public deliberation.*[2] This definition not only combines the classical ideals of eighteenth-century democracy—liberty, equality, and fraternity—but also refuses to set liberty against equality or the needs of the community against both.

The story of how these ideals, which grew from citizens' everyday experience in democratic institutions, diffused and penetrated into all the dimensions of the American community is the story of how democracy became, in Dewey's words, "a way of life." It composes the content of this book.

The idea of democracy has ancient roots, but its modern revival beginning in the eighteenth century had its origins in the release, or emancipation, of people from hierarchical associations given by tradition, often cemented by ties of blood, and sanctified by religion. The first such relationships to be abolished were feudal relationships. Under feudal relationships, everyone had a proper place in a hierarchical chain of personal relationships into which one was born. One was always conscious of who was one's superior and who was one's subordinate and the obligations owed to each. As the hierarchy, inequality, and coercion inherent in feudal relationships (and similar forms, such as slavery and indentured servitude) faded or were overthrown by the first democratic revolutions, free associations of the modern individual emerged, including what we now think of as the market, civil society, and democratic governance. The individual in democratic culture is presumed to be capable of rising above his (and later her) private interests to perceive and act on the common good. Association with other such individuals constituted the self-governing political community.

By the nineteenth century, democratic values were challenging the hierarchy inherent in private property and market relationships, which emerged from the disintegration of the household economy. Property, when it became impersonal and large in scale, was understood to be more than a private affair. It was clothed with the public or common interest, whether that interest be that of the workers whom employers hired or the larger market that was being controlled by large combinations of private properties. The second stage of democratic development occurred when collective bargaining with unions began to reshape the labor market, and government regulations set limits on the actions of corporate managers in their market relationships with each other.

A third phase of democratization grew out of the weakening of the hierarchical bonds of the patriarchal family. The patriarchal family subordinated women, most men, and children under the control of the male head of the household. Patriarchal values governed the personal lives of all family members, including their moral, sexual, and gender relationships and identities. The age-old patriarchal family devolved into the two-sphere system of the nineteenth century and then began to dissolve almost entirely in the late twentieth century. With its dissolution, women emerged as coequals of men in democratic associations; the family itself became a democratic association; new sexual and gender identities took shape; and a new, more democratic culture developed.

More recently, democracy has begun to enter a fourth sphere once thought to be outside human control: the ecosphere. Humanity is recognizing that nature is no longer a relatively distinct sphere, separate from human activities. The "end of nature" came from the realization that within a foreseeable period, global climate change caused by massive, unconscious, and unplanned human intervention in nature would bring catastrophic deterioration in the conditions necessary for civilization. The great question of future generations is whether it is possible to democratically govern the ecosphere for the common good of humanity.

The successive phases of the breakdown of the authority structures in different spheres of life and their replacement to varying degrees with democratic norms, values, habits, and institutions suggest a very different definition of democracy than the one used by modern theorists. The dominant view in political science and the scholarly community sees democracy as a set of rules and procedures for regulating the competition of elites for control of the state. This line of thought strips democracy of its value-laden prescriptions, goals, and ideals. The most widely accepted theory of democratic governance, that of Robert A. Dahl, dispenses with the term *democracy* altogether and replaces it with the term *polyarchy*. But democracy is more than a value-neutral description of that which exists. Because the practice of democracy breeds distinctive values and habits, it is also a spirit, a faith, and a commitment whose embodiment, sometimes progressing, other times regressing, creates a way of life, a type of society, characterized by broad participation and common control of all associations affecting human existence.

Throughout American history, this movement toward a multilayered or "thick" democracy has occurred in *waves*.[3] We discern three major waves in American history, with a fourth wave just taking shape. Each of these waves has followed from the disintegration of older authority structures embedded in feudalism, private property, and the patriarchal family. Each wave has lasted four or five generations, or approximately ninety to one hundred years—a kind of "long revolution"— and each has been followed by a smaller counterwave, which eventually itself may be reversed.

The first wave, which was initiated by the American Revolution, established state and national constitutions and by the early nineteenth century had created a highly developed civil society, mass democratic political parties, and the first mass social movement. It crested with the creation of a more inclusive, democratic basis of the nation-state during and after the Civil War. That wave was immediately followed by a counterwave during the late nineteenth century when African Americans lost many of the political rights they had gained and in which the South lapsed into a one-party oligarchy. Since then there have been two smaller democratic waves expanding democratic governance: a wave in the 1910s that extended the right to vote to women, and a civil rights wave of the 1950s and 1960s that restored and equalized civil and voting rights for African Americans and in other ways expanded the rights of all Americans.

The period from the early to mid-nineteenth century inaugurated the second wave as political democracy in fits and starts became a social or industrial democracy as well. The period after the Civil War witnessed the first durable labor unions and first state social welfare, while the early twentieth century saw the government regulatory agency emerge as a fourth branch of government. By the 1950s, about a third of the country's workforce was organized in unions. The second wave crested during the 1960s' Great Society with the extension of unionization rights to public workers and the expansion of democratic regulation and social insurance. In the last forty years, the country has been living through a strong counterwave that has almost destroyed unions and collective bargaining, significantly weakened regulation of the corporate economy, and created new holes in the safety net for the poor.

The third wave of democracy evident in culture started in the early to mid-twentieth century and gathered enormous momentum from the 1960s' social movements and so-called counterculture. Americans in steadily increasing numbers adopted postmaterial values; women, as well as gay, lesbian, transgender, and queer individuals, liberated themselves from patriarchal institutional, moral, and legal rules; and culture of personal life became significantly more plural in the form of alternative lifestyles, religious and moral beliefs, and ethnic and racial cultures. This third wave or long revolution still has not crested and has overlapped with the launching of the fourth environmental wave.

Historically, the Left (also called at times progressives, liberals, etc.) is defined by four major tendencies. It has questioned, rebelled against, or overthrown old and tottering authority structures in order to maximize the opportunities for the fulfillment of human potential in individuals. It has sought to find ways to include more and more formerly excluded groups of individuals in the democratic community. It has fought to increase participation in decision making in all areas of life. Finally, in doing these things progressive democracy has extended the public into areas of life once deemed private—not to end the private, but to make the two compatible. On the other hand, those who have supported the status quo or fought to reverse the waves of democratic reform have been called "the Right" (also conservatives, reactionaries, and the like). They try to prop up old authority structures, exclude those trying to become part of the democratic community, limit fulfillment of human potential in the name of tradition or authority, limit or reverse broad participation in decision making in all spheres of life, and reduce the reach of the public into the private. In this sense, the Left and Right are not organized sects or parties but broad trends among the American people and within each individual's (often contradictory) consciousness.

Often, the left wing or progressives of an earlier wave become the right wing or conservatives of the next wave, as, for example, with many antislavery Republicans who opposed labor organizing and limits on business in the late nineteenth century. Normally, however, the ideas and commitments of the left and right are cumulative. That is, the definition of the left during an existing democratic wave usually includes the highest level of development achieved in previous waves. Thus, any particular historical embodiment of the left is multilayered. For example, the Knights of Labor in the late nineteenth century viewed the empowerment of labor as a means of restoring the American republic that had been corrupted by concentrated wealth. The black liberation movement of the 1960s combined demands for equal civil and voting rights, antipoverty measures, and efforts to create for blacks a new cultural identity. In the present period, those who today support cultural diversity, women's equality, and postmaterial values also tend to support collective bargaining, unions, government regulation of business for the common good, social insurance, and the fullest participation of citizens in government and politics—though not always.

As might be expected, those who compose the bastion of prodemocratic forces in any period tend to be those who are benefitted by the breakup of older forms of social subordination together with the remnants from previous lefts. In the present period, they have been women, especially those outside existing family structures, blacks, Latinos, and other minorities, and gender and sexual minorities. These groups have been supplemented by the constituencies of the second wave: members of labor unions, low-income workers, and New Deal and Great Society liberals. By the same token, the contemporary right or conservative side of the political spectrum consists overwhelmingly of white males and those, such as employers and the wealthy, who opposed the left in the second wave.

As the diversity of the left and right indicate, it would be limiting and fundamentally elitist to define the Left or Right as embattled tiny minorities with special monopolies on the truth. Left and Right are much broader than organized parties or sects, whether they be abolitionists, socialists, labor activists, or 1960s radicals. The Left and Right include not only leaders and activists but also followers and passive supporters, politicians and those who vote for them, non-elected government administrators, officials, and others. It would also be distorting to imply that individual Americans can be characterized as monolithically left or right. In the large majority of individuals, including political leaders, left and right ideas and policies are part of a complex mix, sometimes contradictory, of democratic, nondemocratic, and antidemocratic ideas.

Still, at most times and with some glaring exceptions, the majority of Americans and the thrust of American history has tended left or prodemocratic. How else can we explain the advance over time of the democratic spirit into new and deeper arenas of life? How else can we explain how the leaders whose names Americans universally celebrate are from the left in their particular era: Thomas Jefferson, George Washington, Abraham Lincoln, Theodore Roosevelt, Franklin Delano Roosevelt, John F. Kennedy, and Martin Luther King Jr.?

Despite the leftward tilt of American politics over its course, in the present period some antidemocratic ideas are present across the political spectrum. Three of these antidemocratic ideas deserve scrutiny.

On the right or conservative side is the belief that democracy, especially because of its belief in equality for all, is an inferior value and often antithetical to liberty or freedom. Among neoliberals (a term we adopt in chapter six to describe an influential contemporary version of conservatism), liberty has replaced democracy as a value and is contrasted with equality. There is said to be an inherent tension, sometimes taking the form of a zero-sum game, between the commitment to equality and democracy on the one hand and liberty on the other. Some say that equality in the form of universal social insurance—for example, old-age pensions, health care, and food stamps—laws that mandate a minimum wage, or laws that protect the right of workers to organize unions dampen the incentive to work and achieve, foster dependency, and impose mediocrity on society and tyranny on the creative individual. It is also said that government regulation of market behavior for the common good restricts the liberty of entrepreneurs and businesspeople in general.

There are two problems with this view. First, if liberty is defined only negatively—the absence of constraint imposed by a superior power—then a conflict *does* sometimes exists, which may require a careful balancing act. But liberty also has a positive aspect to it: the ability to *do* something. To be free to compete for riches and power but to lack the minimal means to do so is worthless. In another example, what good is freedom of speech and the press without education? Positive liberty, without which negative liberty is worthless, is based on the quality of association with others for common purposes—democracy. A second problem is that in practice this point of view elevates the liberty of some people over others. In this case, it values the liberty of a minority, for example, the creative entrepreneur, over the liberty of those who, because they are deprived of an adequate income or health care, lack the liberty to develop their own creative potentials. Without equal liberty or liberty for all, the liberty of a few is a form of privilege and antithetical to democracy. But liberty for all is the very lifeblood of democracy.

A second belief, more widely held on the Left than the Right, is that democracy, including the belief in its reality and power, is a sham or a façade that masks the rule of the corporate elite and the wealthy few. Even with the mask off, democracy is thought to be no match for the power of capitalism, with its concentration of wealth in the hands of a tiny minority and its class hierarchy. From this stand-point, economic democracy in a class-divided society is an impossibility. There can certainly be no doubt that in a capitalist democracy those who own and control the concentrated wealth of society also control the largest part of political power. The problem occurs when those who hold this belief assume that this power is unchallengeable. To believe that unless democracy vanquishes economic oligarchy, democracy is simply a mirage is a dichotomous belief. Such an either-or idea cannot make sense of the historical reality, described in chapters one, three, and five, that democracy was able to expand control over capitalism in some periods, while in others that control declined. It also cannot explain the intermixture of capitalism and socialism in both the private and public sectors that has been a hallmark of the American political economy since the early twentieth century. In short, viewed historically, democracy has forced capitalism and capitalists to compromise and accommodate to the needs and concerns of the larger community and other social groups, even while the results of that compromise have varied, sometimes greatly.

But capitalism and democracy have not only been antagonists and opposing social forces in a zero-sum game. They have also been interdependent forces, secretly cooperating in breaking down old and building up new forms of human community. It was capitalism that laid the basis for and created the possibility of democracy by breaking down hierarchical, coercive relations. As mentioned earlier, the rise of the bourgeoisie and competition from the market broke down feudal relationships, setting the stage for democracy's first wave. Those same market forces undermined the household economy and then partially dissolved private property, enabling competing property interests to merge and consolidate in the form of the modern corporation. In turn, the corporate form allowed for the mix of capitalism, socialism, and democratic governance to penetrate the economy, the hallmark of democracy's second wave. Finally, market forces dissolved the patriarchal household and later the remnants of the patriarchal family, which liberated women from male supremacy and personal life from age-old constraints—democracy's third wave. In each case, capitalism broke down and then redrew the barriers or lines between the private and the public, resulting in the expansion of the public realm, the realm in which human association became subject to democratic governance. That same process is going on today with the environment. In short, capitalism and democracy have been conjoined twins, as well as rival offspring, in modernity's family.

Finally, there is a third antidemocratic belief we must consider. This belief has been shared to some degree by political activists of all stripes, by citizens who have had the benefit of higher education, and by scholars and academics. This is the elitist belief that the largest part of the public is too apathetic, irrational, or ignorant to grasp complicated issues and choose among solutions and is therefore endlessly manipulable by means of the stereotypes present in propaganda and advertising techniques. The view that a government that is simultaneously of, by, and for the people is an impossibility and a dangerous illusion is an old one going back to Plato, who devised a solution in the form of rule by philosopher kings. As mentioned earlier, this view is also prevalent today in the social sciences originating with Joseph A. Schumpeter. The best the public can do in this view is to choose among competing elites with their experts and specialists, who do the real governing in a democracy.

There are two answers to this view. The first is negative. We may start with the words of Winston Churchill, who said that "no one pretends that democracy is perfect or all-wise. Indeed, it has been said that democracy is the worst form of government except all those other forms that have been tried from time to time." But, that view, self-evident as it may seem, begs the question of *why*. Dewey gave this answer: Democracy, as imperfect as it is, forces those who compose society to recognize that there are common interests, which are best discovered and clarified through public discussion. "The man who wears the shoe," wrote Dewey, "knows best that it pinches and where it pinches, even if the expert shoemaker is the best judge of how the trouble is to be remedied." In short, the real problems that are the raw material of governance can best be uncovered by democratic methods. Though experts most certainly have a role in formulating solutions, whether those solutions can fix the pinch is, again, only something the public can decide.

The second answer starts with admitting the realist indictment. All the great theorists who explained and advocated democracy, starting with the founder of the US Constitution, James Madison, and continuing through the great French observer of American democracy, Alexis de Tocqueville, the English philosopher John Stuart Mill and Dewey as well, admitted that counting heads, or majority rule, was by itself a very poor solution to governance. The real solution was to create a robust and representative public opinion free of the fog created by special interests and self-aggrandizing elites. That, in turn, required that the masses be educated in the broad sense of the term. Education to these theorists meant not schooling alone but, as Tocqueville emphasized, extensive participation in the organs of local government and the voluntary associations making up civil society, from juries, school boards, and political parties, to religious associations and advocacy groups. Face-to-face participation in such groups and organs of local government pulls citizens out of their private lives and into the public sphere where notions of the common good are formed. In different words, trusting the masses of citizens with self-rule was possible only if and when they had constant practice and schooling in self-rule. The problem and the solution were one and the same, and its name was democracy.

This book is organized thematically rather than chronologically. Though some repetition results from this choice, we believe that on balance it allows us to develop our argument in more depth and sophistication and with more force. The book consists of seven chapters. Chapter one, "The Three Waves of American Democracy," lays out the major themes of the book. In historical terms, it summarizes, analyzes, and explains the development of democracy in government, the economy, and culture. Chapter two, "Democracy in Culture: American Individualisms," discusses how four types of American individualism have developed in the course of American history and how each type exists in tension with different notions of the common good. Chapter three, "Democracy in the Economy and Workplace," discusses how, beginning in the nineteenth century, workers, capitalists, and other groups began organizing associations to shape market outcomes and how, by the twentieth century, government stepped in to regulate the economy for the common good. The result has been a democratic-tending mix of capitalism and socialism. Chapter four, "Democracy and US Foreign Policy," examines American foreign policy from George Washington to the present era of globalization. Its major theme is that democratic idealism in foreign policy has normally been anchored realistically in America's economic and social interests. American foreign policy has not always prioritized democratic development in its foreign policy, but in recent decades, democracy has moved to the forefront of the country's approach. Chapter five, "The Neoliberal Era: Postindustrial Society in a New Gilded Age," examines the period from the mid-1970s to the present. It explains how the political response of American corporate leaders and working people to the emergence of America's postindustrial or knowledge society created a new Gilded Age characterized by inequality and debt-financed subsidy of aggregate demand. The collapse of that model in the Great Recession of 2008 created an extended economic and political crisis for American democracy, whose end is not in sight. Chapter six, "The Democratic Challenge," enumerates the ways that democratic governance has been stymied and degraded through attempts to keep the rising majority of minorities, women, and voters with postmaterial values in check. It also points to ways that electoral fairness, civil society, and civic culture can be renewed. Chapter seven, "Epilogue, The Environment: Democracy's Fourth Wave," is a historical examination of how nature has become humanized and potentially subject to conscious, democratic control for the common good. Its focus is the rise of environmentalism as a social movement and a contentious issue in politics and government.

# 1

# THE THREE WAVES OF
# AMERICAN DEMOCRACY

*Did you, too, O friend, suppose democracy was only for elections, for politics, and for a party name? I say democracy is only of use there that it may pass on and come to its flower and fruit in manners, in the highest forms of interaction between people, and their beliefs—in religion, literature, colleges and schools—democracy in all public and private life.*

Walt Whitman, *Democratic Vistas* (1871)

Democracy, the theory and practice of self-governing citizens in a community, had its origins in the ancient Greek city-states, notably Athens. But these early forms of democracy limited citizen participation to a small minority of adults, employed direct voting (Rome was a partial exception), and asked citizens to leave behind their self-interest. Democracy acquired new meaning in the modern era during the course of four great revolutions: the English revolutions of 1642 and 1688, the American Revolution of 1776, and the French Revolution of 1789. The modern rebirth of democracy added three crucial new elements—representation of citizen voters in an area of large geographical expanse (the nation-state), equal participation of all as an ideal and growing reality, and the value of individual self-development.

Modern democracy could not be and has not been contained within the nation-state. The experience of citizens participating in a representative democracy creates distinctive values, attitudes, and habits. The political philosopher George Kateb has written that the great lesson of representative democracy stems from the fact that political authority is "at every moment, a temporary, and conditional grant, regularly revocable" through the collective act of voting. Consequently, citizens learn "a pervasive skepticism toward authority." That attitude generates new values that diffuse into the larger society. One is individual autonomy—acting and making commitments based on one's own choices. A second is the tendency to claim the status of citizen in all nonpolitical spheres of life, from the economic to the most intimate relationships. The third moral dimension follows from the practice of majority rule. Insofar as a part of the people—normally a political party—is allowed to stand for the whole, citizens learn that among their fellow citizens there is more than one right solution to a problem. This breeds a tolerance for a diversity of views and respect for the different choices that other citizens make.[1]

As these attitudes and values become habits and institutions, the entire society in the United States has become a terrain for democratic development—that is, a way of life. On that terrain were fought the great moral and political battles to extend democracy. In retrospect, these battles appear as waves, each one a long revolution, though the terrain won for democracy has also been subject to counterwaves. This chapter introduces the reader to the three great waves of democratization in four parts. Parts one and two of this chapter explore the growth of American democratic control over the state; part three, control over economic institutions; and part four, democratic diversity and the liberation of individual potentials in culture and personal life.

## Democracy in Politics and Government: America's First Republic

The American Revolution was the origin and wellspring of democracy in America. Before that signal event, the inhabitants of what is now the United States were largely colonists from Britain with beliefs typical of British subjects of the crown. The colonists adhered to the ideal of "mixed and balanced government," in which each social order—the monarch, the aristocracy, and the people—were to have equal and balanced representation in government. While the English people could claim to be represented in the House of Commons, colonists had their own lower houses—the colonial assemblies—that controlled the power of approving bills that required revenues. American colonists were also fiercely proud of their liberties or British privileges: protection of their persons against arbitrary government action (for example, trial by jury); the right to worship as they chose; and a limited degree of consent in the making of laws (constitutionally limited monarchy).

But this hardly came close to democracy. In a democracy or a republic, only the people are sovereign and an aristocracy and monarch do not exist. Rights are universal attributes of human beings rather than privileges inherited by a small body of citizens within a particular nation. Moreover, the colonists believed that only those white males with sufficient property had the independence of will to participate in elections. This left out women, slaves, white servants, apprentices, laborers, and poor farmers.

Because of its wide distribution of property, and hence its wide participation in the colonial assemblies, its relatively weak aristocracy, and its British heritage of liberty, colonial America was a land of great democratic *promise*. But it would take a cataclysmic event to make the promise an unfolding reality.

It is common to mistake the revolution as the work of great men like Washington and Jefferson or the actions of the military during the War for Independence. But no less an authority than John Adams wrote in retrospect,

> The Revolution was effected before the War commenced. The Revolution was in the hearts and minds of the people, a change in their religious sentiments and their duties and obligations . . . This radical change in the principles, opinions, sentiments, and affections of the people, was the real American Revolution.[2]

The process of "radical change" began in 1765 with Parliament's attempt to tax the colonists without receiving permission to do so from the colonial assemblies. The Stamp Act, which applied to all types of paper, from newspapers and playing cards to public licenses, also allowed someone charged with not paying the tax to be brought before a court without a jury. Americans viewed it as a violation of the colonists' rights as British subjects. After an assembly of delegates from nine colonies denounced the act, Americans resorted to direct action. In Boston, a patriot group calling itself the Sons of Liberty mobilized crowds of lower-class citizens to intimidate royal officials and tax collectors. With the law effectively nullified by civil disobedience, Parliament repealed the tax in 1766.

The pattern of exerted authority and subsequent rebellion was repeated in 1767 after Parliament enacted the Townshend duties on imports into the colonies. This time the Sons of Liberty resorted to nonimportation acts, a boycott of British goods enforced by tarring and feathering, sometimes of rich merchants and notables. Though Parliament repealed the duties, one remained—the tax on imported tea.

In 1773, the Sons of Liberty organized a "tea party" that pitched the boxed tea still on ships into Boston Harbor. Parliament responded angrily with the Coercive Acts. At this point, British authority in the colonies dissolved. Patriot leaders from the popular Committees of Correspondence, which had organized the resistance, planned the first meeting of the Continental Congress in September 1774, which then approved a program of nonimportation. But the people were ahead of their leaders. Conflict between armed American farmers and British regulars began at Lexington and Concord on April 19, 1775, a full fifteen months *before* the Declaration of Independence.

Under the impetus of British intransigence and American direct action, there had occurred a radical shift in "the principles, opinions, sentiments, and affections of the people" referred to by Adams. The response to Tom Paine's popular pamphlet, *Common Sense,* published in January 1776, was the turning point. Written by a poor artisan in unpretentious language, the pamphlet ridiculed kingship: "Of more worth is one honest man to society and in the sight of God than all the crowned ruffians that ever lived." Paine was the first democrat in principle. A Quaker, he did not believe in original sin; instead, he affirmed the perfectability of all. He concluded *Common Sense* by telling Americans that "we have it in our power to begin the world over again. . . . The birthday of a new world is at hand." America, he said, would become a refuge for the fugitives of oppression from all over the world.

Seven months later, the Declaration of Independence (see Documents) stated eloquently to the world the principles behind democratic self-governance. "All men are created equal," it said, and

> are endowed by their Creator with certain unalienable Rights, that among these are Life, Liberty and the pursuit of Happiness. That to secure these rights, Governments are instituted among Men, deriving their just powers from the consent of the governed.

But did the founders really mean all were created equal and should participate in politics and government? After all, many of them held slaves and all believed in male supremacy. Though a full answer is beyond the scope of this chapter, the best answer seems to be yes, they did believe in equality as a principle. If they believed that only white males with property were equal and could govern themselves, they would have returned to a form of expression similar to that which they began the revolution, rights grounded in the British tradition. But too much had changed to do so, even if they had wanted. During the revolution, the people had organized themselves in self-governing associations without authorization from above to protect their existing liberties and then to assert new ones. That self-organization from below had made the revolution a *fait accompli* by 1775 and had created the first Continental Congress whose successor declared independence. This was the substance of democracy as it emerged from the American Revolution. It could not be undone, and the leaders of the revolution accepted that, even if they would resist democracy being applied thoroughly to their vested interests.

Thus, "all men are created equal" was a description of an evolving reality guided by an ideal or principle that would authorize further action to realize it more completely. Eighty-one years later in a speech against slavery, Abraham Lincoln reaffirmed his belief that the words written by the founders meant what they said. The founders, he wrote,

> meant to set up a standard maxim for free society, which should be familiar to all, and revered by all; constantly looked to, constantly labored for, and even though never perfectly attained, constantly approximated, and thereby constantly spreading and deepening its influence, and augmenting the happiness and value of life to all people of all colors everywhere.[3]

In practice, the principle of equality did have an enormous impact on American life. As property ownership began to disappear as a prerequisite for independence of judgment, some states greatly reduced the property qualification for voting, while others replaced it with a taxpaying qualification. White indentured servitude also largely disappeared in the wake of the revolution. Slavery remained in the South, but one by one, the Northern states abolished it, though most denied freed blacks voting and other citizenship rights. Jefferson, who had written the Declaration, authored the Northwest Ordinance eleven years later, banning slavery from the western territories, though Jefferson himself declined to free his own slaves. By 1800, states passed laws providing debtor relief, more equitable taxation, and grants of land to settlers without farms. In language, the word *citizen* replaced *gentleman* and *yeoman,* while *Mr.* replaced titles like *esq.* (esquire) and *His Honor.* Democracy was a spreading reality, not just in government, but also in society and culture.

With the success of the American Revolution, the task of building a modern democratic republic had only just begun. The first form of national government of the new country, the Articles of Confederation, was nothing like a nation-state. The new national government was a loose federation. It had the power to raise an army, make treaties with foreign nations, borrow and print money, request funds from the states, and adjudicate disputes between the states, but its laws were not supreme over the states, and sovereignty remained with the people of the thirteen states. Each state had one vote regardless of population, and it took nine votes to pass important laws.

This weak national government was beset by deep difficulties throughout its existence. Because it couldn't tax, it couldn't fund the country's war debts. It was unable to negotiate a treaty with Britain to remove its forts, which still stood on American soil, because it couldn't order the states to compensate the Loyalists who had fled during the war years. Finally, many of the revolution's leading men were alarmed that state governments, under the influence of poor and middling farmers, refused to levy higher taxes to fund at face value the war bonds that had fallen into the hands of rich speculators. In Massachusetts, Shays's Rebellion in 1786–7 prevented the state from foreclosing on farms. Even though it was suppressed, the state's middle class voted in a new government friendly to their interests.

In 1786, a group of gentlemen nationalists including James Madison, George Washington, Robert Morris, John Jay, Alexander Hamilton, and others now known as "the founders" convinced the Congress to call a meeting to revise the Articles of Confederation. At the closed-door convention in Philadelphia the following year, the prevailing opinion of the delegates was frankly fearful that the democratic influences within the states over the debtor-creditor issue and the Congress's weakness in foreign affairs would disrupt and cripple the new republic. Subsequently, the delegates went beyond their appointed task of revising the Articles and created a constitution for a new national government to be elected directly by the people rather than the states.

The theory behind the new constitution was revolutionary and controversial. It embodied a response to two issues in democratic theory that dominated public opinion at the time. With the dispute over paying states' war debts, Americans quickly discovered that even when rid of monarchy and aristocracy, the people were not a united, harmonious whole. Despite the appeal of the revolution's leaders to citizens' civic virtue, the people invariably split up into factions or interest groups, the most important being those based on different kinds and amounts of private property. Some Americans were creditors, some were debtors; some made money from exporting, others from importing; some made a living from enslaving other human beings who were not part of the political community, while others were independent farmers or merchants; some were rich, and many more were poor with little or no property. How was it possible to prevent a single dominant faction or majority coalition of self-interested factions from corrupting the republic, reducing it to a tyranny, and oppressing the rest of the people or a minority of the people?

A related question was whether a continent-wide nation-state would be too distant from the people to prevent it from being governed tyrannically. Was a viable republic impossible in a large territory? In earlier times, republics had only existed in small-scale, homogenous city-states such as ancient Athens and Rome and the early modern cities of Italy and Switzerland. Those who feared that a vigorous national government would soon degenerate into a tyrannical empire like those run by Europe's absolute monarchs wanted America to remain a loose federation of states. Others, called Federalists, believed that a democracy was possible in a large nation-state. These two concerns preoccupied the members of the convention that met in 1787 to write the constitution for a new federal government.

The answers given to them by the framers of the new constitution embody many of the elements of American democratic governance, which have survived to this day. These answers constituted a revolution in political theory that has convinced the modern world that a democracy is possible—indeed normal—in extended nation-states with heterogeneous populations composed of different classes, ethnicities, races, and religions.

One of the US Constitution's solutions to the previously mentioned concerns was separating the powers of government and allowing the different branches of government—executive, legislative, and judicial—to check and balance each other. For example, the legislative power is mainly lodged in Congress, but the president can veto legislation, though the legislature can override the veto by a two-thirds vote. The courts also have the power to declare legislation unconstitutional and void. By the same principle, even though executive power is lodged in the presidency, the president can be forced to follow the laws by the courts and can be constrained in the expenditure of government funds by Congress. Checks and balances are one way to avoid a majority or minority faction from using the government for oppressive purposes.

The dividing and fragmenting of government to keep it from becoming a ready tool of oppression was extended in the governmental structure of federalism. Though Madison wanted to give the federal government a veto over state legislation, the convention divided sovereignty in the new national state between a national people and a state people. While federal or national laws were to be supreme, including laws to regulate relations with foreign states and interstate commerce, unless a power was expressly granted to the federal government, it was reserved to the states. For example, laws to protect and regulate property, unless involved in interstate commerce, were handled at the state level. Criminal law and the policing of these laws were also handled at the state level. The United States did not and does not have a national police force.

In popular thinking, the idea of checks and balances has been much exaggerated as a solution to these problems. James Madison, the founding father most responsible for the writing of the Constitution, recognized that in a democracy *public opinion* was ultimately sovereign. Checks and balances could not by themselves prevent a tyranny. But, how could public opinion be kept from being distorted in the service of a self-interested majority faction? Madison's answer in "Federalist Paper No. 10" was a major innovation in democratic theory. Rather than accepting the dominant view at the time that nation-states could not be republics because they were distant from the people, Madison argued that the larger the sphere of the republic, the more factions it encompassed and the more difficult each faction would find it to combine with others to dominate public opinion and control the electoral process.

The new view, it could be argued, was intended to protect property from popular majorities. But whatever the intention, Madison's solution could also work *against* the power of property. In a later period, as markets became national, large property interests rather than democratic ones were more easily able to dominate local government. When public deliberation shifted to the federal government where more factions were included, the nonpropertied factions were able to combine to form a powerful check on the power of state and national property interests. As will be seen, the experience of American history is that a powerful national democracy is just as likely an outcome of including more factions as would a pro-property majority.

In retrospect, Madison's approach of embracing a tendency toward a greater plurality and diversity of voices in the public sphere seems progressive and democratic. Shifting power to the national level resulted in the election of more talented, civic-minded, and cosmopolitan office holders. Theoretically, Madison's acceptance that divisions and interests among the people were inevitable and his reliance on that fact to sustain democratic governance were revolutionary. He had inverted the old belief that republics must be small in territory to be viable. To Madison and other founders, democracy was less susceptible to tyranny on the national level than on the state level.

A republican public opinion also relied on rational deliberation. A rational public opinion was to be distinguished from the counting of noses through elections. The founders were especially wary of ephemeral passions and narrowly construed interests. Rather, the public opinion so necessary in a democratic republic was to be guided by the most enlightened thinkers in the direction of the common good. Deliberation, in turn, required widespread education. Like other thinkers of the Western Enlightenment, the founders believed that the ignorance of the masses had allowed kings, aristocrats, and popes to rule in the past. Education was seen as necessary to cultivate civic-mindedness and feelings of respect, trust, sympathy, and common cause with other citizens. Thus, from the beginning of the American republic, the states, particularly in the North, promoted schooling. For example, in 1789 the Massachusetts legislature required all towns and districts to hire schoolmasters and that republican knowledge be taught. By the 1780s, the larger towns chartered the equivalent of modern high schools and the state had its own college, Harvard. However, only in the 1830s and 1840s did public education become universal and professional, starting in the New England states.

Women had a special role to play in the formation of a democratic public opinion. Though confined to the domestic sphere, mothers had the civic duty of teaching their sons independence, ethical character, and the ability to pursue the common good of the republic. Republican mothers themselves were expected to be rational, independent, literate, and politically knowledgeable. For this they needed to be educated, and the commitment to female education followed. The first female academies were formed in the 1790s.

Notwithstanding these relatively enlightened and modern elements of democratic governance, the fact that it was elected by the people rather than the states, and the reality that it was by far the most advanced democracy in the world at the time, the American nation-state founded by the Constitution of 1787 was only partially democratic when compared to the commonly accepted features of contemporary democracy. Thus the founders mandated that only the House of Representatives was to be directly elected by the people. State legislatures selected members of the US Senate, and an Electoral College of wise men was to elect the president. In practice, when it came to nominations for offices, local notables and their followers, rather than common people, made political decisions. While the founders understood the importance of public opinion, they believed that an "aristocracy of virtue" should filter and refine the thinking of the people, who in turn should defer to them in public matters. These virtuous men were thought by the founders to be synonymous with the wellborn and wealthy classes. The founders also viewed the press mainly as a means to inform rather than discuss contentious issues, laws, and fundamental principles. It would not be an exaggeration to say that America's founders wanted the new republic to be guided from above by the wellborn, wealthy, and better educated. Political facts mirrored this view, as voter turnout was low—well below 40 percent of eligible voters.

One of the most important elements of modern democracy is civil freedom. But the founders only added the Bill of Rights (the first ten amendments to the constitution)—which included the rights to freedom of speech, freedom of the press, freedom of association, freedom of religion, the right of habeas corpus, the right to own guns (a protection against a standing army), and the right not to be forced to testify against oneself—as a way to appease and win the support of opponents of the new government. Moreover, these limitations on government's ability to oppress the people only applied to the federal government and did not extend to the state governments until the twentieth century.

The limits on the extent of American democracy were starkly evident in the restrictions on who could participate in elections and hold public office. State laws kept over 80 percent of the inhabitants of the new country—women, African Americans, American Indians, other racial minorities, and some white males who didn't own property or pay taxes—walled out of the polity. The capturing of millions of Africans and transporting them to America to be enslaved doing the work whites refused to do and the genocidal treatment of Indians were America's original sins (women's oppression was much older). The treatment of both groups as subhuman was inherited by American democracy and largely accepted. Until the Civil War era, the major advances for democracy occurred only among white males.

Americans tend to have a blind spot about the oppression of minorities–it is in America's shadow. We either deny it, ignore it, or minimize it as an exception to the rule of equality. One major reason is what some call the "myth of innocence." In this long and deeply held story Americans tell about themselves, the United States was the country where people from the old world could come to throw off their oppressive pasts and begin anew in a land where each man (women were not initially included) could rise by his own efforts and where everyone got what he deserved. If anyone failed, he had no one to blame but himself. Under this vision of reality, America and Americans have no guilt and nothing to apologize for or fix because all achievement is based on merit.

As an aspiration, such a myth has its virtues, but as a description of America's history, it is an illusion. It takes little effort to realize that much of the white male equality that Americans boasted of was built on a foundation of inequality. The free land that attracted immigrants to America and allowed them to assume a position of independence and equality with each other was predicated on the US government's expulsion of American Indians from their ancestral lands and their confinement in concentration camps called reservations. A major factor in American industrialization—in addition to America's vaunted ingenuity—were the profits made by American slaveholders from the brutal exploitation of African American slave labor. Those profits coming from the export of cotton allowed Americans to borrow the capital from abroad necessary to build the canals, roads, and railroads required for the Industrial Revolution. Later in the century, these same industrial profits depended on the cheap labor supplied by immigrant working people. In short, understanding the prosperity, success, and the very shape of American democracy is not conceivable without confronting the American myth of innocence and accepting the hidden truths of American history.

That American history from its beginning was far from democratic and that democracy remains as much an aspiration as it is a fact is also evident in the way early elections were carried out. America's founders were unwilling to countenance competing political parties, a generally recognized hallmark of democracy. That there was not yet a concept of the loyal opposition was evident in 1798 when the ruling Federalists passed the Alien and Sedition Acts, which removed freedoms of the press and speech from their political opponents. Though the election in 1800 of the Democratic-Republican leader Thomas Jefferson ended this early threat to freedom, the Federalists quickly declined and disappeared, leaving the country again without a legitimate opposition party. Until the 1830s, the American polity was governed on the national level by a loosely structured one-party system dominated by notables.

Another important element of American democracy, which is now taken for granted, was also largely absent at first. The idea that society could largely govern itself and the government should serve that society emerged only gradually in the first half-century following the revolution. Americans did not accept the idea of citizens forming voluntary associations, whether founded for profit or not-for-profit activities. Much like the new nation-states established by twentieth-century revolutions in less developed countries, revolutionary-era Americans feared that allowing private citizens to organize for self-interest would undermine the close relationship between the people and their new government and create special interests that could thwart the people's will.

The early American government carefully guarded the privilege of forming voluntary associations. Only if they were manifestly in the public interest and authorized by legislation could they be tolerated. Thus state governments chartered corporations to build bridges and canals and create banks. They also chartered charities, colleges, and state churches. But citizens were not supposed to combine on their own to form corporations, political parties, or associations to influence the government. In his last presidential address of 1796, President George Washington warned citizens against "all combinations and associations, under whatever plausible charter, with the real design to direct, control, counteract or awe the regular deliberation and action of the constituted authorities."

In current thinking, the body of voluntary associations known as civil society, which constitute the economy and society independent of the state, are thought to be essential to a functioning democracy. It is now a commonplace assertion that the values nurtured in civil society of respect for the views of others, civility, equal opportunity, and a commitment to social justice are as important for the success of a democracy as its institutional features, such as voting rights, competitive elections, and the rule of law. Voluntary associations pull people out of their private orbits where they pursue their self-interest as solitary individuals and demonstrate that they can make a difference through common endeavors. People learn to overcome differences in race, ethnicity, religion, gender, political party, and the like to deliberate together on public business. As pointed out by Theda Skocpol, democratic association independent of the state also serves as a springboard to mobilize citizens for electioneering, voting, lobbying, and service in government.

In America, it took two generations for such a civil society to emerge. It occurred in two stages. First, as Americans broke up into political factions, those who originally chartered the state corporations faced a loss of control over these institutions when they were voted out of office and new officeholders were installed. As partisan conflict over control of the government and these chartered associations became the norm, Americans abandoned their opposition to voluntary associations. The government would extend the right of free incorporation to *all* businesses and grant free association to all religious and other associations. Replacing the old distrust of independent voluntary associations formed at the grassroots and the reliance on granting special privileges to business interests or an educated elite, the new idea was that *competition in the market and civil society* among a multiplicity of business corporations and private associations would keep special interests or factions from dominating the state.

A second stage occurred from below. The United States experienced an explosion of church-related voluntary association between 1810 and 1830. Born-again Christians attempted to make America a Christian nation by distributing Christian tracts and Bibles, advocating temperance (in drinking alcohol), Sabbatarianism (keeping Sunday free from work), and rescuing "fallen women" (prostitutes). By the 1830s, many Americans had learned the skills and habits necessary for creating and maintaining voluntary associations, including writing constitutions and bylaws, electing officers, paying dues, distributing association newsletters, and creating state- and nationwide parent organizations. Volunteering in associations had become the primary tool Americans used to make their voices heard in the public sphere.

The most significant example of a new voluntary association influencing national politics came with William Lloyd Garrison's antislavery society, whose members he recruited from other Christian reform associations. Founded in 1833, Garrison's association sparked the nation's first mass movement intended to transform the character of American democracy.

Social movements are democracy in motion, its most dynamic element, though they are often held in public disrepute. Nor have all social movements been prodemocratic or progressive—think of the anti-Catholic Know Nothings or the Ku Klux Klan. But the large majority of them have fought to expand the scope of civil society and recast discussion in the public sphere by empowering groups that have been excluded or marginalized. Social movements generally share the understanding articulated by the black abolitionist Frederick Douglass, who said that "power concedes nothing without a demand." Social movements generally rely on controversial, often disruptive methods in bringing new issues, grievances, and standards of freedom and democracy before the public. They employ leaflets, newspapers, books, petitions, mass meetings, marches, boycotts, strikes, nonviolent civil disobedience—even occasional violence. Once their claims are accepted as legitimate, however, social movements disappear or become part of organized civil society.

In 1831, Garrison burst onto the public scene with the intent of repudiating gradual manumission by slaveholders and the colonization of the freed slaves to other nations. Convinced by free black leaders that colonization was intended to deport free blacks and strengthen slavery, Garrison's society came out for immediate abolition and the acceptance of blacks as citizens. The American Anti-Slavery Society (AAS) mounted a fierce moral assault on the foundations of slavery. It called attention to the breakup of black families by the selling of black children on the auction block, the rape of slave women by white slaveholding men, and the inability of black men to improve themselves economically.

Though its white leaders never fully overcame a paternalistic attitude toward blacks, the AAS enrolled large numbers of black members and leaders and for the first time gave significant numbers of women an opportunity to engage in politics. Eventually, abolitionist women, notably Elizabeth Cady Stanton and Lucretia Mott, would found the woman's rights movement at Seneca Falls in 1848 (see Documents).

By 1838, the AAS had 1,350 local chapters and a quarter of a million members. But in the 1840s the abolitionist movement split, and its political impact dwindled. Its demand for immediate abolition and its openness to women's public activism were too controversial, and it was unable to work within the new mass-democratic political parties that had appeared.

Political parties were another kind of voluntary association. Before the 1830s, political parties, like other associations, were not quite legitimate. However, the spread of market relationships replacing older forms of hierarchy, the rise of civil society (voluntary associations outside the state), the lowering of voting qualifications so that propertyless white males could vote, and the dissatisfaction of average Americans with rule by the wellborn and wealthy opened the way for permanent political parties. New Yorker Martin Van Buren formed the first political party between 1817 and 1821. This early party machine countered the political connections that local notables had used to wield power with the use of patronage—distributing government offices to party loyalists. With patronage as the party glue, the party boss could enforce discipline in voting by officeholders and attract a slice of the electorate. Van Buren argued that patronage, or the "spoils system" (rotation in office), was democratic because it reflected the preference of the majority of voters.

The first national political party was the Democratic Party formed under the leadership of President Andrew Jackson (1829–37); the opposition Whig Party soon followed. Permanent parties performed critical democratic functions. They educated and mobilized voters, recruited candidates and linked them with voters, served as the center of voter identification, formulated public policy, and provided the arguments to legitimize it. The new parties checked the political power of wealthy notables and provided a vehicle for the political power of the common man. American political parties were the world's first mass political parties, a major innovation in democratic practice.

On the eve of the Civil War, America's first republic, which had been characterized by elite-run, one-party politics, limited civil liberties, thin participation
in electoral politics, weak civil society, and the exclusion of nonwhite males, had
been transformed. The United States had made important strides toward becoming a fully modern democratic polity. A vigorous civil society served as a school
for democracy, mobilized citizens for public discussion and electoral politics, and
embodied the idea that society was largely self-governing independent of the
state. These developments in turn created the foundation for the world's first
mass-democratic political parties. At the same time, the country's first mass social
movement, that of the abolitionists, demonstrated that blacks and whites, women
and men could cooperate in the advocacy of equal access to citizenship, a positive
omen for the future. But American governance was about to become even more
democratic and national.

## America's Second Republic: The Civil War as a Turning Point

The Civil War (1861–5) was the decisive moment in the democratization of the
American nation. The emergence of mass political parties and other voluntary
associations with a public and national focus, including the antislavery movement, made the divisive issue of slavery incapable of being resolved by party
elites. During the Missouri Compromise of 1821, the Compromise of 1850, and
the Kansas-Nebraska Act of 1854, political elites of both sections intervened to
impose temporary settlements of the irrepressible issue of the expansion of slavery
into the western territories. But by 1854, the fusion of antislavery with free-labor
ideology and the mass democratic nature of the new political parties rendered the
American polity incapable of sustaining support for another grand compromise.
The Northern Democratic Party split in two, while the Northern Whig Party dissolved. The new Republican Party that emerged combined Northern Whigs and
many Northern Democrats under the banner of no compromise with the "Slave
Power" in its drive to expand slavery into the West.

There is a popular notion today that the Republican Party was dominated by
industrial capitalists. But, Northern capitalists were split over the issue of slavery.
Larger capitalists, typified by New England textile magnates and New York bankers, had strong ties with Southern slaveholders. The emergence of a significant
group of antislavery manufacturers in the North, who needed help from the
federal government to accumulate capital, created the basis for a broad antislavery
alliance. That democratic coalition of Northern industrialists, commercial farmers,
and skilled workers constituted the base of the new Republican Party. In other
countries undergoing industrialization and state building in the nineteenth century, notably Japan and Germany, the industrial bourgeoisie followed the lead of
the old aristocracy and that alliance charted an authoritarian path to modernity.
In America, a large-enough segment of the Northern capitalist class united with
the middling and lower orders to produce a cross-class democratic movement

to oppose the expansion of slavery and open the way for the further spread of democracy.[4]

With the election of the Republican Abraham Lincoln in 1860, the Southern slave states seceded (border slave states remained in the union) to protect their "peculiar institution." Though slavery was the underlying issue of the conflict, in political theory, the South relied on the states' rights theory propounded three decades earlier by South Carolina senator and onetime vice president John C. Calhoun. In contrast to Madison, Calhoun was the first to recognize that majorities were as likely or more likely to threaten property interests—in this case, property in human beings—on the national level as on the state level. To check that majority and reconcile slavery and union, Calhoun responded with his theory of the concurrent majority. That theory rejected the belief of nationalists that once the people of the states had ceded part of their sovereignty to the national people in 1788, it could not be withdrawn. Calhoun argued that a state could nullify federal law simply by assembling in another constitutional convention, which would effectively restore its full sovereignty. Though he had not supported it before he died, the right to secede was the logical conclusion of Calhoun's theory that the people on the state level were ultimately sovereign.

Lincoln's response cut to the heart of democracy. For majority rule to truly represent the sovereign will of the people, the minority must accept the right of the majority to rule. The legitimacy of the majority to rule depends on public deliberation in which a majority faction in public opinion emerges only by taking into account the views of those who hold minority positions. The minority accepts the right of the majority to rule in the expectation that if the majority becomes oppressive, the minority can appeal to public opinion with the prospect of becoming the majority at some later point.

Nullification or secession cut short that continuous process of public deliberation that is at the heart of democracy. As Lincoln put it, once the Southern states began seceding,

> It is now for [Americans] to demonstrate to the world, that those who can fairly carry an election, can also suppress a rebellion—that ballots are the rightful, and peaceful, successors of bullets; and that when ballots have fairly, and constitutionally, decided, there can be no successful appeal, back to bullets; that there can be no successful appeal, except to ballots themselves, at succeeding elections.[5]

The secession of the Southern slave states and the start of the Civil War was, according to Lincoln, a test whether the democratic United States "or any nation so conceived and so dedicated, can long endure." But at first, the goal of the Union was only to reaffirm majority rule and restore the status quo as to slavery. With the Emancipation Proclamation of 1863, the war became something else; it became a revolutionary upheaval. The emancipation confiscated without compensation about half the wealth of the South, and it authorized a mass rebellion consisting of a half-million slaves, over 12 percent of the total slave population in the United States. In response to Lincoln's edict, these slaves cast aside the legal bonds that shackled them to their masters and made their way under difficult conditions to Union Army lines. There they were employed first as laborers and then as soldiers. That armed slaves were engaging in battle against the military forces of their masters with their freedom in the balance was nothing short of the overthrow of a legal property system with the active participation of those it had subordinated: a revolution. The emancipation had turned the Civil War from a blood feud among white men into a multiracial democratic struggle against one of the most horrific forms of labor and racial exploitation the modern world has known. The result would forever change the identity of the United States, making it a civic rather than an ethnic (Caucasian) nation.

At the same time that America had a new birth of freedom, it became a modern nation-state. Before the Civil War, Americans did not view themselves as a nation but instead referred to their national government as a "union." Most government intervention in the economy was done at the state level where legislatures chartered corporations for special public purposes and established state boards to regulate education, health, and agriculture. On the national level, the old fear of central government dating from the revolution still held sway. Eleven of the first twelve amendments to the constitution were negative, in that they restricted the powers of the federal government. The war upset and reversed that older balance between the states and the federal government, making the federal government the focus of the people's sovereignty. That shift was reflected in the fact that six of seven amendments to the Constitution passed during and following the war expanded the power of the federal government in relation to the states.[6]

During the war, the federal government greatly expanded its size, functions, authority, and reach into all areas of life. It not only set precedents in taxing internally, conscripting citizens, and suppressing dissent but also in actively redistributing property and income. The most dramatic example was the expropriation of the wealth of the Southern slaveholders in the form of human beings, the granting of the vote to the freedmen, and passage of the Fourteenth Amendment, which nationalized citizenship. The American people acting at the federal level had become the most important single force for democratization in American history.

A large factor in that democratization was the new relationship between the federal government and civil society. The war forged strong links between federal authority and the activism of voluntary associations, including the associations of liberated slaves. For example, 87 percent of the members of the Union Army were volunteers from local and state militias, not conscripts; only a minority were draftees. On the Union Army's home front, female-led voluntary groups, notably the sanitary commissions, coordinated medical, social, and spiritual support for the soldiers. Northern abolitionist groups worked closely with the Freedman's Bureau.

The close of the war brought a great expansion of civil society. Building on the war's idealism and the national networks it had created, Americans formed new voluntary associations. Some were insurance-oriented fraternal orders such as the American Order of United Workmen and the Knights of Pythias. Other workers founded labor unions to strike for higher wages. Among farmers, Oliver Kelley created the Patrons of Husbandry or Grange using his Masonic ties. Clara Barton got Congress to charter the American Red Cross, and temperance women founded the Woman's Christian Temperance Union. Notably, African Americans formed dozens of new fraternal and mutual-aid federations after the war, at rates even higher than whites. Not least, Union Army veterans formed the Grand Army of the Republic, which was closely allied with the Republican Party and lobbied tirelessly for the expansion of federally funded military pensions.

In his Gettysburg Address (see Documents) President Lincoln famously redefined American democracy by calling the new nation-state "a government of the people, by the people, for the people." This was a far more robust definition than the minimalist and passive one contained in the Declaration of Independence, which only required the "consent of the governed" and the protection by government of the individual's unalienable rights. While the old definition fit well with Americans' deference to local and regional elites during the early republic, the new definition presupposed the active participation of the nation's poor and middling farmers and working classes through the medium of civil society and mass political parties at all levels of government.

In fits and starts, America was also becoming a democracy of a new type—a *social* or industrial democracy. Social democracy, which will be discussed in more depth in the next section and in chapter four, reflected the fact that a growing majority of the workforce was engaged in wage labor and no longer required access to property in the form of a farm or an artisan workshop. Instead, workers required a rising standard of living and protection from the vagaries of the market. That normally entailed some regulation of the national market and some redistribution of income and wealth. Thus, immediately following the war, the federal government funded the Freedman's Bureau, which provided education, health care, basic welfare, and supervised the labor contracts of the emancipated slaves. In the North, it created the system of military pensions for Civil War veterans, which by 1894 took up 37 percent of the federal budget.

Most redistribution, however, was upward rather than downward. Throughout the war, the new nation-state actively promoted industrialization by redistributing resources to capital accumulators. Land grants for transcontinental railroads and state colleges and universities subsidized the infrastructure and human capital necessary for a modern industrial society. The federal government enacted a protective tariff to aid infant manufacturing and a national banking system to promote a national market. More long term, the Fourteenth Amendment federalized the legal protection of that national market. Defining corporations as persons, subsequent court decisions authorized the government to intervene in the regulation of that market, usually in ways that protected large national business enterprises. The changes in federal power were so stunning and transformational that historians often refer to the post-Civil War nation as the "Second Republic."

During Reconstruction, a period lasting from 1865 to 1877, the nation's lower orders expanded democracy not only by joining new voluntary associations but also by forming political advocacy groups, which demanded that government meet their pressing needs and lofty aspirations. In the North, farmers asked for cheap money and low interest rates to retain their farms and maintain their incomes. In this period, the basic political elements that would flower in the 1880s and 1890s as agrarian Populism took hold. Feminists, after failing to win Congressional support for universal suffrage, created a durable national woman's suffrage movement. Urban workers formed trade unions and citywide trade assemblies, which mounted massive citywide strikes in Chicago and New York and mobilized votes for the eight-hour workday. The nation's first socialist parties took root among German-speaking immigrants and created a political presence in the cities.

The nation's major focus, however, was in the South where the defeated Confederate leadership sought to maintain the freed slaves in a subordinate relationship similar to slavery. In response, Republicans forged a precarious majority in the North on the premise that securing the nation's new freedom required federal protection of civil freedoms and the right to vote of freedmen in the South. Embodied in the Fourteenth and Fifteenth Amendments, this nationalist majority created the framework of the modern democratic nation-state by nationalizing citizenship rights, while preventing the reenslavement of blacks.

But the practical effect of the new commitment to liberty and equality for all was greatly diluted if not completely wiped out by the white supremacist reaction in the South during the 1870s. Despite the establishment of new, federally sponsored state governments in the South, which allowed blacks to vote, hold office, and enjoy civil rights, the former plantation owners, with the help of the Ku Klux Klan and other such groups, were soon able to overthrow these governments through terror and intimidation. "The Yankees helped free us, so they say," said one former slave reminiscing a half century later, "but they let us be put back in slavery again."[7] Still, there were enormous gains. The slave driver and his whip as a goad to labor were eliminated. Also eliminated was the pervasive rape of black women by white slave owners and the auction block that separated black families. In place of the horror of slavery, there grew up a mix of small-holding farming, wage labor, and the most prevalent form of labor, sharecropping. With the advent of the crop-lien system, a form of debt slavery, African Americans became quasi-peasants, whose labor was subject to the coercive of power of local elites backed by state governments.

These governments remained firmly under white control because they found ways to eliminate blacks' right to vote. In the 1890s, the Populist Party tried to unite black and white sharecroppers against the leading property-owning classes of the South. The fear that a biracial majority might undo the prerogatives of property led the ruling Democratic Party in the South to enact a series of laws removing blacks' right to vote and to some degree poor whites' right as well. Mississippi had an understanding clause in which the registrar asked each prospective voter to interpret a clause of the state constitution to his own satisfaction before he could vote. Other states had literacy tests or poll taxes as a requirement for voting. In many states, overt violence kept blacks away from the polls. Southern voter turnout was cut in half. With blacks and their political allies disfranchised, the real election occurred in the all-white Democratic primary. This powerful reverse wave undid most of the democratic gains of Reconstruction. In the words of one historian, Reconstruction was "America's Unfinished Revolution," not to be completed until the civil rights movement over eight decades later.[8]

In other ways, however, the expansion toward an ever-more-inclusive democracy gathered steam after Reconstruction. Its underlying sources were the diffusion of redistributive issues and concerns into the public sphere, the growth of national voluntary associations, from fraternal orders and women's temperance associations to labor unions, and large national projects that mobilized the energies of masses of citizens and focused them on the federal government. The critical events were the two world wars, the recovery from the Great Depression of the 1930s and the Cold War.

During these crises, patriotism merged with democracy, and even the conservative economic elites of the North learned to appreciate grassroots democracy. During World War I, for example, the federal government implemented conscription using 192,000 volunteer workers, the War Industries Board relied on 250,000 volunteers; and the Committee on Public Information had a volunteer army of 150,000. These and other parastate organizations made unnecessary state command systems based on elaborate state bureaucracies. Wartime mobilization went hand in hand with state support for redistributive democracy. During the war, women suffragists conducted a struggle for the right to vote, winning it in 1920. Organized workers won wartime protection for the right to organize, a minimum wage, and the eight-hour day, which served as a precedent for permanent legislation during the New Deal. Immediately following the war, women's groups lobbied successfully to win congressional enactment of the Sheppard-Towner Maternity and Infant Protection Act establishing matching funds for "mothers' pensions" (later, "aid to dependent children" and still later stigmatized as "welfare").

It would have been difficult to accomplish many of these things with any effectiveness through state-level democracy. Because states had to take into account businesses' ability to move out of state in response to higher taxes or regulatory burdens, they were normally hamstrung. However, in the era before a globalized market, the federal government was not subject to this limitation. In addition, unlike the federal government, states lacked the ability to control the money supply and run budget deficits as a way of stimulating the economy. As a result, social programs were often scrapped during business downturns or not expanded to meet rising demand. Finally, most state governments were under the stranglehold of economic elites whose businesses determined the prosperity of state economies.

The high point of federally sponsored democratization came in the mid-1960s. The Civil Rights Act of 1964 forbade discrimination in employment and public accommodations based on race, religion, nationality, or sex. It was soon followed by the Voting Rights Act, which gave the federal government the responsibility of protecting the right to vote against discriminatory practices at the state level. For the first time, women, African Americans, Latinos, and other minorities had a voice in the public sphere. Eventually, what became known as the "rights revolution" established positive rights guaranteed by federal legislation and enforced by the federal courts. The most notable example was affirmative action in hiring, but the new emphasis on empowerment through legislated rights also created the right of children in families to be protected against abuse, workers against unsafe and unhealthful working conditions, all employees from sexual harassment and age discrimination, disabled people from discrimination, and private sector employees to take a leave from work for family and medical reasons without being subject to discipline or firing. The rights revolution represented the high point of nationalized democracy. At the same time, it heralded a shift away from reliance on the national administrative state back in the direction of individual rights, with the implicit understanding that these rights did not originate in a state of nature but in the democratic polity itself.

All the while however, powerful countertrends gained in force, which would eventually weaken the link between mass mobilization from below and democratic nationalization. During the first twenty years of the century, Americans reacted against the political party. It was thought that a would-be aristocracy of corrupt bosses (party leaders who dictated nominations and appointments to office and brokered deals between business and government) had taken power through political parties. Rotation in office or patronage came to be viewed as a means of securing the power of these party bosses over the people and the power of businessmen to corrupt the bosses. During the Progressive Era, the period from the 1890s to the 1910s, governments at all levels enacted reforms to undermine the power of the party over the polity. Civil service laws made it difficult or impossible for elected leaders to fire and hire government officials for political purposes. Government-run primaries to nominate candidates took over from party-run caucuses. New laws made the ballot secret so that no one could know how each citizen voted in an election. The new model of citizenship called for voters who were well-informed and autonomous rather than loyal to a political party and willing to march to the polls and vote for it.

In practice, the individual citizen's vote did not become more enlightened. Rather, the lobbying in civil society of interest and pressure groups, which represented considerably less than a majority of citizens, became more pervasive and powerful, while the ability of political parties to offer inducements like patronage to mobilize the citizenry to vote declined. By the late twentieth century,

Americans faced the problem of special interests, especially those funded by large corporations, corrupting the political process and dominating the unelected administrative agencies of government through their superior access to resources. As a result, the American majority came to suspect the results of voluntary organizing in civil society.

Just as important as a factor undermining mass democratic mobilization was the decline of mass-membership voluntary associations. Such associations, including fraternal orders, women's clubs, veterans' organizations, and labor unions entered an extended decline beginning in the 1960s. Recently, even churches have joined the trend of decline. Mass voluntary associations have been replaced by professionally managed advocacy organizations, which demanded only that members pay dues. This new type of organization was a logical response to the rise of the regulatory state, which rewards continuous lobbying by interest groups. America's civic life was becoming remarkably oligarchic. The one major segment of American life that retained a vibrant civic life until very recently was the Christian right wing. However, the right wing's political thrust tended to be anti-federal government and favored the return of powers to the states.

Perhaps the turning point in American citizens' loss of faith in federal power came with two enormous shocks felt by the system in the late 1960s and early 1970s. A mass movement of millions of citizens arose in opposition to the government's prosecution of the war in Vietnam. For the first time since the nineteenth century, a war elicited angry democratic opposition from a large portion of its citizens rather than a mass patriotic revival. A few years later, it was revealed the President Richard Nixon had abused his presidential powers by spying on the opposition party and lying to the American public to cover it up. By the end of the 1970s, many white working people abandoned their longtime support for federal social legislation, which, since the 1960s, they believed had helped blacks and poor people at their expense. Since then, polls indicate a persistent and widespread disaffection from government in general, but mainly the federal government. When the Cold War ended in 1991, no new national project emerged to take its place. Even the 2001 War on Terror following the shocking bombings of the World Trade Center and the Pentagon by terrorists in hijacked airliners elicited only a short burst of patriotic fervor and even less democratic action at the grassroots level.

Whither American democracy? Will it return to a new version of the elite-dominated early republic, or can there be a national democratic renewal? That topic will be addressed in more depth chapters five and six, which examine the period from the 1970s to the present.

## Democracy in the Economy

The second wave of democratization involved challenging the abuses, inequities, and dysfunctions involved in modern capitalism. Starting during the early period of American history, the rise of large-scale, for-profit enterprises employing significant numbers of wageworkers aroused suspicion and often outright opposition.

In the first phases of capitalist development, the concerns came from the holders of small-scale property. Family farmers, artisans, and small merchants feared that the concentration of property in the hands of the few would shift power and resources away from the large majority. Most Americans believed that a republic needed to be based on a large middle class of self-sufficient yeomen. Thus Thomas Jefferson proposed in his draft constitution for Virginia that each poor citizen be provided by the government with forty acres of farming land. Jefferson's Democratic-Republicans, the dominant party in the first quarter of the nineteenth century, sought to expand the land available to would-be family farmers in the expectation that it would perpetuate America's republican distribution of wealth.

The decline of agriculture and the rise of wage work concerned American leaders. Writing in the 1820s, Madison was pessimistic about the future of the republic because he foresaw a "dangerous social inequality" arising from "the connection between the great Capitalists in Manufactures and Commerce and the members employed by them."[9] The popular suspicion of what today would be called "capitalism" centered on the opposition to the accumulation and concentration of wealth in the hands of the few. It was widely believed that if the property arrangements were left intact, a natural equality would result. Only political intervention in society could upset this republican balance and reintroduce aristocracy. Government policies that raised taxes on the producing classes (farmers and artisans), that established an unproductive bureaucracy in the form of a standing army, that manipulated the currency to create high interest rates for debtors, and that established market monopolies were all ways of siphoning off the fruits of the labor of producers. When that wealth was transferred to a parasitic elite, the republic was corrupted and could devolve into an oligarchy.

The presidency of Andrew Jackson highlighted new policies designed to prevent the concentration of wealth. A self-identified "democrat," Jackson founded the Democratic Party with its slogan "equal rights to all, special privileges to none." Jackson scaled back the tariff, viewed as a tax on producers, though he vigorously rejected his vice president's idea that states could nullify a federal law. Jackson also vetoed the rechartering of the Second Bank of the United States, which he labeled a nest of special privilege and monopoly, though it only stabilized the national currency. He also enabled the Southern states to forcibly remove Native Americans from their lands to open up settlements for white farmers. Finally, Jackson appointed Judge Roger B. Taney as Supreme Court chief justice. Taney's rulings expanded the constitutional authority that states used to legislatively limit the claims and regulate the operation of capitalist property. Jacksonian politics inaugurated an enduring ideological thread in American politics, a majoritarian, but often backward-looking, Populism that feared an economic elite.

The Civil War was a great turning point in the democratic response to the impact of capitalism on American life. Before the war, the nation-state gathered the land necessary for widespread property ownership from *outside* the democratic polity and redistributed it to those within. Maintaining a republican distribution of wealth did not normally require tampering with property or the market *within* the polity. During and after the Civil War, the federal government shifted to redistributing income and property and regulating the market *inside* the national polity.

The politics of redistribution evokes reflexive opposition among many Americans. It seems as if government is taking income or property from those who earned it and giving it to those who didn't. This seems to be a commonsense violation of justice. There are two problems with this unexamined common sense. The first is that it assumes that the wealth and income returned to the individual by the operations of the market are equal in measure with the quality and quantity of one's efforts. But the market masks a myriad of decisions made by those who run large-scale business institutions that distribute wealth and income for purposes *other* than justice. For example, when an employer installs more productive machinery in his factory and decides how much to distribute the increased income derived from that machinery to his employees, how much to shareholders, how much to his consumers, and how much to profits, he is making a decision whose justice or injustice is hidden by the market. When CEO pay rises in relation to wage earner income from a 20:1 ratio to a 200:1 ratio as it has in the last forty years, is that hundredfold increase in the ratio the result of the greatly increased efforts of the CEOs or the result of the self-interested decisions made by those CEOs? In short, what is called the market invariably distributes and redistributes the results of labor according to criteria that usually have little to do with justice.

Second, in addition to the market, almost all budgetary actions by government redistribute income. When the federal government used tax revenues to fund the National Road, which helped open up the western territories, it redistributed income from taxpayers in the east to pioneers in the west. Likewise, funding education redistributes income from the general community to those with school-age children. It is very difficult for government to do anything without redistributing in some way. The turning point for redistributive actions on the federal level occurred during the Civil War. Not only did the federal government confiscate the slave property of secessionist Southerners, but it used the protective tariff, inflationary fiscal policies, and special subsidies to spur the industrialization of the country. These policies transferred wealth and income from the general community to manufacturing and transportation capitalists. In short, government taxing and spending almost always redistributes income.

Following the Civil War, Americans began to question the market outcomes of capitalism and industrialization. That questioning would eventually give rise to new forms of government action redistributing and regulating market practices. Americans became aware of three great social problems that seemed to attend the rise of capitalism: monopoly, a permanent working class, and the recurrence of depressions. These problems made it clear that the threats to a republican distribution of wealth could come from *within* society, not merely from the unjust actions by government. Eventually, a revised public opinion would propel the national government to interfere extensively in the workings of the market.

The rise of big business was the first sign that something had changed from the prewar economy of small producers. Using superior access to credit, more efficient and innovative technology, new methods of business organization, and predatory pricing, large firms appeared that dwarfed their competitors. John D. Rockefeller's Standard Oil, Andrew Carnegie's Carnegie Steel Company, and Gustavus Swift's Swift & Company (meatpacking) were examples of what contemporaries called "trusts" or "monopolies." They were so large that it was almost impossible for smaller business rivals to compete or consumers to buy somewhere else. The new market structure called into question the old belief in social mobility, which reconciled capitalism with democracy. The faith that in America each man was the architect of his own fortune had two versions. In the mid-nineteenth century, the idea was that if someone who started as a wageworker did not become an independent proprietor or a prosperous skilled worker, it was his own fault. That belief had become obsolete. The revised belief was that the existing distribution of wealth was democratic because everyone had the opportunity to become a Rockefeller or Carnegie: the rags-to-riches fable. But how common was it really?

It was becoming increasingly clear after the Civil War that the status of the wage earner was permanent. It was not a mere way station on the road to property ownership. To some degree, the fact that workers were a permanent class was masked from the public by the fact that most of the new factory, railroad, and other industrial workers were newcomers, immigrants from foreign lands. But the existence of urban slums with their public health problems and vice became undeniable once they were investigated and publicized by the early social settlement-house workers such as Jane Addams and Florence Kelley. The great railroad strikes, riots, and social upheavals that periodically convulsed urban centers such as Chicago in the late nineteenth century also had a profound public impact. There was little escaping what was called "the labor problem."

Americans also became aware of a third issue. Periods of prosperity were regularly followed by periods of depression—the business cycle. Investment in new factories and railroads and the production of consumer goods regularly seemed to outpace the ability of buyers to purchase them. Supply was supposed to be balanced by adequate demand, but in the real economy, supply seemed to regularly exceed demand, a phenomenon called "overproduction." When this happened, prices fell, businesses closed their doors, workers were laid off, and human misery was compounded. There were depressions in 1873–8, 1883–5, and 1893–8. All told, during the last quarter of the nineteenth century there were more months of depression than of prosperity. All classes were harmed by extended depressions, and all had an interest in ending or mitigating them.

In dealing with the new problems of capitalism—the monopoly question, the labor problem, and the ubiquity of depressions—Americans were forced to reexamine older beliefs. Americans and those in other Western nations believed that the laws of the market, as first articulated by the British economist Adam Smith in the late eighteenth century, were natural and inviolable, and any interference in them would be unjust and socially detrimental because it would deny some individuals the results of their labor. Just as Americans believed that natural law mandated governing by the consent of the governed, so it was thought that the laws of economics governed market activity.

But were these laws timeless and immutable—self-evident laws of nature as eighteenth-century thinkers viewed them—or were they subject to conscious human intervention? Could they be transformed by rational, instrumental values into a further development of democracy? The answer could be found in the revolutionary transformations of the nineteenth and twentieth centuries. Just as the great bourgeois revolutions and the act of constitution making asserted the rule of the citizen over the state, so in the nineteenth century did the rise of working class and other social movements assert the conscious control of the workers, farmers, and other producers over the economy. This was the second great thrust: democratization of the economy.

At this time, some Western social thinkers started to argue that the rise of a capitalist economy was a historical rather than a natural phenomenon and that its regulation signified a new and expanded definition of freedom. The interest of society as a whole would now take precedence over the laws of the market and the interest of individual private profit. As the great democratic revolutions of Europe and America transitioned from dealing with monarchy and aristocracy to dealing with capitalism and its monied aristocracy, they fashioned new terms for the movement to assert democratic control over the economy: social democracy, cooperative commonwealth, socialism, and still later, industrial democracy. In different words, while democracy is human freedom applied to the state, social democracy can be viewed as human freedom applied to the economy.

By the late 1880s, there was a reaction among all classes of people against the unfettered market. Businessmen worried that cutthroat competition would lower their market returns to the point where profit evaporated, workers wanted to regulate competition in the labor market in order to have shorter hours and higher wages, and consumers wanted government protection from the principle of *caveat emptor* or buyer beware.

To achieve the previously mentioned goals, workers and capitalists turned to self-organization to secure collective influence over the market. Workers turned to unions and collective bargaining. Only a few groups of workers were able to win collective bargaining in the extremely competitive conditions of the late nineteenth century. But this didn't prevent hundreds of thousands of workers from participating in mammoth labor upheavals during this period. In 1877, a nationwide railroad strike sparked general walkouts that shut down Pittsburgh, Baltimore, Chicago, St. Louis, Kansas City, and a host of smaller cities. The federal government had to call out troops to break the strike. Over one hundred workers were killed. In 1886, three hundred thousand workers, mainly in Chicago, struck for the eight-hour day on May 1. At the end of the decade, the international socialist movement adopted May 1 as its official labor holiday. In 1894, the American Railway Union shut down the country's railroads from Chicago to the West Coast for two weeks. The Pullman Strike was led by Eugene V. Debs, a man who would soon become America's most renowned socialist leader, running five times for the presidency. By the early twentieth century, the labor question had become America's most polarizing and explosive issue.

The associations formed by workers were more than matched by those formed by America's capitalists. America's capitalists combined to form large firms to limit price competition, better plan future investment, and reduce costs. Between 1896 and 1904, America's economy came to be dominated by large corporations. The small-to medium-sized family-owned firm was becoming marginal to the economy. The great impersonal corporations in steel, railroads, shipping, electrical generation, meatpacking, and other industries separated ownership of property from control of it.

Were these large corporations dangerous monopolies whose power threatened to corrupt and destroy the republic? This view was a remnant of older thinking in which the laws of competition were thought to be inviolable. New thinking identified a middle ground between pure competition and pure monopoly. This new ground was compatible with the existence of associations of workers (unions) and associations of capitalists (corporations). Thus, rather than view unions as labor monopolies, what was called the "new liberalism" viewed them as giving workers a collective voice that bargained with the collective voice of employers within an industry. Both voices were limited by what the market would bear. In different words, the new associations didn't destroy the market but reshaped it.

The same view could be applied to large corporations. These new firms combined the savings of hundreds of thousands of investors. They were usually so large that they were able to change the structure of the market. What had once been competitive was now oligopolistic. In other words, these large firms became pricemakers rather than pricetakers. But only if these firms were able to prevent competitors from entering the market were they pure monopolies. Like unions, they reshaped and restructured labor markets. For example, the corporations' professional managers sidestepped the labor market by doing most hiring and training within the company. Workers became used to climbing job ladders within a corporation to achieve social mobility. The labor market was largely internalized. In different words, corporations in the words of America's leading business historian, Alfred D. Chandler Jr., replaced what Adam Smith had called "the invisible hand" of the market with the visible hand of business organization.

Just as unions were semisocialist in that they operated against the profit principle and pushed to redistribute income from profits to wages, the big corporations had similar power over the market. By dispersing stock shares to the public, they distributed ownership of the nation's economy to larger and larger segments of the public, thereby partially socializing ownership. Their ability to raise prices above the competitive level allowed them to use the extra income for public uses such as government taxation, philanthropy, research and development, higher wages, and eventually corporate-supplied pensions, safety programs, leisure activities, profit sharing and health care.

In standing aside and allowing corporations and, to a lesser degree, unions to significantly influence market pricing and therefore the allocation of scarce resources, democratic governance had taken a crucial step. In the early nineteenth century, when the government gave up regulating the economy as it had done in mercantilist days, the courts adopted the common law principle that the competitive market was justified because it served the public good. By legalizing the activities of the large corporation, therefore, the state was transferring its public powers over the market to the corporation. But legalizing corporate power created a problem. Because the large corporation was a concentration of private power that often dwarfed the power of the market and even rivaled the power of government, the public interest was threatened. How was it possible to have the efficiency of the large corporation while maintaining the sovereignty of the people in their republic?

In the early twentieth century, Americans came up with a typical liberal solution: set up regulatory commissions to look over the shoulder of the corporation so that it did not abuse its special powers. In other words, while the corporation retained its price-setting and investment-allocating powers, thus vindicating the principle of private-sector self-regulation, the government set up watchdog commissions to establish minimal market standards, keep market concentration from becoming a pure monopoly, and prevent exploitation of consumers and the public at large. For example, the Interstate Commerce Commission set maximum railroad shipping prices and outlawed certain practices, such as rebating to favored large shippers, but did not interfere in the day-to-day operation of the railroad business. Later the same solution would be applied to labor unions with the National Labor Relations Act. By the 1930s, an expanded regulatory state had emerged as an integral part of the liberal state.

From the founding of the nation through the nineteenth century, Americans had been divided into parties of activist national government (the Federalists, Whigs, and Republicans) and parties of small government with activism limited to state-level affairs (Democratic-Republicans and Democrats). The activist parties, originating with Alexander Hamilton, wanted to redistribute wealth upward in order to economically develop the new nation, even if it meant creating a monied aristocracy. The parties of small government, originating with Thomas Jefferson, feared rising inequality so much that they wanted to keep national government limited and small so that capitalists couldn't use it.

In the early twentieth century—the Progressive Era—these two political tendencies with their different means to different ends underwent a startling reversal. Once large corporations were able to restructure the economy and society, Americans recognized that the goal of protecting democracy, including a large-enough middle class, required not maintaining a status quo of small producers but using activist government to restrain and regulate the market behavior of the large corporations (later to provide Americans with social insurance). By the same token, once national majorities were willing and able to use an activist federal government to regulate large business enterprise, the spokesmen of the corporate interests became advocates of small government. In the words of contemporary political thinker Herbert Croly, the first type of party employed Hamiltonian (big government) means to achieve Jeffersonian (democratic) ends, while the other political tendency used Jeffersonian means (limited government and states rights) to achieve Hamiltonian ends (as defined by large corporations). This great political reversal of the late nineteenth and early twentieth centuries has given us what are now called our liberal and conservative political wings.[10]

The rise of the corporation's visible hand and a federal regulatory apparatus supervising market activity can be viewed as the flowering of a democratic mix of capitalism and socialism, both in the private and public sector. In the private sector, large corporate firms began to voluntarily provide welfare benefits to their employees. By the 1970s, these benefits covered most American workers and included pensions, health coverage, and paid sick and vacation days. Even though these were private benefits, they represented a shift from profits to the pool of compensation accruing to workers; hence they were as socialistic as government benefits. Of course, not all Americans were covered by corporate-supplied benefits; the advantage of government social insurance is that it is universal. By the end of the 1930s, corporations were also bargaining collectively with industrial unions. Under the influence of unions, corporations set up grievance procedures and other rules that extended the rule of law to the nation's workplaces.

At the same time, the federal government was intervening in the private economy in ways to better secure the public good. For example, the Federal Reserve Act of 1913, a private-public partnership, allowed the board of the Federal Reserve to set interest rates and control the supply of money, thus evening out the business cycle and limiting the severity and length of depressions. The Sherman Anti-Trust Act (1890) and the Clayton Act (1914) restricted anticompetitive business practices that tended toward monopoly. In the 1930s, a plethora of government acts regulated the economy or established the right of workers to join unions and engage in collective bargaining. The Social Security Act (1935) and Fair Labor Standards Act (1937) established a social safety net. By setting a floor under the competitive labor market under which no one should fall—for example, the minimum wage or old-age pensions—the American public established the democratic principle that no one should be driven into destitution, that the American community was not only for the wealthy and prosperous middle class, and that all deserved equal opportunity. In different words, the New Deal was about the expansion of positive liberty to balance negative liberty.

Throughout history the meaning of freedom or citizenship has been subject to expansion; it has been cumulative. It took until the mid-nineteenth century for Americans to accept the right to form voluntary associations, and the enforcement of civil liberties by the federal government only occurred in the twentieth century. The new ideal that emerged from the 1930s was *social citizenship*. Government, collective bargaining, and not-for-profit cooperative enterprises would provide public goods like pensions, health care, and low-interest mortgages that were not being provided by the for-profit sector. In doing so, citizens would claim rights (sometimes called "entitlements" by critics) defined by the expanding social standards of a developing democracy (see Franklin Delano Roosevelt, State of the Union Message to Congress in Documents).

The arc of the second wave continued through the 1960s, but in the following decade, it ran into powerful headwinds. A reverse wave restored many of the inequalities in authority, income, and wealth that had been weakened or moderated in the previous century. New policies of government and corporate management reined in workers' power and through deregulation restored the freedom of corporate leaders to restructure and reduce employee benefits, limit wage increases, and raise profits. That era in which class inequality began to grow again is explored in chapter five.

## The Democratization of Culture

The mid-twentieth century began a third wave of democracy, an era extending into the present in which democratic values, beliefs, and ways of life extended into cultural realms not normally viewed as a terrain for its development. But if democracy is about the equal opportunity to develop and fulfill one's potential, then those institutions that deny, limit, or distort that opportunity, whether they be governmental, economic, or in the realm of culture, must be rethought and reconstructed. The 1960s saw deep and lasting challenges to family institutions, race relations, gender relations, sexual expression, moral standards, and the way personal identities were constructed and defined. The result was a long revolution whose shorthand definition was the 1960s slogan of women's liberation: "the personal is the political." In different words, personal life was becoming democratized.

The third wave was a response to fundamental changes occurring in the conditions underlying the family and personal life. One development occurred within the capitalist economy, while the other occurred within the family.

In the early twentieth century, the American economy underwent a fundamental transformation. Not only did it become corporate dominated, but it entered a postindustrial phase of development. In this "new era," as President Herbert Hoover called it, less and less capital and human labor were required for the expansion of productive capacity and output. The declining requirement for labor as a result of the new technologies that contributed to mass production meant that the old industrial working class started its long decline as a percentage of the workforce. By the early postwar period, employment in the service sector had overtaken employment in manufacturing, transportation, and mining and is now over 80 percent of employment.

The decline in capital requirements added another dimension to the postindustrial economy. If capital was becoming less necessary for economic prosperity, then consumption no longer had to be restrained in order to expand investment and grow the economy. For the same reason, oversavings or surplus capital, rather than the old problem of not enough capital, became the central issue of the postindustrial economy. Under these new conditions, investment of savings in new means of production atrophied, and consumption replaced investment as the major component—now over 70 percent—of aggregate demand for goods and services. This was the state of things recognized by the British economist John Maynard Keynes when he published his masterwork during the Great Depression of the 1930s.

The solution to depression taught by Keynes and his American followers was expanding the *demand* for goods and services; the *supply* of them would follow from increasing demand. At first, this demand took the form of investment in war goods during World War II, which helped jumpstart the struggling economy. But after the war, consumer spending took up the slack. America's postindustrial capitalism became consumer capitalism. Through higher wages and consumer lending, large segments of the country's poor and working people became part of an expanding middle class. A single statistic can stand in for this success story. At the start of World War II, the home ownership rate was 43.6 percent; by 1960, it had reached 61.9 percent.[11] Though almost a third of all Americans remained in substandard conditions, in the words of economist John Kenneth Galbraith, America had become an "affluent society."

The sociologist Daniel Bell was one of the first to write convincingly about the consequences of postindustrialism and consumerism. Bell wrote that work and accumulation, instead of being ends in themselves as they were in the industrial period, had become a means to the end of a rising quality of life. As early as the 1920s, the bourgeois character structured by self-restraint, savings, hard work, and achievement began to give way to the once-bohemian values of pleasure and play. Traditional morality gave way to psychology; guilt was replaced by anxiety. By the 1960s, culture had become the most dynamic element in American society, replacing the economy.

Bell and other critics, many of whom became neoliberals (see chapter five), were alarmed that the new values threatened the work ethic as the moral basis of the capitalist social order. This may well be, but since then observers have cast the new values as the basis of a new social order. The political scientist Ronald Franklin Inglehart views affluence and a consumer-based morality as the foundation for postmaterial values (see Documents). In this book we draw on Inglehart's theory, though we differ in one important respect.[12] Freed of the need to attend to economic and physical security, middle-class Americans and those with a similar status in other advanced societies have adopted the values of personal autonomy over deference to authority, a greater concern for personal growth than security, environmental protection as a higher value than exploitation of nature, and the life value of self-fulfillment through personal expression and personal growth. These were non-economic, quality of life values, whose expression in American life is explored more in depth in chapters two and seven.

The first mass expression of the new values came with Lyndon Johnson's Great Society and other 1960s movements, including the sexual revolution, counterculture, environmentalism, and women's liberation. It is hard to escape the conclusion that postmaterial values represent a new phase of democratic aspiration. Insofar as the structures of government remain tethered to material values, postmaterialism also helps explain the large disconnect between government and its citizenry in the present era.

The postindustrial economy that created consumerist and postmaterial values dovetailed with changes in the family that liberated personal life from the constraints associated with older patterns of patriarchal subordination. When the economy was not separate from the family but rather was embedded within it in the form of a household economy, typically on a family farm, relations within the family were constricted by the overriding necessity of making a living. The family was a zone of survival. Sexuality was restricted to and oriented toward procreation. Emotions were to be held in check, and spouses related to each other with great formality; children were supposed to strictly obey parents—to be seen and not heard. Marriages required the approval of parents, since marriage determined the passage of income-producing property from family to family; women in particular were under tight patriarchal control within the family since men were in the household. These attitudes toward gender, family, and sex have been widely shared across early modern cultures undergoing the transition to industrial capitalism regardless of religion or culture.

With the separation of work from family, the family as a zone of physical and economic survival and its materialist values gave way to the modern nuclear family with separate spheres for men and women and its value of intimacy. As patriarchal controls over marriage decisions eroded, and women's household labor became less necessary, spouses married for love and happiness. Children's relationship to parents was also expected to be one of intimacy; indeed, living in urban areas, parents had fewer children and lavished affection on the smaller number. Children came to be idealized and romanticized instead of exploited for their agricultural labor. The family came to be seen as a refuge from work, "a haven in a heartless world," as the historian Christopher Lasch put it. This was the Victorian family culture that emerged in the mid-nineteenth century and influenced ideals into the mid-twentieth century.

By the early twentieth century, the family as a zone of intimacy had generated values that led to the first great sexual revolution. Chaperoning of young men and women was replaced by unsupervised dating. The rates of pregnancy among unmarried women rose. The prevailing veneration of women as wide-hipped, slightly buxom mothers gave way to the glorification of women as young, slim, sexually attractive flappers. Divorce rates almost doubled between 1890 and

1910 as women began to expect more of marriage than just financial support for children.

During and following World War II, large numbers of married women entered the workforce for the first time. Before this, the large majority of women in the workforce were single, and when they married, they left it. But family-based labor was becoming less and less necessary. Mothers were having significantly fewer children per family and living longer (the average age at death for women in 1900 was 49.7 years, while by the decade of the 1980s, it was in the low eighties). Women now had the time to think about the possibility of fulfilling themselves outside the home rather than only through their children. The postindustrial shift of work to the service sector opened up jobs that were more suited to women. These jobs dealt with the public in sales and often involved activities such as cooking, nursing, teaching, and interacting with the public, skills that women had in abundance. The new consumerism also pulled housewives into the economy in order to supply the additional income to meet the rising family standard of living. By 1970, 40 percent of married women were in the workforce, but that figure rose to 58 percent in 1990 and 62 percent in 2009. The old idea of separate spheres for men and women was at an end. Gender identities were freed up; sexuality began to be formed more by societal expectations than parental guidance, and women as well as men had joined the rush toward postmaterial values. The sphere of personal life, instead of being formed by the older morality of the family, was now ripe for politicization.

The older bourgeois character type structured around self-restraint and the two-sphere, male breadwinner family ideal had been the basis for a single identity that defined what it was to be an American. This identity, which lasted into the mid-twentieth century, constituted what it was to be an individual. But this purportedly universal identity—the pot into which everyone was invited to melt—was based on the privileged experiences of whites, males, and middle-class Americans. Politicians, businesses, and school textbooks depicted the ideal citizen, socially mobile individual, or community leader as a white middle-class male. The life experiences of blacks, women, and others outside the norm were rendered invisible, and social expectations structured around this ideal put these groups at a disadvantage. The boxer Muhammad Ali put it this way:

> We've been brainwashed. Everything good is supposed to be white. We look at Jesus, and we see a white with blond hair and blue eyes. We look at all the angels; we see white with blond hair and blue eyes. . . . Where are the colored angels? They must be in the kitchen preparing milk and honey. We look at Miss America, we see white. . . . Even Tarzan, the king of the jungle in black Africa, he's white.[13]

Stokely Carmichael in his justification for Black Power (see Documents) argued that blacks couldn't rely on whites' definition of the American Dream. They had to begin to define it for themselves. By the 1970s, the universality of the old identity lay in ruins. The old industrial and family relationships and rise of post-material values opened the way for the movements of the 1960s that questioned that identity.

The great variety of 1960s movements are commonly divided into the civil rights, Black Power, antiwar, feminist, gay, Chicano, Native American, environmental, and the counterculture. But these movements had something in common. They shared the fact that they were preeminently democratic movements. They were democratic in that they challenged existing authority structures in all realms of life. The political scientist Samuel P. Huntington wrote,

> People no longer felt the same compulsion to obey those whom they had previously considered superior to themselves in age, rank, status, expertise, character, or talents. Within most organizations discipline eased and differences in status became blurred. Each group claimed its right to participate equally—and perhaps more than equally—in the decisions which affected itself. . . . The questioning of authority pervaded society.[14]

In this great third wave, the previous two democratic waves gathered renewed impetus. Most 1960s movements combined the aims and demands of the three waves. The civil rights movement started as a project to complete the first wave's democratic tasks that Reconstruction had left unfinished—that is, the legal protection of civil liberties and voting rights for African Americans and all Americans—but then moved on to the other two waves.

The walls of Jim Crow, the first great challenge to the civil rights movement, did not fall easily. Led by the Rev. Martin Luther King Jr., the movement employed the disruptive tactic of sit-ins and freedom rides. King justified defiance of existing authority in the name of a higher truth by invoking the pacifist philosophy of nonviolent civil disobedience.

Nonviolent direct action revived the old idea that democracy, even representative democracy, required participation by ordinary citizens. But direct action was not about governing. It was about oppressed people learning to overcome their own fears and passivity to take part in a struggle against their own oppression. Direct action reinvigorated the old democratic principle that freedom needed to be won by the oppressed themselves rather than handed to them as a gift from above. The sit-ins, which involved tens of thousands throughout the South in the early 1960s, allowed blacks to transgress the grinning, accommodating, decorous behavior they were expected to perform before whites but without inviting violent retaliation. By refusing to physically resist the police, they kept that retribution to a minimum, thus opening up a relatively safe path to resisting unjust authority. At the same time, they appealed to the democratic community to adjust its standards. As King put it in his famous "Letter from Birmingham Jail," "Nonviolent direct action seeks to create such a crisis and establish such creative tension that a community that has constantly refused to negotiate is forced to confront the issue." The approach that the new 1960s student organization Students for a Democratic Society called "participatory democracy" would spread to the antiwar movement, feminist movement, and other minority movements with explosive consequences.

Scarcely had the task of legalizing civil rights been completed, when, under the impact of the ghetto riots, the movement and its allies in government turned to a second-wave goal: the eradication of poverty. Even before this, the civil rights movement had built alliances with the progressive unions. Quickly thereafter, the new third wave took center stage: questioning the white, male, middle-class identity that masqueraded as universal. Malcolm X took the radical step of disaffiliating from the sanitized textbook view of American identity. "We didn't land on Plymouth Rock," he said, "the rock was landed on us." Malcolm exhorted blacks to throw off their submissiveness and lack of ambition, which he associated with the word "Negro," and be proud of their skin color and heritage. This was symbolized by the new term to designate that new status, "black."

The advent in the mid-1960s of feminism also combined the concerns of the three waves, with the third wave emerging after the first two were established. Feminism was predicated on the claim first made at Seneca Falls in 1848 that women were entitled to the same eighteenth-century rights that men were. Women were individuals with the right to life, liberty, and the pursuit of happiness, including the right to a career outside the home and control over their own bodies. The movement began to organize when the federal agency designed to implement the 1964 Civil Rights Act did not enforce equal workplace rights for women. The National Organization of Women (NOW) demanded, among other things, that male-only jobs be opened to women, a second-wave demand.

In 1968, the third wave of democracy appeared when members of the women's liberation movement picketed the Miss America Pageant on the boardwalk at Atlantic City. Women challenged the "degrading mindless-Boob-Girlie Symbol" portrayed by the pageant. "Women in our society," said their leaflet, are "forced daily to compete for male approval, enslaved by ludicrous 'beauty' standards we ourselves are conditioned to take seriously." A hundred women protesters threw symbols of the beauty industry—wigs, false eyelashes, and makeup—into a "freedom trash can" and staged a ceremony crowning a live sheep as Miss America.[15]

Women's libbers, as the media called them derisively, challenged the patterns of day-to-day relationships between women and men and also the smiling, self-abnegating, subordinate identity that women had accepted during three thousand years of patriarchy, a new concept popularized by the movement. The slogan that encapsulated the new cultural terrain on which the movement struggled was "the personal is the political." As with the black liberation movement, the third wave claimed the sphere of personal life for democratic politics. In the language and tone that had been used to confront political tyranny, radical women confronted men's refusal to do housework; the self-sacrificing within the family that women did for men but men didn't do for women; male domination of the church; the view of God as a father rather than a mother figure; the unwillingness of the culture to take violence against women seriously; the criminalization of abortion; and the many daily small ways that women were objectified, trivialized, depreciated, and exploited. They championed a new identity appropriate to a postmaterialist era—that of the liberated woman.

In 1969, the homosexuals joined the parade of movements following their rebellion at the Stonewall Inn in the Greenwich Village neighborhood in New York City. Homosexual patrons at bars were accustomed to being harassed, extorted for money, and beaten by police. But now they drew a line in the sand; urged on by transgender women they resisted, sparking a full-scale community uprising. Following the affair, many homosexuals threw off their shame and fear and publicly challenged the widespread belief that being homosexual was a psychological disorder and that they deserved their public condemnation as perverts. Just as African Americans refused to be called Negroes and adopted a new identity as blacks with the slogan "black pride," and feminist women created the identity of the liberated woman, homosexuals claimed a new identity as gay. In the new parlance, they were "out of the closet." They were gay and proud.

Identity movements with their postmaterial-values politics were able in significant ways to enlarge the rules and norms of the democratic community through the rights revolution. The unlikely site of the revolution was the US Supreme Court. Rarely in American history had the Supreme Court been a paragon of defense of individual rights other than property rights. But in the 1965 *Griswold* decision, the Warren court created the right of privacy based on already-existing constitutional rights. The new right to privacy created a legal gateway for the expansion of individual freedom. It was the basis for declaring unconstitutional laws that limited access to birth control and laws against sodomy that criminalized homosexuality. It was also the basis for the 1973 *Roe v. Wade* decision, which gave women the right to abort fetuses up through the second trimester of pregnancy. These developments, along with legislated no-fault divorces and protections for children, fundamentally changed the institution of the family into another voluntary association composed of legally autonomous individuals.

Jurisprudence surrounding the 1964 Civil Rights Act further developed the rights revolution. Individuals now had the court-enforced right to be free of discrimination on the basis of race, religion, national origin, and sex in employment and public accommodations. Later court decisions legalized a mandate for affirmative action for blacks and women and codes to prevent sexual harassment, which also protected homosexuals. The rights revolution of the 1960s also included expanded rights for criminal defendants, the right not to be discriminated against on the basis of age, and the right to a safe and healthy work environment. It continued into the 1980s and 1990s with laws establishing rights for the disabled (1990) and the right of employees to family and medical leave from employment (1993).

The rights revolution did not depend only on the courts or the agencies of the federal government. Within corporations, human resource departments took over vigorous enforcement of nondiscrimination in hiring and firing, maternity leaves, and the like. Other corporate departments set up rules to implement federally mandated health and safety and pension rules. In this way, the rights revolution found expression within the more established practices of the mix of capitalism and socialism. The federal government set the guidelines and remained a watchdog, but rule setting and day-to-day enforcement occurred in the corporate sector, thus guarding against statism.

Identity politics went hand in hand with the expanded sphere of democratic individuality given backbone by the rights revolution. It rejected an older, one-size-fits-all culture to which all were expected to conform and replaced it with a new ideal of multiculturalism; it provided a new psychological space from which to appraise, question, and defy existing institutional authority; and it liberated individual potentials. These new energies and creative potentials have been evident in music, arts, literature, academic scholarship, and new lifestyles. But the politics of identity and expanded individualism was also extremely controversial. Liberal communitarians criticized it for denying individual responsibility to the larger American community; conservatives thought the new politics would destroy family values, and they have characterized "rights talk" as a self-pitying appeal to victimization; some from the old (second wave) left criticized it for disuniting and fragmenting the left.

The most telling criticisms of identity politics or multiculturalism came from within the new movements. First, blacks, then lesbians, then women from less developed countries criticized feminists for defining *woman* and what her concerns should be by filtering them through the experiences of white, heterosexual, middle-class women. Later, the queer movement criticized the lesbian and gay movement for perpetuating the binary in which people had to choose between being a woman or a man and between being a homosexual or a heterosexual with no alternatives in between. In short, identity movements seemed to be creating their own new but still limiting and distorting structures. In postmodern terms, identity movements were essentialist. The term *queer* was an attempt by gay, lesbian, and transgender individuals to construct a nonnormative umbrella identity to remedy this difficulty. By the 1990s, the new trend was to break down, destabilize, or deconstruct all identities, even alternative identities. Among lesbian, gay, bisexual, transgender, and queer (LGBTQ) individuals the only common denominator seems to be that people should have the freedom to forge their own identities, lifestyles, and other forms of personal expression without most of the limits provided by traditional morality.

From a democratic perspective, what seems to be of lasting value from the history of the identity movements are not the specific redefinitions of identities but the authorization given by a new kind of democratic community to individuals to define their own lives and to make of themselves what they will, which qualifies as an enlarging of the sphere of democratic individualism.

The explosion of new identities that shattered a unitary cultural ideal and its replacement with nonnormative identities, the expansion of democratic individualism along postmaterial lines, and challenges to authority in all realms of life, including the family, made up a perfect storm that roiled and rent American society. As the wave subsided in the 1970s, it was succeeded by an enormous conservative counterwave. That decade inaugurated a long period of cultural contention, sometimes simmering, sometimes flaring into bitter battles, between traditionalists with their material values and cultural progressives with postmaterial values that shaped electoral politics from the 1970s through the early 2000s.

There were two wings of the new conservatism. One wing attempted to reverse the welfare shift in federal spending (new programs like Medicare and Medicaid and the War on Poverty), the rights revolution, and the loss of faith in the national government. The new conservative politics, which we have termed neoliberalism, will be examined in more depth in chapters five and six. The other wing, social conservatism, tried to salvage the remnants of the patriarchal family, the values of traditional authority, and a unitary national culture, all grounded in orthodox religion. Conservatives shared a worldview that the family, morality, and America itself were on the verge of an apocalypse with only their activism preventing complete collapse. Conservative leader Patrick Buchanan characterized it this way in a famous speech to the 1992 Republican convention: "There is a religious war going on in our country for the soul of America. It is a cultural war, as critical to the kind of nation we will one day be as was the Cold War itself." The new issues that social conservatives targeted for cultural contention—women leaving the family for work, legalized abortion, moral permissiveness, pornography, frank and open talk about sex, and gay and transgender rights—resulted from the expansion of the realm of the public into spheres previously thought to be private. The very fact that public deliberation since then has so often turned on issues emerging from personal life is a testament to the success of 1960s movements in politicizing that realm.

The social conservative reaction began in 1972 when Phyllis Schlafly inaugurated a grassroots campaign to oppose a constitutional amendment that would guarantee American women equal rights (known as the Equal Rights Amendment or ERA). In that year, the ERA had already been ratified by thirty of the necessary thirty-eight states. As a result of her campaign, the amendment was defeated. In 1977, Anita Bryant began a successful campaign to overturn an amendment in Miami, Florida, which banned discrimination on the basis of sexual orientation. She broadened her effort into a national antigay movement in cities across the United States. Her success led to an effort to pass the Briggs initiative in California, which would have made pro or neutral statements regarding homosexuals or homosexuality by any public school employee cause for dismissal. It was defeated.

These movements were the tip of the iceberg of a resurgence of Protestant fundamentalism, which had its strongest base in the South and had been growing since the 1950s, while the mainline, more liberal denominations had been in decline. Previously an apolitical religious trend, fundamentalism had by the 1970s become a highly politicized religious doctrine. The first major public vehicle of the Christian right was the Moral Majority headed by Jerry Falwell. The group wanted to make abortion and homosexual acts illegal, censor those media outlets with an antifamily agenda, and support Republican Party candidates. Since the 1980s, the Moral Majority has given way to Pat Dobson's Focus on the Family and Pat Robertson's Christian Coalition and Christian Broadcasting Network.

From the 1970s onward, the Republican Party has increasingly accommodated the conservative movement until it has practically become synonymous with it. The success of Republicans in winning national elections between 1968 and 2004 and the partial acceptance by Democrats of conservative ideology and policies has convinced many observers that the last four decades can be characterized as a triumph of conservatism. This is seriously misleading, at least when it comes to the sphere of culture.

Despite its electoral strength, cultural conservatism has steadily lost its attraction, as the tectonic shifts in the economy and family discussed earlier continue to spread and deepen. In turn, postmaterial values have taken the place left by the retreat of a lifeless orthodoxy. According to Inglehart, the leading scholar of postmaterialism, in the 1970s materialists substantially outnumbered postmaterialists, but by the turn of the twenty-first century, postmaterialists were double the number of materialists (see Documents). One indication that the 1960s democratic upsurge was not a flash in the pan but the dawn of a new era was that, since the 1960s, what sociologists called "new social movements" (NSMs) have proliferated. NSMs challenge the authority and hierarchy embedded in the norms governing everyday relationships and personal life and seek to expand individual choice and personal growth. They often bypass electoral politics and material questions focusing on the distribution of wealth. NSMs are based in the educated middle class and thrive in loose networks rather than formal organizations. The NSMs that have grown since the 1960s include environmentalism, especially the part that includes green living (see chapter seven); consumer activism; support for healthy and natural foods; alternative health care, the LGBTQ movement; New Age or alternative spirituality; pacifism; and feminism.

Despite their cultural emphasis, there has also been a political side to the new movements. By the 1970s, civil rights and Black Power activists—for example, John Lewis, Marion Barry Jr., Andrew Young, and Jesse Jackson—were moving seamlessly into politics and government. Something similar happened with antiwar activists. John Kerry, the 2004 candidate for president and later secretary of state, began his political career as a prominent antiwar activist in 1970–1. Tom Hayden, a founder and leader of Students for a Democratic Society, became a major figure in California politics. More important, post-1960s organizations such as the National Association for the Advancement of Colored People, the National Council of La Raza and other Latino groups, the National Organization for Women, Planned Parenthood, the National Abortion and Reproductive Rights Action League, League of Conservation Voters, the Sierra Club, the National Gay and Lesbian Task Force, People for the American Way, and the Children's Defense Fund have emerged as powerful voices in the Democratic Party for new thinking. Together with older groups, such as labor unions, they constitute the country's political left.[16]

The strongest evidence that the movements and beliefs of the 1960s and early 1970s have had an electoral consequence is that the groups they mobilized— blacks, Latinos, sexual minorities, women (especially single women), and college-educated professionals—have grown in size and make up the core of the new majority coalition that has come to national power under President Barack Obama in the 2008 and 2012 elections, a topic discussed in more depth in chapters five and six.

The long revolution unleashed by the 1960s, which is still in process, has been part of the ongoing movement of democracy in American history. In challenging older authority structures and enlisting broader participation in decision making, democracy has continually broadened the sphere of the public so that it takes in areas of life once deemed private, while also expanding the private into the public. In the first half of the nineteenth century, the emergence of civil society and mass political parties redefined the public to include elements of private life. At the same time, the self-interest pursued in private life became part of the public. From the mid-nineteenth century through the mid-twentieth century, the economy increasingly became a sphere with public characteristics as the corporation took on public functions once relegated to the market and in turn was regulated by government as the semipublic institution it had become. Since then, the sphere of personal life has become politicized as older family structures have broken down under postindustrialism. The overall result has been a kind of democracy that can no longer be understood simply as a form of government. It has become and is becoming a *way of life*.

# 2

# DEMOCRACY IN CULTURE

## American Individualisms

*If a man does not keep pace with his companions, perhaps it is because he hears a different drummer. Let him step to the music which he hears, however measured or far away.*

Henry David Thoreau, *Walden (1854)*

If there is such a thing as an American character or an American secular religion, it is indelibly stamped with the idea and practice of individualism. Individualism, along with liberty and equality, is also one of the core ideas of democracy. American history is a record of the defeat or erosion of ideas that have competed with individualism. Today, the ideology of individualism, though not always the practice of individuality, reigns supreme in American life.

When Americans think of freedom, they think of the autonomy and independence of the individual from all forms of coercion, starting with the democratic state. The distinction between the individual and government is the beginning of democratic individuality. The very fact that an authority exists outside oneself but is nonetheless limited—by rule of law, constitutional liberties, and recurring elections of those who wield political power—establishes for the modern individual a distance and independence from authority. That distance breeds the values of autonomy, independence, and a willingness to be critical of authority. As these values have spread into the rest of American life through the waves of democracy described in this book, individuality has itself become more complex and multidimensional.

Despite the cultural consensus on individualism and its necessity in a democratic society, Americans throughout their history have been concerned about the individual's relation to the larger community. On the one hand, they have feared that the individual's freedom would be taken too far and detract from the common good of the community. On the other hand, they have worried that individuality would be unduly stifled.

All democratic theorists have identified the pursuit of personal liberty without regard to common good as a major, if not the main, danger to democracy. Madison worried that individuals who united passion and interest would create dangerous factions in the body politic. Five decades later, the French observer Alexis de Tocqueville observed that Americans were able to contain the tendency for individualism to become overly selfish and private by participating in the organs of local government and voluntary associations. It seemed that in aristocratic societies people were so tightly bound together by tradition and class that they did not require association. But in a democratic society, individuals were so weak and separate from one another that they could accomplish nothing without association. Tocqueville thought that associating together would produce a flow of common feelings based on the realization that by benefitting others, individuals would benefit themselves—what Tocqueville called "enlightened self-interest."

Understanding the individual's relation to the larger community also requires us to distinguish between individuality and individualism. The former refers to the fulfillment of one's potentialities, balanced by the ability to say no, when necessary, to authority and conventions. On the other hand, individualism is a powerful ideology or myth. It is susceptible to the illusion that individuals can fulfill their potentials without the community, can pursue their self-interest without regard to others, and owe little or nothing to others. In the self-made-man myth, individuals often believe that they have achieved or can achieve wealth or high position completely by their own efforts and are justified in curtailing any obligation to the community. They use their ingenuity to game the system so as to maximize their benefits from the community and minimize their own contributions. They ignore the way they have benefitted from family connections, from the continual improvement of science and technology, and from the democratic community itself, which has provided them common goods such as education, infrastructure, and the defense of the nation. In this way, individuality is set against the many forms of democratic association.

The opposite fear has also periodically preoccupied Americans. Americans have sought to free themselves from the overbearing weight of authority relationships, which people in many other countries take for granted as being necessary for a viable society—participation in family, kin, and village institutions governed by tradition. Democracy itself has sometimes been viewed as a threat to individuality. This can take many forms. Government can impose stifling regulations on creative enterprise. It can limit freedom of speech due to excessive fear of an external or internal enemy. It can also prohibit forms of behavior—for example, partaking of harmless, recreational drugs—which unnecessarily intrude on personal life. What is called "tyranny of the majority" can also take the form of socially prescribed standards of behavior. Given the near absence of tradition and the weakness of government in the United States, Americans typically rely on norms to govern personal behavior. These socially prescribed patterns of everyday behavior can at times take on the same oppressive power that state or religious tyrannies have in other societies and create a culture of conformity and regimentation.

Two of the best-known American novels, which have had critical acclaim and great popularity, celebrate individualism in the face of stifling social norms. In the nineteenth century, Mark Twain's *The Adventures of Huckleberry Finn* (1884) and, in the twentieth century, Jack Kerouac's *On the Road* (1957) explore the theme of individuals finding freedom by escaping civilization. Each in its own way celebrates the individual liberated from the demands of family, work, and community and relying on oneself.

In the following examples, it is possible to glimpse the tensions inherent in American individualism:

- Compared to most other countries, American individuals enjoy an unrestricted right to freedom of speech. Americans can publicly criticize the government and its officials, even call for its overthrow, and publish and purchase literature deemed pornographic by virtually all cultures. Even when a form of speech is clearly immoral, it will not be censored. Only when there is demonstrable harm to others—as in personal libel or hate speech—is legal recourse against speech possible, after the fact.

- A visitor to the United States, arriving by airplane, would notice that in any city, even the largest, the bulk of population lives in single-family dwellings sprawling outward from the central city, where the large skyscrapers are concentrated. In 2009, 67 percent of American households resided in single-family dwellings that they owned. A similar pattern can be found in agriculture and rural life. Homes are located on the farm itself. American farmers are relatively isolated from each other, in contrast to the inherited patterns in Europe and much of the rest of the world, where the farm population lives in villages or small towns.

- Though it may seem odd to others, American corporations are considered to be legal persons having many of the same rights, protections, privileges, responsibilities, and liabilities under law as natural persons do. Most advanced countries have similar provisions, but in the United States, this legal fiction is carried further in that corporate entities have the right to freedom of speech in elections, advertising, and other matters. So pervasive is the equation of the corporation with individualism that many Americans treat government regulation of corporations as equivalent to an assault on individual freedom, notwithstanding the fact that corporations are creatures of government.

- Still another face of American individualism is the right to own guns of all types, not merely to hunt, but to defend themselves against other individuals. The courts have recently reinterpreted the Second Amendment to the US Constitution to mean that the right to keep and bear arms is a fundamental right, making it difficult to regulate firearms. The United States has the highest individual gun ownership rate—39 percent—in the world. It also has by far the highest rate of gun-related deaths in the world—thirty thousand per year—with two-thirds being suicides.

- Americans have not always privileged individualism in relation to the state. There have been notorious examples of government infringement on the basic rights of individuals. These examples are often referred to as the "tyranny of the majority." One example was the internment during World War II of 110,000 Japanese American citizens living on the Pacific Coast. Even though only ten Japanese Americans were convicted of spying for Japan, Americans feared their collaboration with a threatened Japanese invasion. Another example was the denial of basic rights to many during the Red Scare or McCarthy period from the late 1940s to the late 1950s. Thousands of government officials, entertainers, educators, and union leaders were targets of government investigations and were fired and blacklisted. More recently, the fear of terrorism has led Americans to tolerate roving wiretaps of phone calls and secret searches of records, which many believe are an invasion of the basic right of privacy.

The fear of individuality eclipsing the needs of the democratic community, as well as the opposite worry that individuality might be buried under the dictates of social norms or institutional elites, is one major theme of our discussion. Another is the sheer variety of individualisms available in American democracy. The rest of this chapter examines four models of individualism. Contemporary Americans choose among them and often combine them in ways that suit their personalities and circumstances. Each model has its unacknowledged shadow side; each has its critics, as well as advocates; and each has had a problematic relation to the larger democratic community.

## The Rise of the Self-Made Man

During colonial times, individualism was strictly contained. In seventeenth- and eighteenth-century New England, a man gained personal fulfillment through performing public duties, his role as head of the household, and the social status of his family, rather than individual achievement. Early New Englanders valued those who carried out their social obligations, learned submission or deference to superiors, and presented an amiable personality by closely governing their passions. They considered pride, ambition, and self-assertion to be sins, not virtues.

For example, the head of the household was responsible for the religious devotion of his family and was expected to deal benevolently and fairly with his wife and all those who depended on him. He would answer to the community if he failed to perform his duties. Wives and children were supposed to be submissive. A husband could be fined or ducked in the village pond for allowing his wife to usurp his authority.

The American personality of self-abnegation began to dissipate in the middle part of the eighteenth century. During the Great Awakening (a religious revival), preachers of low status challenged the authority of their betters in the established churches. Those who followed them into new Protestant denominations, most notably the Baptists, had to stand up for their beliefs against those they had submitted to. The challenge to the social order was also evident in the new belief that personal behavior, not class or status, determined whether someone could be saved.

The American Revolution significantly accelerated the pace of change. Revolutionary leaders such as Sam Adams and Thomas Paine encouraged Americans to refuse to submit to British tyranny. Americans largely abandoned the tradition that every relationship had to have a superior and a subordinate and embraced equality. By the early 1800s, Americans adopted the belief that all men (though not yet women) should be individuals, independent of others' wills.

Much of the inspiration for the revolution came from republicanism. Republican thinking focused on the need for citizens to rise above their self-interest and passions and learn to think foremost of the public good. Yet, notwithstanding the strength of the period's republican ideology, it was clear in a multitude of ways that the pursuit of self-interest, once deemed a vice, was simply unavoidable. For that reason, the new US Constitution, accepted the pervasiveness of individualism, and tried through the structure of government (checks and balances), the creation of larger electoral districts that would include a greater number and variety of factions, and the development of a more refined and cosmopolitan public opinion, to channel, check, and control it.

It would take until the nineteenth century for the first form of modern individualism—possessive individualism or the self-made-man myth—to unfold. The basis of this type of individualism was the spread of a market economy in which individuals competed with each other in the pursuit of their self-interest. The market was expected to be self-regulating. Those individuals who were more efficient, innovative, and industrious would be rewarded by the market, while those who were not would fall by the wayside. The result would be the continuous increase in societal wealth—the new definition of the common good. In the 1830s, the French observer Tocqueville noted, "It is a strange thing to see how feverishly the Americans pursue prosperity and how tormented they are all the time by a vague fear of having missed the fastest way of achieving it."[1]

Using the new model of self-interested action in the market, Americans rethought all social relationships. Society was deemed to be an association of separate and independent individuals, each finding his (not yet her) place by his own efforts. Rather than stifle his passions, the new individual was expected to channel his sexuality, ambition, and self-assertion into the drive for achievement. This became known as the ideal (or myth) of the "self-made man." The ethic was one of self-discipline, sobriety, industriousness, competitiveness, purposefulness, and a willingness to sacrifice present pleasure for future achievement. This was also the "work ethic," originally the "Protestant work ethic," but now shorn of its original goal of glorifying God through one's "calling" (occupation). In the work ethic, labor and the accumulation of wealth was not a means to an end (life, enjoyment), but an end in itself.

America's first great self-made man and apostle of the work ethic was Benjamin Franklin. Born to a candlemaker and the fifteenth of seventeen children, Franklin struck out on his own by going to the big city (Philadelphia) and starting a successful printing business. His *Poor Richard's Almanack* became famous for its character-building sayings, which quickly found their way into the English language. Among them were "Time is money"; "a penny saved is a penny earned"; "God helps those who help themselves"; "honesty is the best policy"; "a place for everything, everything in its place"; and "early to bed, early to rise makes a man healthy, wealthy, and wise." Over two hundred years later Americans still learn and use these proverbs.

Franklin followed his own advice. A man of ceaseless energy, he became one the world's outstanding scientists and inventors and served the REVOLUTION as signer of the Declaration of Independence, ambassador to France, and contributor to the US Constitution.

The rise of the individual went hand in hand with the triumph of democracy in American political life. Before Andrew Jackson's election in 1828, all American presidents were well-born, well-educated men of social standing. But the election of 1828 saw voter participation double over 1824 and quadruple over 1820. Jackson himself symbolized the rise of the common man who could make something of himself by his own efforts. Jackson came from a poor family, was orphaned by age thirteen, and was injured fighting in the American Revolution. But through a career in law and politics, military prowess, and a fortuitous marriage, he rose to wealth, fame, and eventually the presidency.

By the time of the Civil War, presidential candidates were expected to boast of being self-made men. President Abraham Lincoln was born in a log cabin on the frontier and had only a few months of schooling. But Lincoln gained wealth through his skill as a lawyer and speaker and in 1860 was elected president on an antislavery ticket. When the Southern states seceded, setting off the Civil War, his Emancipation Proclamation changed the goal of the war to ending slavery. Meanwhile, his skillful leadership kept the Northern states united until its armies could defeat the Southern Confederacy. Though he was almost completely self-taught, Lincoln wrote and delivered some of the greatest speeches in the English language. Martyred by an assassin less than a week after the surrender of the Confederacy, Lincoln is now revered as America's greatest president.

Lincoln popularized more than anyone the free labor doctrine, sometimes referred to as the American Dream. According to this widespread belief, property was the result of human labor and good character mixed together with nature's bounty. As Lincoln put it,

> The prudent, penniless beginner in the world, labors for wages awhile, saves
> a surplus with which to buy tools or land, for himself; then labors on his

own account another while, and at length hires another new beginner to help him. This, say its advocates, is *free* labor—the just and generous, and prosperous system, which opens the way for all—gives hope to all, and energy, and progress, and improvement of condition to all. If any continue through life in the condition of the hired laborer, it is not fault of the system, but because of either a dependent nature which prefers it, or improvidence, folly, or singular misfortune.[2]

Free labor ideology was an attempt to describe, justify, and celebrate a social reality that still existed. In the middle of the nineteenth century, American society was one in which the majority of white males could expect to accumulate property, usually in the form of a small farm. But the expansion of capitalism and wage labor after the Civil War would soon eclipse independent property ownership. Free-labor ideology rationalized this new reality by emphasizing social mobility. Those who remained as workers had failed in the race of life. They had no one to blame but themselves because the free enterprise system had afforded them opportunity.

The Civil War not only defeated the slaveholders and freed the slaves. It also resulted in the passage of the Fourteenth Amendment to the US Constitution. Complementing the Declaration of Independence with its promise that the protection of the pursuit of happiness was the first goal of government, the new amendment became part of the charter of American economic individualism. It committed the federal government to protecting each person's right to due process under the law and equal protection under the law. America's courts soon interpreted the new law as protection of the individual's right to compete in the market and to be secure in his property. The courts included the new privately chartered business corporation in the definition of personhood deserving legal protection.

On this new legal basis, both capitalism and free-labor ideology came into their own following the Civil War. No man better symbolized the new order and its ideology than Andrew Carnegie. An immigrant who came from Scotland with his poor family in the mid-nineteenth century, Carnegie took his first job at age thirteen as a bobbin boy changing spools of thread in a cotton mill twelve hours a day, six days a week; still later, he was telegraph messenger boy. The turning point occurred when he became a secretary to one of the most powerful men in corporate America at the time, Tom Scott. Throughout his rise, Carnegie's passion for education, his indefatigable commitment to work, and his ability to grasp opportunity in the form of personal contacts fueled his rise into entrepreneurship and accumulation of wealth. Eventually, Carnegie built the largest steel company in the world and became the world's richest man. Then, at the height of his fame, Carnegie sold his firm to the banker J. P. Morgan and used his enormous wealth for philanthropic purposes. He endowed libraries all over the United States and established the Carnegie Endowment for Peace.

Carnegie's rags-to-riches story became one of the most popular versions of the American Dream and gripped the imaginations of large numbers of young Americans in the late nineteenth century. His life also exemplified Social Darwinism, the application of Darwin's theory of evolution to society. In this belief, the struggle for supremacy in the competitive market was merely the working of the universal principle of the survival of the fittest. To have pity on the poor or to bring down the rich would undermine social progress. But Carnegie didn't advocate ignoring the poor. He argued in his "Gospel of Wealth" that the rich should use their wealth as trustees for society and generously bestow charity on the less fit.

The myth and reality of the self-made man, the autonomous individual using the virtues of the work ethic to accumulate wealth, helped make American society democratic, develop its economy, and advertised the United States to would-be immigrants all over the world as "the best poor man's country." But it never characterized the life paths of most Americans, least of all immigrants, nor could it adequately explain the rise of big business. The myth also could be used to justify the most shameless exploitation of labor and public resources by the wielders of wealth. Carnegie, for example, used all the forces at his disposal to crush a union in his factories.

The myth also exaggerated the autonomy of its male practitioners. The great secret of the first form of American individualism was that male independence required female dependence and subordination. In the colonial period men held the responsibility for the religious education and the instilling of virtue in children. But the new male individual, specializing as he did in the virtues of the self-made man, had left that realm behind and required a counterbalance. Women were expected to supply what male individualism lacked: the care and nurture of communal values, including personal morality, social bonds, and religious piety. In keeping a home free of discord and dedicated to comfort and relaxation, their goal was to provide men with a refuge from the rat race of the market.

Not only did women take over home-based religious education, they also dominated the attendance at religious revivals and dragged their husbands and male relatives along with them. Beginning in the 1830s, they even moved into the public sphere to reform male vices by crusading against saloon culture, advocating temperance (in drinking alcohol), campaigning against sexual violence and prostitution, limiting employers' exploitation of children, and providing charity for poor and fallen women (prostitutes).

American culture at this time conceived men and women as opposites and complementary in their natures and as having separate spheres of action. Men were aggressive and autonomous individuals operating in work, business, politics, and government. Women were self-sacrificing, pious, innocent of sex, and accommodating to men. But in their sphere of home and family, they were supreme. As a popular 1865 poem put it, "the hand that rocks the cradle rules the world." According to another popular saying, "behind every great man is a great woman."

Mothers had the noble task of instilling in men the dedication to the common good necessary to sustain the republic. Mid-nineteenth century women may not have been full individuals—the main paid occupation open to women then was that of housemaid—but they were essential to *men's* individualism.

Despite the limitations for women inherent in the two-sphere system, it was a significant advancement for them. Women were no longer seen as inferior to men, but had a transcendent moral worth, which entitled them to be placed on a pedestal and take on the new position of manager of the family. Moreover, according to the new norms, the relationships of women and men in marriage and between parents and children in the family were to be governed by love and reason rather than force and tradition. The two-sphere system represented a distinct softening of male supremacy and a step forward for women.

The saga of the self-made individual ascending to great wealth still inspires many Americans and has many billionaire exemplars, including Bill Gates, Warren Buffett, Donald Trump, Sam Walton, Martha Stewart, and Oprah Winfrey. American politicians testify to the popularity of this value when they ritually brag of their humble origins and celebrate a system that enabled them to rise by their own efforts. Many self-made businesspeople continue to accept the corollary to the rags-to-riches myth: that great wealth has its duties and should be returned to society as philanthropy. For example, beginning in the 1970s, private individuals began to give their private land as gifts or sell it at below-market value to land trusts, such as the Nature Conservancy, for environmental purposes. In another example, in 2010 a group of forty wealthy families, led by billionaires Gates and Buffett, pledged to donate at least half of their wealth to charities and philanthropies. Still, by the turn of the twentieth century, the old individualism was failing badly as an ideology.

## The Era of the Social Individual

The old individualism could not explain the rise of big business, the central institution of which, the corporation, embodied the consolidation of individual ownership into a single impersonal entity. In the two decades before 1900, Americans viewed the size of new business institutions and their ability to outcompete individually or family-owned businesses and farms with great dismay. But over the first two decades of the twentieth century, they came to terms with the fact that large corporations had replaced the individual as the prime unit of market competition. One reason was that Americans recognized that large concentrations of capital provided the most efficient way of producing wealth and competing in international markets. By having regulatory commissions oversee corporate behavior, many Americans were reassured that corporate abuses would not be tolerated.

But there was another reason more critical for Americans' acceptance of the new reality. The large majority of Americans were no longer self-employed and therefore less inclined to view personal property ownership as an essential condition of individual autonomy and achievement. The percentage of self-employed Americans in the labor force had fallen from 58 percent in 1800 to less than 20 percent in 1920. By then, well over 80 percent of all Americans were employees.

The new nation of employees worked in large bureaucracies. The self-made man's characteristic of independence was superfluous in a bureaucracy; other characteristics, such as risk-taking behavior and self-assertion, could be downright counterproductive. The highest goal of a bureaucracy was efficiency, and the most effective means to that end was the impersonal and standardized application of regulations and procedures. Because most large business firms, educational institutions, political parties, churches, unions, and the organs of the executive branch of government operated as bureaucracies, Americans had to adapt their older individuality to new conditions. A new individualism arose that has been termed the "organization man" or "social individualism."

In the words of the sociologist David Riesman, the new American character was neither traditional (colonial period) nor "inner directed" (the nineteenth-century self-made man) but rather "other-directed." On the typical job the most important value was the ability to get along, to work well with others, and to see oneself as part of a team. The other-directed person was an organization man or woman, adapting and conforming to the needs of the larger whole. The new individual was constantly looking for cues from his or her fellow workers and the boss about what to think, do, or express.

The other-directed individual was evident in job interviews, where attitude came to be viewed as equal to or more important than virtuous character, knowledge, or individual achievement. A popular self-help book written by Dale Carnegie in 1936, titled *How to Win Friends and Influence People,* offered those seeking success the advice to "make people like you"; "win people to your way of thinking"; and "change people without giving offense or arousing resentment." In the twenty-first century, the most popular American self-help book for success in life, written by Steven Covey, offers "seven habits of highly effective people" (for example, "think win-win"). Practicing these habits elevates people from "dependence" to "independence," and finally to "interdependence," the realization that "cooperation [is necessary] to achieve something that cannot be achieved independently."[3] These manuals gave very different advice than that advocated a century and a half earlier by Ben Franklin.

But for blue-collar workers, and increasingly for lower white-collar workers as well, the new workplace was far less interesting and no longer a terrain for the expression of individuality in any way. Their experience represented the shadow side of the new organization man. Using the principles of scientific management, individual decision making based on custom, common sense, or hunch gave way to the dictates of management based on what studies had shown to be most efficient and effective. Increasingly, individual autonomy on the job gave way to the one right way to do things. Managers subdivided tasks into their simpler components, standardized their operations, and then coordinated them. The conceiving or thinking part of work was to be concentrated in management, while the execution of management's orders became the job of the worker. The new employee was told, "Don't do things the way you think they should be done, but the way you are told." As a result, the typical employee usually required significant training when hired and close supervision subsequently.

It may be objected that the new American character was not individualistic at all. The modern organization and workplace seemed to demand conformity and accommodation far more than autonomy. But much of what made up the older individualism remained in new forms. Social mobility still existed, but instead of ascent into property ownership through saving and hard work, it involved climbing the organization's job ladder, rung by rung. With each rung, there came more complex tasks with greater difficulty, additional responsibilities, and higher pay. Competition still existed, but instead of occurring in the market, it was within the organization. What was new was that competing successfully meant not producing a product or service more cheaply, but being able to read other people, make alliances, neutralize enemies, and play office politics. The new individual still had to save, but savings took the form of accumulating shares of the firm's stock or the compulsory payroll deductions mandated by the 1935 Social Security system.

The most inviting arena for the new individuality was not in work at all but in consumption. The best way to display to one's fellows one's income, status, and unique style or taste was through the purchase of an increasingly diverse array of products and services. Individuality could be expressed as a particular style manifested in one's choice of clothes or automobile, vacation spot, preferred sport, or home furnishings. As the standard of living of Americans rose, the amount of leisure time increased, and the array of consumer goods expanded, the act of going shopping became an essential expression of one's individuality in relation to others. Studies confirmed that shopping had become one of Americans' most time-consuming activities outside of paid work and watching television. It was also among the most pleasurable, as indicated in a popular women's term for shopping, "retail therapy," and the slogan "When the going gets tough, the tough go shopping."

Yet, here too the pressures of ubiquitous advertising in the mass media and the norms of one's peers tended to create an ever-changing mass style, which constrained individuality. Americans' consumption patterns were largely determined by the socially produced standard of living and enforced by the need to "keep up with the Joneses." Thus, one's individuality was largely circumscribed by income and class, ethnicity, gender, and one's choice of peers. As social scientists and philosophers often noted, it had become impossible to separate modern individuality from the social terrain in which it existed. It had become a truism that the old rugged individualism was a myth, an outmoded ideological belief.

Who were the new organization men and women? One of the most respected CEOs is Jack Welch formerly of General Electric. Unlike earlier self-made men,

Welch had the benefit of extensive education, receiving his PhD in chemical engineering in 1960. Within a ten-year period, he rose steadily through GE's ranks from vice president, to senior vice president, then vice chairman and finally GE's youngest CEO in 1981. As its top officer, Welch dismantled excessive bureaucracy and prodded his managers to be more productive. Each year, he fired the bottom 1 percent of his managers and offered the top 20 percent bonuses and stock options. He believed that if a company owned by GE was not number one or number two in its field, it should be upgraded or closed. When Welch took over GE, it was worth $14 billion, but when he left it in 2004, its market value was $410 billion, making it the largest company in the world.[4]

Labor leader George Meany took a different life path, but he was nonetheless an organization man. He began his career as a plumber, joined New York City's plumbers' union and served as its business agent. Having proven his worth to the city's Central Labor Federation and the State Federation of Labor, he was elected president of the latter in 1934. During World War II, as an officer of the American Federation of Labor (AFL), he helped found the federal government's War Labor Board, which promoted the growth of union membership. In 1955 as the AFL's president, he unified the country's fractious labor movement by merging the AFL with the rival Congress of Industrial Organizations. Under his leadership, which lasted until 1979, America's unions became a powerful political voice, speaking on behalf of not only union members but also all working people.

During the first half of the twentieth century, American women began in significant numbers to join their male counterparts in public and social life. In the 1890s "the new woman"—later known as the "liberated woman"—appeared. As more and more family functions were socialized, increasing numbers of women left the cloistered confines of the family and home to participate in all levels of schooling, government administration, department stores, and labor unions. A new female individualistic personality began to supplant the traditional one. According to one description,

> The New Woman typically values self-fulfillment and independence rather than the stereotypically feminine ideal of self-sacrifice; believes in legal and sexual equality; often remains single because of the difficulty of combining such equality with marriage; is more open about her sexuality than the "Old Woman"; is well-educated and reads a great deal; has a job; is athletic or otherwise physically vigorous and, accordingly, prefers comfortable clothes (sometimes male attire) to traditional female garb.[5]

To one conservative in 1907, women's traditional commitment to family had given way to "the worship of the brazen calf of Self."

Though not an organization woman, Amelia Earhart was unquestionably a new woman. She dressed in slacks, wore her hair short, and only accepted marriage when assured she and her husband would be equal partners. In the 1920s, she took up flying and her adventuresome spirit quickly put her in the forefront of those challenging the boundaries of flight. In 1928, she became the first woman to fly across the Atlantic and, in 1932, became the first woman to fly solo nonstop across the United States. In 1937, attempting to fly around the world, she and her plane were lost and never recovered. Her iconoclastic lifestyle, risk-taking adventuring, and personal courage in arenas where women had not ventured before has made her a role model for young women and an exemplar of feminism, which is essentially the idea that women deserve individuality as much as men.

The shift from propertied individualism to the social individual living and working within a large-scale organization had its defenders and detractors. To its defenders, notably the pragmatist philosopher John Dewey, the new acceptance of interdependence seemed to presage a democratic socialist reconstruction of the American community. Armed with a new social intelligence, freely associating individuals would move beyond private property and create the "great community." For a while, something like that seemed to be happening. The American labor movement, with its call for the solidarity of all workers, endorsed the ideal of social unity. Most of the twentieth-century achievements of social justice—unemployment insurance, old-age pensions, minimum wage, the forty-hour work week, health care insurance for the elderly and poor, and civil rights for women and minorities—occurred in the era when the social individual was the norm.

But eventually the detractors ruled the day. As early as the 1920s, Walter Lippmann argued that American public opinion was determined more by "stereotypes" and propaganda than by rational discussion.[6] The worldwide struggle against fascism during World War II and communism afterward discredited the idea that the common good could be determined for everyone else by a virtuous elite. Totalitarianism—the control of all life outside the state by a one-party dictatorship—led to the destruction of any semblance of individuality. Other critics of American life decried increasing conformity and the transformation of Americans into "cheerful robots."[7] In the 1960s, critics on the left termed the large corporation and its consumer culture a "soft totalitarianism" that enslaved Americans. The stage was set for a resurgence of the ideology of autonomous individualism.

## Expressive Individualism and Libertarian Individualism

Autonomous individualism took two new forms: a partial revival of the self-employed individualism within the competitive market, and a more widespread and revolutionary type of individualism, which has been termed "expressive individualism," also referred to by academics as "postmaterialism" (see Documents).

Expressive individualism is the idea that each individual should follow his or her unique passion or passions, which may not be immediately evident to oneself or acceptable to conventional society. By paying attention to, discovering, and following these promptings of the sacred inner self at whatever cost, the new individualism promises that people can achieve happiness, creativity, and personal fulfillment.

The roots of expressive individualism go far back in American history. It started with a rebellious woman. Ann Hutchinson, among the first generation of Puritan settlers in colonial America, decided to hold her own Bible study classes. What was most controversial was that she freely interpreted the Bible in the light of what she called her divine inspiration. The idea that religion could be fundamentally personal in nature threatened the authority of church and the cohesiveness of the early Puritan community. Following a trial in 1638, Hutchinson was exiled from the Massachusetts Bay Colony for the sin of "antinomianism." She, along with Roger Williams, who was similarly banished, has become known as the progenitor of American religious freedom. Their belief that religion needed to be personally interpreted and that churches should be composed of small face-to-face associations of "seekers" would become widespread and result in the splintering of American Protestantism into multitudes of denominations.

In the mid-nineteenth century, antinomianism became a form of secular individualism under the influence of the transcendentalists. This small group of writers and intellectuals included the great essayist and philosopher Ralph Waldo Emerson, the poet Walt Whitman, and the proto-environmentalist Henry David Thoreau. The transcendentalists, influenced by fellow Western romantics, Western mysticism, and the ancient texts of the Hindu religion, affirmed the priority of one's soul over the authority of all human institutions.

One day while in his formative years, Emerson went to a valued elder advisor and asked him, "What have I to do with the sacredness of traditions, if I live wholly from within?" His friend replied, "But these impulses may be from below, not from above." Emerson's response typified the new individualism: "They do not seem to me to be such; but if I am the Devil's child, I will live then from the Devil." Emerson continued, saying that

> no law can be sacred to me but that of my nature. Good and bad are but names very readily transferable to that or this; the only right is what is after my constitution, the only wrong what is against it.

Later in the classic essay "Self-Reliance," Emerson offered this aphorism: "Trust thyself: every heart vibrates to that iron string." Emerson's influence is suggested by the fact that by the 1850s he was the most popular lecturer in the United States. Whitman had the same thing in mind as Emerson when in his poem "Song of Myself" he deified the personal soul: "nothing, not god, is greater to one than one's self is, . . . Nor do I understand who there can be more wonderful than myself."

During the nineteenth century, expressive individualism had been severed from the culture of the self-made man. Expressing feelings, passions, and the promptings of the imagination was the province of middle- and upper-class women and "happy-go-lucky" blacks. To the self-made man, such expressiveness was the sheerest self-indulgence. It was not until the 1960s that expressive individualism become possible and legitimate for millions of Americans. The prime reason was the spread in the United States and other advanced industrial democracies of material abundance brought by the postindustrial economy. When people's basic needs for survival and security were met, the higher, postmaterial needs for personal fulfillment and quality of life took priority. It also helped that most Americans enjoyed increased leisure time from work, married women were less occupied with family responsibilities as the number of children per family declined by almost half from its nineteenth-century peak, and young people's phase of life before work and marriage was extended into their twenties.

The new expressive individualism of young baby boomers (a large cohort resulting from the increase in births between 1946 and 1964) was initially modeled on the bohemian lifestyle lived by "the beats" of the 1950s. The beats listened to jazz music because its improvisational character inspired the spontaneity they desired. The beats were often "on the road" (the title of Jack Kerouac's famous novel) in search of some ineffable peak experience they could define only as "IT." The hippies of the 1960s and the many millions who were influenced by the counterculture followed in the beats' footsteps, but in place of jazz they took up rock 'n roll music, with its primal beat and antiauthority ethos. They combined rock with the search for the elusive inner self via hallucinogenic drugs, notably LSD. They also rejected the prevailing norms of sexuality by engaging in casual sex, living together out of wedlock, and openly discussing sex. Sex was not dirty to the hippies but was a holy act.

Conformity to the social norms, the old enemy of individualism, also took a beating in the 1960s from new social movements. Black nationalist leader Malcolm X denounced the ways American culture emasculated African Americans by making them ashamed of their own race. Feminists pointed out how women were taught to hide their intelligence and abilities. While boys were told they could grow up to be president, girls were told they could grow up to be Miss America. Gay advocates refused to hide their sexuality any longer and asserted their gay pride. Eventually, a new ethic of multiculturalism would challenge the older idea that America was a melting pot in which ethnic and other differences would dissolve into a single individual type with minimal variations. Now, there could be a variety of different lifestyles available as options to expand one's individuality.

By the 1970s, the counterculture of the hippies and the criticisms of the dominant culture coming out of 1960s movements were seeping into American culture in diluted form as expressive individualism. The new individualism was particularly strong among college-educated professionals on the coasts. It was premised on a suspicion of social conformity, respectability, and especially the overriding emphasis on success and the work ethic, which had led earlier generations of Americans to sacrifice present happiness for future accumulation and achievements. For much of the new generation, work was not to be valued as an end in itself but only insofar as it produced happiness and self-fulfillment. The goal was for the boundary between work and play to fall away. Paradoxically, those who viewed work in this new way devoted themselves to their careers in their search for happiness as passionately as their self-made-men forbears.

The benefits of expressive individualism have been greatest for women. There has been an enormous rise in women's workforce participation, which has recently come close to that of men. Women can now choose to seek personal fulfillment, as well as relief from being around children all day, in a career or job. Greatly loosened divorce laws and the end of the social stigma of a woman being single has allowed them to leave unhappy marriages as independent individuals. Freely available and highly effective birth control and easy access to abortion has greatly eased the consequences for engaging in uninhibited sexual activity. A woman who cannot find a husband now has the option of having children alone. Forty percent of all children born to unmarried women were intentionally conceived. The number and variety of life choices for women are incomparably greater than in the period before the 1960s.

Expressive individualism is present today in many forms. It won legal support when the Supreme Court established privacy as a constitutional right and on that basis legalized women's right to an abortion, despite furious opposition. Significant numbers of Americans:

> now place a high value on personal choice;
> are tolerant of different lifestyles, including gay and transgender ways of living (together termed the "queer" lifestyle);
> adopt informal modes of personal expression;
> show a greater concern for their health, well-being, and fitness;
> believe in the sacredness of nature and strongly support environmental protection;
> show an interest in different cultures and religions;
> and support New Age spiritual trends based on the search for direct spiritual experience.

In the decades following the 1960s, successive generations modified, adapted, and further developed expressive individualism. One of the first signs it had become mainstream was the US Army's recruiting slogan adopted in 1980 (lasting until 2001): "Be All You Can Be." Other signs are evident in widespread casual dressing in public, including the wearing of jeans, shorts, sandals, and T-shirts. Most Americans now use informal modes of communication in everyday speech, such as dispensing with formal titles like Mr., Mrs., or Ms. and addressing people by their first names. By 2012, marijuana had become legal in two states, while medical marijuana is legal (with a doctor's authorization) in eighteen states, and small amounts have been decriminalized in fifteen states and many cities. Meanwhile, once disreputable forms of music, first rock 'n roll and now hip-hop, are mainstream. Censorship is almost nonexistent, and different kinds of sex, including gay sex, can be depicted and discussed frankly on television and in film.

More significantly, marriage, once the gateway to adulthood, is no longer the central organizing institution for sexual behavior, living arrangements, and child rearing. Divorce ends over 40 percent of all first marriages. There is a thriving sexual culture for single adults, hetero- and homosexual, and cohabitation (living together outside of marriage) is socially acceptable. These couples now benefit from laws that give them some of the same legal privileges as married couples. Increasingly, individuals opt to remain single. One-half of all US households contain unmarried people and one-quarter only one person. One in three children are born to unmarried women. According to one demographer, there is no longer a standard life course; an individual now "composes his or her history a la carte."[8] Despite greater options for the individual, marriage is not fading away. It has been democratized by adapting itself to meet the needs of the individual. Spouses in marriage share child rearing and breadwinning as never before and enjoy far greater equality.

The new individualism is also present in religious attitudes that reflect New Age trends. A 2009 Pew survey of American religious attitudes found that while Americans remain overwhelmingly Christian, two-thirds reject the traditional idea that there is only one path—Jesus—to eternal life. Roughly a quarter of all Americans believe in reincarnation, in astrology, in yoga as a spiritual practice, and that spiritual energy resides in nature.

The new trends that point to a much more pluralistic culture now characterize all advanced countries. But in the United States they have been vigorously resisted by fundamentalist Protestant and conservative Catholic church leaders and their followers. The model of culture they once knew and still identify as God given is crumbling before their eyes. Many conservative Protestants believe that Armageddon (the end of time prophesied in the Bible) is close at hand. But their efforts to reverse history have been to little avail.

As it has spread, expressive individualism has elicited criticism and predictions of its demise. Conservatives, both religious and secular, are especially incensed because of the new individualism's disregard for traditional morality predicated on the sacrifice of the present for the future. They charge the defenders of expressive individualism with hedonism and moral relativism. A newly influential group known as Communitarians criticize it for privatizing Americans and making them neglectful of their public obligations. In that vein, social scientists have demonstrated that voluntary associations, which constitute the civil society vital to democracy, have been on the wane. There can be little doubt that Americans have become much more private and less enmeshed in family and public obligations. Has individualism gone too far? One answer is that the private-regarding aspect of expressive individualism is a reaction to the unresponsiveness of democratic institutions to the new individual potentials shaped by postmaterial values. One has only to look at increasingly regimented schools, repressive drug laws, mass incarceration, the lack of significant progress in protecting the environment, and the struggle of sexual and gender minorities to win full equality to understand the frustration and alienation of many Americans from the larger democratic community. In that case, the loss of faith in American government and civil society is not the fault of the new individualism but of unresponsive public institutions.[9]

Past expressions of individualism have had mechanisms for reconciling the individual with the large community. The era of the self-made man had the stay-at-home wife to nurture a respite from the cutthroat competition of the marketplace. Social individualists operated within the confines of the corporation and benefitted from unions and government regulation. Both individual types participated in a dense net of voluntary associations, which has now withered. What new postmaterial institutions will emerge to mediate the relations of expressive individuals with the democratic community? The answers are still emerging. One thing is certain. The new expressive individualism has not faded and is getting stronger as postmaterial values spread.

Despite its success, expressive individualism has not fundamentally altered the large corporate structures, the managed workplace, or consumerism. Nor has it replaced, but has at most combined in various ways with, the first two forms of individualism: the self-made man and the other-directed individual.

Meanwhile, a very different kind of individualism has developed, which has real roots in the economy and is rationalized by conservative religion. Like expressive individualism, what might be called market individualism or libertarianism is suspicious of large-scale organizations, especially government, and seeks a return to autonomous individualism. Both speak the language of individual choice, rights, and opportunity. But, unlike expressive individualism, it retains the traditional work ethic, seeks to sustain the older family system, and finds autonomy in a return to the self-employed individual inventing him- or herself in the flux of market competition. The supporters of this kind of individualism blame government provision of welfare and regulation of business, not the rise of the corporation, for the decline of old-style, rugged individualism. They believe that government provision of social insurance creates a psychology of dependency. These libertarians seek a return to individual responsibility (rather than shared responsibility) and independence (rather than interdependence) and view the discipline of competing in the market as a way of promoting these values.

But the new entrepreneurialism has not changed the fact that the United States is still a nation of employees. The most pervasive manifestation of the new individualism has come rather in a *compulsory* form, resulting from new policies of corporate employers and government. One of the most notable changes has been the rise of the contingent workforce. Facing heightened global and domestic competition and the need to cut costs and become more flexible, corporations and other institutions have loosened the social safety net (provision of health care, pensions, and other benefits) they once offered their employees. They have resorted to jettisoning large numbers of their permanent employees and hiring them back on contract or subcontracting the job altogether. Variously termed freelancers, independent professionals, temporary contract workers, or simply consultants, these former employees are now considered self-employed individuals competing in the market to sell their services. Very few enjoy health care or pension benefits or rights on the job. The Government Accounting Office reports that in 2005 almost one-third of all US workers were contingent. In American higher education, two-thirds of all faculty members are contingent in this sense and lack tenure, participation in shared governance of the university, or a decent salary. Though there is no commonly accepted figure, there can be little doubt the number of these workers has grown enormously. One estimate is that 20 percent of the average company's workforce is contingent. The US government has followed suit. In the Department of Homeland Security, the number of contractors equals the number of permanent employees: more than two hundred thousand.

Libertarian individualism is also present in the new way of financing the university. Public universities used to be almost wholly financed by state governments. But the conservative opposition to taxes and government spending, combined with competing budget priorities in state government, has led to a continuous decline in the state-supplied share of university budgets. To replace revenue, universities rely on tuition increases paid by students and their parents. Since the late 1970s, tuition and fees have grown approximately four times faster than the cost of living. Meanwhile, government grants to students have declined and been replaced by loans. The average American college student graduated in 2009 with a loan debt of over twenty-three thousand dollars. The justification for this has been that education should be viewed less as a public good than as an individual good. It is argued that the enormous earnings differential—one million dollars over a lifetime—between those with a college education and those without justify this. Borrowing is an investment in one's self whose returns more than defray the principal and interest. Libertarians argue for a further reduction in government funding, even for student loans, as it would foster greater individual responsibility for one's education. The assumption is the nineteenth-century belief that the market creates self-discipline and is the best measure and guarantor of the common good.

Liberals have scathingly criticized this new type of individualism because it has decreased opportunities for those with less income, has increased social inequality, and has undermined the social safety net. But regardless of its controversial nature, it is a broad and powerful trend in American life and has influenced the financing of health care, private pensions, public education at all levels, tax policy, and the nature of employment.

As we have seen, American individualism has evolved over time and can be broken down into four forms. Each is reconciled with the public good in different ways. Each has its strengths and weaknesses. Each has been heavily criticized. Part of the pluralism of contemporary American culture is that Americans can choose from these forms of individualism as from a buffet and combine them in various ways. For example, many Americans are corporate men and women on the job but expressive individualists off the job. The rise from humble beginnings still motivates many Americans, but it may take the form of rising through the organization's ranks or supplementing one's living as a consultant and contain elements of expressive individualism in consumption. In the end, however, all forms have in common the belief that the common good should not be determined in advance for the individual but rather must follow from his or her voluntary actions.

# 3
# DEMOCRACY IN THE ECONOMY AND WORKPLACE

*The true friend of property, the true conservative, is he who insists that property shall be the servant and not the master of the commonwealth; who insists that the creature of man's making shall be the servant and not the master of the man who made it. The citizens of the United States must effectively control the mighty commercial forces, which they have themselves called into being.*

Theodore Roosevelt, speech at Osawatomie, Kansas (1910)

*"Necessitous men are not free men." People who are hungry and out of a job are the stuff of which dictatorships are made.*

Franklin Delano Roosevelt, State of the Union Message (1944)

Among many inside and outside the United States, there is a widely held view that American capitalism goes largely unchecked. The American state and its relationship to the economy are often contrasted with that of the European welfare states and other states with a deeper socialist influence. The latter are viewed as more responsive to the interests of those with little wealth and income, while the US model is condemned as excessively individualist and heartless toward those with little wealth. The same contrast is often made with regard to the influence of corporate leaders and concentrated wealth in politics. Indeed, there can be little doubt that in recent decades US big business and concentrated wealth have a greater influence on democratic politics than in most other advanced countries or in America's past and that the American welfare state is not as broadly available to its people as in many advanced capitalist democracies.

But these contrasts are typically drawn too starkly and lead people to miss the ways that Americans have gone about democratizing their economic system. In the United States, despite the enormous influence of concentrated wealth, Americans have continually relied on democratic values and procedures to broaden the benefits of capitalism, check its abuses of the common good, and prevent the wealthy from closing down avenues of opportunity. This is not a straightforward story of government against business or the people struggling against and then either triumphing over or being defeated by concentrated wealth. The real history in the United States reveals a much more complex picture, one in which government and business, workers, farmers, professionals, and business leaders have cooperated far more than they have fought. Thus, movements from the grassroots have usually triumphed only when their goals have coincided significantly with the needs and purposes of those at the top. For example, a major reason that unionism and social insurance programs won support from social strata outside the working class was because the higher wages brought by unions promised to raise consumption levels and prevent business downturns, which hurt all Americans.

Another level of complexity resides in the broadly held American value that sovereignty resides in the people rather than the state. That value has had the effect of limiting support for *state* action to contain capitalism, while allowing and even encouraging *private* action to modify the reach of the profit motive. Thus those looking for the complete picture of democratic reform of the economy must also look outside American government and take notice of how private sector activity has itself been democratized: for example, the not-for-profit sector of the American economy, the rise of unions and collective bargaining, employer-provided pensions and health care, and tax breaks to subsidize and direct business activity toward the public good.

## Producers' Democracy

Only a review of American history can provide an understanding of the complexities involved in the relationship of democracy and the American economy. Contrary to the belief that America was always capitalist, it is important to understand that such a system was not always dominant and pervasive. While America had a very weak aristocratic heritage, before the Civil War (1861–5), a majority of Americans conducted work in one of two noncapitalist property-production systems. The majority of whites in the North and South worked in a mode of production without the wage-labor relationship characteristic of capitalism. In what scholars call a "producers' economy," farmers, artisans, and merchants controlled their own labor through small-scale property ownership. In the other system, African American slaves labored in a hybrid mode of production, combining slave labor with production for an international market. Both property-production systems lacked the hallmarks of capitalism: an orientation toward capital accumulation and wage labor.

Though limited to white males, democratic values and beliefs and government policies infused the system of self-employed property ownership from the late eighteenth century through the mid-nineteenth. As Thomas Jefferson put it:

"[I]t is not too soon to provide by every possible means that as few as possible shall be without a little portion of land. The small landholders are the most precious part of a state."[1] During this period, the policy of the federal government was to purchase or take by force western lands and distribute them to would-be white farmers. It was widely believed that a republic could only exist if there was a balanced distribution of property in society. As long as the majority of citizens had the means to establish their independence and have a stake in society, the republic was deemed to be safe. This early American value of individual independence through ownership of a family farm or artisan workshop was the cornerstone of both democracy and the economy.

The American thirst for land was seemingly unquenchable. In 1803, the American "apostle of democracy" Thomas Jefferson completed the Louisiana Purchase from France, doubling the size of the country with the acquisition of a vast territory west of the Mississippi River and east of the Rocky Mountains. The purchase ended France's stake in North America and, just as importantly, provided the means for the independence of future generations of Americans. The purchase, predicted Jefferson, would make America an "empire of liberty." Meanwhile, Congress steadily reduced the per-acre price and the size of allotments of federal land to be sold to settlers and allowed payment in installments. The Preemption Act of 1841 allowed settlers to purchase at a low price up to 160 acres of federal land if they had built a house on the land and improved it. Finally, the Homestead Act of 1862 granted up to 160 acres of federal land to settlers without payment.

Initially, American democracy did not include women, African American slaves, or American Indians. Long native to the American continent, the American Indians still occupied and controlled much of North America west of the Appalachian Mountains. To build a democracy of white male settlers meant pushing these hunter-gatherer—and in the South, agricultural—tribes off their traditional lands. But the American Indians resisted, often fiercely. The early American state used its military forces to battle American Indians who refused to move west. In 1794, the army defeated the Western Indian Confederacy at the Battle of Fallen Timbers (near what is today Toledo, Ohio), and in 1811, a small force under William Henry Harrison defeated Chief Tecumseh in what is now west-central Indiana. The War of 1812 constituted the great defeat for the American Indians east of the Mississippi. While the war is sometimes considered a draw, it resulted in the defeat of an alliance of the British and the American Indians, both of whom sought to stem American expansion. The inability of the British to maintain a military presence in the American West opened that vast territory for settlement and an expansion of agrarian democracy.

Andrew Jackson's miraculous victory over a far superior British force at the Battle of New Orleans in 1815 secured that city as a port for the export of the crops of western farmers. It also catapulted Jackson to fame as the first democratic president, a champion of the common man.

In the next four decades, Americans continued their expansion across the continent. In 1819, Spain ceded Florida to the United States following a series of military skirmishes. Texas, which had become independent from Mexico in 1836 following a slaveholders' revolt, was annexed by the United States in 1844. The 1846–8 Mexican-American War led to the cession by Mexico of what is now the American Southwest, including the state of California. The present boundaries of the United States reached final form with the purchase of Alaska from Russia in 1867 and the annexation of Hawaii following the Spanish-American War. Expansion was popular among many Americans, who viewed it as their "manifest destiny"—a God-granted blessing bestowed on the new American nation.

While Americans were securing new means for landed economic independence, they moved away from state mercantilism and toward the idea that the market should be free of state-chartered monopolies. Given the broad distribution of land and wealth in America, this new policy had democratic implications. It eliminated state government grants of monopoly charters to the wealthy and well connected and opened up the formation of corporations to all who applied. This, too, helped democratize the economy.

The settlement by the masses of American farmers of the American West had a major sticking point: the question of slavery. Since 1821, the US government had drawn a north-south line, extending west from the southern border of Missouri, dividing territories that could enter the Union as slave states or free states. In 1854, Senator Stephen A. Douglas was able to pass a bill through Congress that repealed that dividing line and opened up much of the West to slavery. The question was of enormous importance because the Southern slave states were on the verge of being outvoted in Congress by the representatives of the free states. The ability of slavery to expand anywhere in the West threatened the belief of most Northerners that the future of the country would be freedom not slavery. In opposition to Douglas, a new party was formed on the basis of opposition to the expansion of slavery anywhere in the West. This new party, the Republican Party, ascended to power in 1860 with the election of its candidate for president, Abraham Lincoln.

Lincoln espoused better than most a new form of democratic thinking: "free labor ideology." Its basic idea was that freedom consisted in the *opportunity* that wageworkers had to raise themselves up from wage labor to independent proprietorship. The ideology emphasized the necessity for a moral personal character in the form of the "work ethic": hard work, thrift, self-control, abstinence from intoxication, and constant self-improvement and ambition. But free labor ideology was also a rationale for reconciling millions to a subordinate and dependent market position. If a wage laborer did not raise himself (herself would come later) into a position of property ownership, he had only himself to blame, said this new ideology.

Americans viewed free labor ideology, more recently called "the free enterprise system," as a social reality; and to a significant degree, it was in the mid-nineteenth century. The democratic element was the conviction that under the American brand of capitalism everyone had the opportunity to go into business for himself. Unlike societies groaning under feudalism, there was social approbation for rising above the social station one was born into. As one aristocratic Polish visitor put it, "In Europe to say of someone that he rose from nothing is a disgrace and reproach. It is the opposite here. . . . It is the highest recommendation."[2]

To encourage social mobility, the Republican Party supported the Homestead Act, which gave away land to farmers seeking to establish farms in the West. In the late nineteenth century, the Sherman Antitrust Act sought to prevent monopolization of markets by big business, and in modified form is still on the books.

The election of Lincoln on the plank of opposition to the expansion of slavery led the Southern states to secede. When the Northern states refused to let them go, a civil war ensued, the bloodiest of such wars in the nineteenth century. The Civil War was a watershed in a momentous transition occurring within the country. Notwithstanding the abundance of open land available for independent farming, an economy based on wage labor was becoming dominant throughout the country. In 1800, only 12 percent of the nation's labor force consisted of wage workers, while 57 percent were self-employed family farmers, shopkeepers, and artisans, and 31 percent were slaves. However, by the eve of the Civil War in 1860, 40 percent were wage earners, while only 37 percent were self-employed, and 23 percent were slaves. By the start of the twentieth century, 78 percent were wageworkers, and only 22 percent were involved in the self-employed mode of production.[3] The American Civil War was the crucial turning point in this transition because it put state power in the hands of procapitalist elements of society and removed it from the representatives of small producers, Southern slave owners, and Northern merchants and bankers who were profiting from these declining modes of production.

The Civil War–era Republican Party introduced new policies that included a protective tariff for American manufacturers; subsidies for the railroads, the major form of American big business; and a national banking system to make commodity production more viable across the entire nation. The expropriation of the property of the slave owners of the South, combined with the tariff, the issuance of a national currency—greenbacks—and the removal of the economy from the gold standard resulted in a massive transference of wealth from Southerners and the Northeastern merchant and banking elite to rising manufacturers and other entrepreneurs. Meanwhile, land grants for transcontinental railroads and state colleges and universities subsidized the infrastructure and human capital necessary for a modern industrial society. More long term, the Fourteenth Amendment federalized protection of a national market. Defining corporations as persons, subsequent court decisions authorized the government to intervene in that market, usually in ways that protected large national business enterprises from the type of regulation supported by small producers and workers.

## Progressive Democracy: The Mix of Capitalism and Socialism

The newfound nationwide dominance of capitalism in its modern industrial form created the social context for a new kind of democracy, what historians call a "progressive democracy" or "industrial democracy" as opposed to the old producers' or agrarian democracy based on individual proprietorship. The hallmark of the new democracy was collective organization to regulate the market. Both workers, capitalists, and later, middle-class professionals cooperated among themselves in organizations and with the sanction of government, set rules, minimum standards, and stable prices in the face of market competition.

The development that spurred this new era of cooperation in the market was the prevalence of depressions during the late nineteenth century. The new circumstances of industrialized production created high fixed costs for many businesses and led them to resort to cutthroat competition to cover those costs. The result was a series of periodic crises of generalized overproduction, something that classical political economy said was impossible. If the downturns of 1873–98 are added together, there were more months of contraction than of expansion, leading some at the turn of the twentieth century to portray the 1873–98 period as an extended "great depression." Falling profit rates and falling prices, together with rising bankruptcies and economic instability, characterized this period. Capitalists responded by combining in order to reduce costs and limit cutthroat competition.

They formed large corporations and resorted to other forms of cooperation, such as gentlemen's agreements, also known as cartels, to limit competition and raise prices and profits. Between 1896 and 1904, America's economy came to be dominated by large corporations. The great impersonal corporations in steel, railroads, shipping, electrical, meat-packing, and other industries separated ownership from control. They were operated by professional managers, and ownership was dispersed to the public in the form of stock offerings. The new firms were so large that they were able to change the structure of the market from competitive to oligopolistic. In other words, in each industry a small number of large firms were able to become price *makers* rather than price *takers*. They also sidestepped and internalized the labor market by doing most hiring and training from within the company (instead of through the market). Workers became used to climbing job ladders within a corporation. In short, corporations, in the words of America's leading business historian, partially replaced the invisible hand of the market with the "visible hand" of business organization.

Capitalists were not the only group to organize to influence market outcomes. In response to their position in the labor market and on the job, America's working people began to organize unions.

From a democratic point of view, the inequality of bargaining power in the labor market and lack of autonomy in the workplace under "at will" employment (the legal doctrine that an employee can be hired, fired, promoted, or demoted at the will of the employer) constrains the opportunities for self-development of the large majority of people. The lack of opportunity, stunted individuality, and dependence on those with power over their lives cannot help but have a distorting and limiting effect on democratic citizenship. James Madison and other founding fathers feared a nation of wage workers because they viewed wage labor as a form of dependency. With the old agrarian democracy fading, strong unions and the public acceptance of collective bargaining became vital in strengthening democracy.

To its advocates, having an institutionalized voice on the job educates workers and enables union members to overcome the fear, cynicism, and apathy so typical of working-class life. That, in turn, enables them to supplement individual strategies for self-improvement with collective strategies to improve working conditions. In the words of the popular 1940 labor song, "Talking Union," joining a union was a way for otherwise disempowered people to assert their needs through forming their own associations:

> If you want higher wages, let me tell you what to do;
> You got to talk to the workers in the shop with you;
> You got to build you a union, got to make it strong,
> But if you all stick together, now, 'twont be long.
> You'll get shorter hours,
> Better working conditions.
> Vacations with pay,
> Take your kids to the seashore.
> It ain't quite this simple, so I better explain
> Just why you got to ride on the union train;
> 'Cause if you wait for the boss to raise your pay,
> We'll all be waiting till Judgment Day;
> We'll all be buried—gone to Heaven
> Saint Peter'll be the straw boss then.
> Now, you know you're underpaid, but the boss says you ain't;
> He speeds up the work till you're 'bout to faint,
> You may be down and out, but you ain't beaten,
> Pass out a leaflet and call a meetin'
> Talk it over—speak your mind
> Decide to do something about it.
> . . .
>
> You got a union now; you're sitting pretty;
> Put some of the boys on the steering committee.
> The boss won't listen when one man squawks.
> But he's got to listen when the union talks.
> He'd better, be mighty lonely
> Everybody decide to walk out on him[4]

Besides affording workers collective power in relation to their employers, participation in unions enabled workers to have a robust voice in the formation of public opinion and to mobilize for political action in electoral politics and government lobbying. As pressure groups, labor has used its muscle not just to protect their own organizational interests but also to support civil rights, voting rights, women's equality, and antipoverty legislation. The experience of the late twentieth and the early twenty-first centuries, when unions have greatly declined, suggests that it is difficult to assemble progressive democratic political coalitions and win real gains without a strong working-class component.

America has been home to the most ferocious class conflict in the world. Among the many violent clashes between workers and their unions and capitalists and the government that backed them, the greatest strike of the nineteenth century was the Pullman Strike led by Eugene V. Debs. Even though he was a skilled railroad worker, Debs realized that unions needed to bring together all railroad workers, skilled and unskilled, in a single consolidated union. The American Railway Union (ARU), which he founded in 1893, did this. It was the first labor organization to be able to stand on an equal footing with the large railroad corporations.

The two sides clashed in the great Pullman Strike and boycott of 1894. Pullman was a company town, south of Chicago, which manufactured Pullman sleeping cars. In response to the 1893 depression, George Pullman cut the wages of his workers more than 30 percent but would not reduce the rents at the homes he rented to workers or the prices he charged them at his stores. The Pullman workers joined the ARU and went on strike. In solidarity, the ARU called a boycott of all trains carrying Pullman cars, and this quickly escalated into an all-out showdown between the union and the nation's railroad corporations. At its height, the boycott and strike closed the rail arteries connecting cities and towns in half the nation. It led the president of the United States, Grover Cleveland, to dispatch ten thousand troops to the strike's center in Chicago to defeat it. Meanwhile, the courts declared the boycott an illegal conspiracy to control the market and ordered Debs to call the strike off. When he refused, he was sent to prison.

The strike was defeated, but American working people did not forget the way the government had been used to side with capital against labor. Debs became America's first great working-class hero. While in prison, Debs read Karl Marx, eventually became a socialist, and played a major role in forming the Socialist Party of America in 1901.

One of the new developments in the labor movement of this period was the organization of women. In 1909 and 1910, thousands of New York garment workers, mostly immigrant women—Russian Jews and Italians—spontaneously walked off their jobs to protest starvation wages, twelve-hour days, unsafe working conditions, and sexual abuse by male supervisors. The strike was sparked by a twenty-three-year-old socialist—and later communist—immigrant woman, Clara

Lemlich. She electrified an audience of workers by calling for a general strike when none of the unions would do so. The crowd responded enthusiastically and, after taking a traditional Yiddish oath—"If I turn traitor to the cause I now pledge, may this hand wither from the arm I now raise"—voted for a general strike. Approximately twenty thousand out of the thirty-two thousand workers in the shirtwaist trade walked out in the next two days; this would become known as the Uprising of the 20,000. Lemlich went on to fight for women's right to vote, which was won in 1919, and consumer rights.[5]

Many Americans of that time period wanted to restore the old producer-proprietor republic and viewed organization to regulate and control the market in the terms of the old agrarian democracy: the equivalent of monopoly and aristocracy. The growth of big business seemed to be crowding out the small farmers and artisans. Advocates of returning to this older form of democracy called themselves "Populists." They sought to break up or nationalize (have the government own) big business, which would limit its ability to outcompete farmers and other small-scale or would-be businesspeople. They also wanted to supply credit to small producers by expanding the currency through the free coinage of silver and lowering interest rates. The high tide of the Populists came in the 1896 presidential election, when Democratic Party candidate William Jennings Bryan lost to Republican William McKinley.

McKinley represented a new political grouping known as Progressives, which tried to build a democracy suited to the new world of the large corporations. Unlike the Populists, they sanctioned organizational cooperation or collectivism in the market with appropriate government oversight. Thus, workers forming unions, capitalists forming corporations, and middle-class professionals forming professional associations were all forms of collective regulation of market activities. Insofar as this collectivism supported profit making through private property, this new democracy was procapitalist, but insofar as it channeled market activity into the public good, they were socialist tending. In short, progressive democracy was a mix or partial reconciliation of the two (see the "President's Strike Commission Report" in the Documents).

To most Americans, *socialism* is a scary term. That is because they see socialism as existing only in the government and originating from outside the market and society. It seems to be a form of state control over society. There is some truth in this. In Russian Communism, the state, monopolized by a single party, exercised unchecked command over the economy and society.

But, not all socialism is statist. At least two forms make up what might be called liberal socialism. The first form, which is common in the West, is the social control of capital, which has taken the form of limited state enterprise (Tennessee Valley Authority, government-owned utilities, etc.) and government oversight of markets through regulatory agencies. In that version, public power has always been checked and balanced by the institutions of democracy: the courts, the legislative and executive branches of government, and ultimately the voters.

There is still another liberal socialist tradition. That is the long tradition of *private*-sector socialism. That tradition includes the British, European, and, to a lesser extent, American cooperative movements (for example, nonprofit food co-ops or credit unions) and private, not-for-profit enterprise (for example, hospitals, charities, foundations, colleges, social welfare groups, advocacy groups). In this tradition, socialism exists in the form of an enterprise outside the state. In the American context, the principle of a self-regulating and self-developing society superior to the state has dictated that Americans do many of the things that other societies have done using the state through societal institutions in order to preserve the maximum amount of individual initiative. The corporation is another such institution.

To call corporations a mix of the principles of private profit and public good is to say they were a mix of capitalist and socialist modes of production. Many people view socialism and capitalism as monolithic systems that cannot have a partial existence in the form of a blend with other property-production systems. But throughout history, most economic systems have been intertwined with different systems at one time or another. For example, in early modern Europe, feudalism and capitalism intricately combined in markets and in absolute states. To say that socialism is an all-or-nothing proposition is to create a utopian construct that is outside of history.

Let us look more closely at the ways the corporation acted for the public good, because to most observers, the ways it served profit interests are already obvious:

- By separating ownership from control, the corporation partially socialized and democratized ownership through dispersing property to a larger public through stock ownership. Today, some segments of the working class, as well as the middle class, own corporations through pension plans.

- Separating ownership from control created a managerial class of functionaries trained in universities according to the latest scientific, technical, and social scientific knowledge. This new class had a relative independence from property considerations.

- The oligopolistic market power of corporations allowed managers to set prices at levels beyond those needed to cover operating and overhead costs. The significant divergence between price and cost, coupled with rising productivity, gave managers much greater leeway than the old proprietary capitalists to allocate funds for social purposes. For example, when pushed, the corporation could fund higher wages, shorter hours, and benefits, whether negotiated or not by unions; scientific research and development; employee safety; health benefits; job training; recreation activities; workplace redesign; philanthropy; charity; and taxes for public goods such as education. These and other socially disposed allocations of resources came to be folded into the price system and passed along to producers and consumers through the market price. One result was that by 1980 most medium- to large-scale employers paid 100 percent of the premiums for employee's health care, while 80 percent of such firms provided their employees with defined benefit pensions.

- The new market power enjoyed by large corporations allowed their managers to plan investment, product development, marketing, and other functions in such a way as to adjust supply and demand over the long term. The anarchy of uncontrolled market competition, surplus capital, and depressions was mitigated by planning based on foresight. Today's diversified corporations consist of multiple divisions or firms in many different industries. With their enormous amounts of retained earnings, they do not need to rely on credit markets but can allocate capital among their different divisions based on a variety of criteria. For example, during the first decade of the twenty-first century, General Electric owned firms in the financial service, information technology, petrochemical, television and film-making, green technology, and health care sectors.

- Insofar as corporations in many industries became significantly "clothed with the public interest," they invited government intervention in ways that family-owned firms within the old competitive economy did not, thus laying the basis for greater public control over the economy through regulatory agencies, Keynesian deficit spending, and social welfare reforms such as old-age pensions and unemployment compensation.

In the early twentieth century, a new and growing body of regulatory agencies emerged. Many conservatives then, as well as today, view almost *all* state regulation of market behavior as equivalent to state despotism. According to this belief, every accretion of state power is a loss for individual freedom. There are several major problems with this view.

First, American political philosophy from the eighteenth century onward has never viewed a democratically elected and constitutionally limited government as an enemy of freedom. While the democratic principle of the state serving society limits the reach of the state, it can also sanction an exceedingly active or positive state (while still being limited). State action can enhance individual liberty, as with the emancipation of the slaves or, more recently, the legislation of rights to prevent discrimination based on race, sex, age, or disability. At other times state action can enhance community by limiting individual freedom in a way that ultimately supports it, as with state laws that prevent child labor except under certain circumstances and compel parents to enroll their children in school or demonstrate that they are homeschooling their children.

Second, participation in the market is not individual. America's economy since the turn of the last century has been organized in large corporations, a response to the dysfunction of markets widely evident in the late nineteenth century. These corporations have become the centers of power in society. The large business corporation has taken on the market functions of planning investment, setting prices, creating internal labor markets, and allocating funds for public purposes.

Thus the invisible hand of the market, which was thought to be sufficient to produce the common good, has been supplemented by the visible hand of business organization. The power of the corporations quickly arose to the point of controlling state power itself. To keep that visible hand from sacrificing the public good, that concentration of market power required a watchdog, which consisted of the regulatory agencies of government. The only alternatives to regulation would be breaking up the large corporations and returning to individual, small-scale enterprise or accepting the ability of unlimited corporate power to control the larger democratic community.

Third, government regulation is not in theory incompatible with competition. The late nineteenth-century progressive economist Henry Carter Adams showed that regulating the market did not abolish or distort competition but merely limited its reach.[6] To ban child labor, for example, was merely to put a floor under competition so that competition in the labor market still occurred but excluded certain categories of labor. From this standpoint, regulation for the public good and the competitive market were not mutually exclusive institutions and could coexist. This is not to say that a line cannot be drawn between regulation that is unproductive and hampers democracy and regulation that is productive and enhances democracy. In any era, Americans will have different views as to where that line exists.

The turning point in public acceptance of broad national regulation came during the Theodore Roosevelt years from 1901 to 1909. Roosevelt came from an upper-class family with a legacy of public service. But, except at the start of his career, he did not rely on his wealth and instead created a reputation for living the strenuous life. Though he suffered from asthma as a child, he moved out West and through sheer force of will reinvented himself as a cowboy on the frontier. Returning to New York City as police chief after his stint out West, he reformed its corrupt police force. Roosevelt also became a well-known historian. His college thesis on the naval War of 1812 is still used in the US Naval Academy. Later, he wrote a four-volume history of the American West. He was an avid reader, usually completing several books a day even as president. When the Spanish-American War broke out in 1898, Roosevelt assembled a band of cowboys into the famous Rough Rider cavalry regiment whose exploits made him a war hero. His fame won him the governorship of New York and then the vice presidency under McKinley. When McKinley was assassinated at the start of his second term in 1901, Roosevelt became president of the United States.

Roosevelt was not a Populist. He believed that big business resulted from the natural evolution of societal forces and was more efficient than small business. But he did believe that people should come before profits and that the corporations needed to be regulated on the federal level. He became the people's tribune in using his office to respond to the public clamor for reform.

A good example came with the scandal about the way sausages were being produced at large corporate-owned factories. In 1906, Upton Sinclair wrote a book called *The Jungle* that exposed the conditions under which meat was being butchered and packed. According to Sinclair,

> There was never the least attention paid to what was cut up for sausage; there would come all the way back from Europe old sausage that had been rejected, and that was moldy and white. It would be dosed with borax and glycerine and dumped into the hoppers and made again for home consumption. There would be meat that had tumbled out on the floor, in the dirt and sawdust, where the workers had tramped and spit uncounted billions of consumption germs. There would be meat stored in great piles in rooms, and the water from leaky roofs would drip over it; and thousands of rats would race about on it. It was too dark in these storage places to see well, but a man could run his hand over these piles of meat and sweep off handfuls of the dried dung of rats. These rats were nuisances and would die, and then packers would put poisoned bread out for them; they would die, and then rats, bread, and meat would go into the hoppers together. . . . All of their sausage came into the same bowl, but when they came to wrap it, they would stamp some of it "special," and for this they would charge 2 cents more a pound.[7]

Out of the public outcry came the Meat Inspection Act and the Pure Food and Drug Act (both in 1906). Significantly, large meat-packers were one of the major interest groups supporting regulatory legislation. Federal supervision helped certify their beef as fit to eat in foreign markets, and the cost of making the production process safe could drive smaller competitors out of the market. The involvement of business interests in the Meat Inspection Act was typical. Normally, all segments of the national community have shaped and assented to regulatory passage.

Other public regulatory bodies established under the Roosevelt administration included a strengthened Interstate Commerce Commission, which could act against discriminatory rebates, set maximum rates, examine railroad books, and prescribe uniform bookkeeping; the establishment of the Federal Reserve Board, America's central bank, which could control the money supply and set interest rates, thereby containing the business cycle; and the Clayton Antitrust Act, which specified which anticompetitive practices of corporations were legal.

The great expansion of the regulatory state came during the Great Depression of the 1930s. Gross national product fell 30 percent and unemployment rose to almost a quarter of the workforce. There was a widespread loss of faith in the management of the economy by leaders of the large corporations and banks. As the newly elected president, Franklin Delano Roosevelt (FDR), a distant cousin of Theodore, put it in his inaugural address,

> The rulers of the exchange of mankind's goods have failed through their own stubbornness and their own incompetence, have admitted their failures

and abdicated. Practices of the unscrupulous money changers stand indicted in the court of public opinion, rejected by the hearts and minds of men.

Roosevelt's administration responded to the crisis with a flurry of legislation offering Americans a New Deal (as in a reshuffling of playing cards). Congress established new agencies:

- to protect workers' rights to form unions with the National Labor Relations or Wagner Administration (1935);
- to fund public works projects and employ the unemployed with the Work Projects Administration (1935);
- to create old-age and disability pensions and aid to dependent children with the Social Security Act (1935);
- to regulate air travel, insure and regulate banking, grant low-interest mortgage loans to poor homeowners, and build public housing for the poor;
- to establish and enforce the eight-hour workday, set a minimum wage, and ban child labor with the Fair Labor Standards Act (1938); and
- to subsidize American soldiers returning from World War II to attend college, buy homes, or start businesses with the GI Bill (1944).

In public opinion the New Deal established two things. First, it created what FDR called America's second bill of rights (see his 1944 "State of the Union Message to Congress" in Documents), the idea government would guarantee minimal or basic living standards—education, food, shelter, work, and health care—necessary for full participation in an advanced democratic society. Second, the New Deal's regulatory apparatus reinvented America's corporate economy as one serving the public good, as well as profits. Roosevelt was hated by America's wealthy, many of whom would not even use his name in private conversations. But America's working people loved him.

By the mid-1930s, the labor movement grew into a mighty force to support the aspirations of working people for security, justice, and power. The great test between the unions and the nation's employers occurred in Flint, Michigan, in the plants of General Motors, the largest corporation in the United States and the world. In 1936, unionized workers took over several key plants in a sit-down strike and refused to leave until they had won collective bargaining. When the Michigan governor and US president refused to send in troops, as had been done to crush Debs's Pullman Strike in 1894, GM capitulated. In the next few years, America's largest corporations accepted collective bargaining.

Unions won much more than the right to bargain for all workers collectively. They won something called "industrial democracy." Unions now had a say in many of the ways the large corporation operated the workplace. They set up grievance procedures, which established the workplace rule of law. Much in the same way that the state and the market were governed by the rule of law, the workplace from the 1940s through the 1970s came to be governed by a series of precedents arising from settled grievance disputes. The arbitrary decisions of company managers were being eliminated in the same way that the new democratic state had abolished the arbitrary rule of the old aristocracy. During World War II, more millions joined the labor movement. By the end of the war, fifteen million workers belonged to unions as compared to three million in 1933. By 1954, over a third of all American workers belonged to a labor union.

In one area, the New Deal fell far short of facilitating the equality necessary for democracy. That was the sphere of race relations. While the Civil War and the Thirteenth Amendment had abolished chattel slavery, the South's landed elites soon restored racial subordination in agriculture through the sharecropping and crop-lien system and debt peonage. By the early twentieth century, most Southern blacks were also denied the right to vote. In America's cities, North as well as South, blacks became subject to humiliating laws and customs that segregated them from other citizens in civil society. Such practices were backed by openly racist attitudes. A late 1930s' poll reported that eight in ten Americans thought that blacks should be kept out of white residential areas, while a 1940 poll showed that half of all Americans believed that whites should have the first chance at an open job.[8] When racist attitudes did not suffice, the Jim Crow system was enforced by concerted terror, the apex of which was lynching.

The New Deal largely acquiesced in racial subordination. The Social Security Act excluded agricultural and domestic workers, the majority of whom were black and female. In the South, New Deal public-works projects did not hire blacks, and throughout the country, local officials kept federal housing racially segregated. An antilynching act failed in the New Deal Congress due to the strength of the Democrats' Southern wing.

During the 1940s, the labor movement was the most promising prospect for challenging the racial subordination and segregation of African Americans, as well as for improving the living conditions for working Americans. African Americans in unions spearheaded the first mass movement for civil rights and economic justice. A. Philip Randolph, the socialist president of the all-black Brotherhood of Sleeping Car Porters, called for a march on Washington in 1941 to protest racial discrimination in defense industry hiring. When President Roosevelt threw his support to a Fair Employment Act that soon passed Congress, Randolph called off the march. Meanwhile, Randolph organized bus boycotts against segregated busing. Many unions in the American Federation of Labor were segregated, but the appearance of the Congress of Industrial Organizations (CIO) in 1935 started the trend toward an integrated unionism. CIO unions such as the United Auto Workers and the Mine, Mill, and Smelter Workers made racial equality an important part of their organizing and bargaining strategies in the 1940s. In the South, CIO unions fought to register black voters.

But these efforts could not break through the powerful institutional forces behind Jim Crow racism until the 1950s. Then, Martin Luther King Jr. and his church-based movement employed the direct-action method of nonviolent civil disobedience. The civil rights movement combined all three dimensions of democracy. It pushed for legislative enforcement of equal civil and voting rights with the Civil Rights Act of 1964 and the Voting Rights Act of 1965 (the political and governmental dimension). The movement went beyond color-blind justice by supporting programs to supply jobs and economic justice for all poor people (the economic dimension) and by challenging white paternalism and black deference that characterized everyday race relations (the cultural dimension).

The combined impact of the militant labor and civil movements created the conditions for the legislative advances of the 1960s. The administrations of John F. Kennedy and Lyndon B. Johnson (LBJ) added another layer of regulatory agencies to those created during the New Deal. They included those ensuring workplace safety, environmental protection, and civil rights enforcement. The 1960s also witnessed major advances in America's welfare state, raising the floor under the standard of living, which in turn helped all working Americans. The food stamp program offered free food to America's poor. Pell grants subsidized children from low-income families to attend college. Federal aid flowed to school districts educating the children of poor families, including the provision of free lunches. Perhaps most importantly, the federal government established health insurance for the poor (Medicaid) and senior citizens (Medicare). LBJ justified government policies to abolish poverty and bring blacks into the mainstream of American society in his Howard University speech (see Documents). Johnson said, "It is not enough just to open the gates of opportunity. All our citizens must have the ability to walk through those gates."

The 1960s and early 1970s culminated a thirty-year period in which the US government became a major agent of social insurance. In the ten years from 1965 to 1975, federal transfer payments for old-age pensions, dependent children, disability, health care, and the like doubled as a share of total personal income from 6.5 percent to 13 percent. As a result of these payments, the prosperity of the consumer economy, and the new responsibility of the federal government to minimize unemployment through Keynesian deficit spending (the use of government deficits to make up for the lack of private demand for goods and services), large swaths of the working class were able to adopt a middle-class lifestyle. By many measures, the percentage of those living a comfortable, affluent lifestyle doubled between World War II and the mid-1970s. The mix of capitalism and socialism, far from being inherently unstable, had proven during this period to be relatively harmonious.

The implications for democracy were immense. With one-third of the US workforce protected by strong unions, poverty levels cut in half, corporations providing health care and pensions for those employed, wages linked to productivity increases, and the government ensuring that a Great Depression would not return, working people could participate in public life, gain a quality education, and pursue happiness as individuals as never before. America had truly become a middle-class democracy. But unlike the nineteenth century when middle class status was based on land ownership, democracy was now available to those who worked for wages.

It is important to understand America's middle-class democracy from an international perspective. America's welfare state has remained less developed than that of Europe. According to the Organisation of Economic Co-Operation and Development, in the late 2000s, the US government spent about 10 percent less on transfer payments than France, Germany, and the UK (16 percent of gross domestic product [GDP] vs. an average of 26 percent of GDP). As a result, the share of the workforce that remains in poverty—17.3 percent, when taxes and transfer payments are taken into account—is almost twice the average of these other three countries.[9] In part, the differences reflect America's continuing preference for private, societal action in the form of social insurance provided by corporations over government action. In this and other cases, private benefits are subsidized by the federal government through the tax system. For example, a high level of home ownership would not be possible without the mortgage interest deduction on federal taxes. Employer-provided health care and retirement benefits are also subsidized by a federal tax deduction. There is a similar deduction for student loans taken out to attend college. These tax expenditures come to 7.4 percent of GDP. Altogether, when employer- and private sector–provided social benefits are taken into account, the United States is on par with Canada and Australia and just below the Netherlands and Denmark.

The differences between Europe and the United States have been accentuated by the greater strength in the United States during recent decades of the neoliberal or conservative reaction to the long wave of economic democracy cresting in the early 1970s (covered in depth in chapter five).

In the 1970s, American business leaders mounted a fierce ideological and political assault on the regulation of business, social welfare spending, and collective bargaining. According one of the most influential Wall Street analysts, Henry B. Kaufman, "Fundamental change has been taking place in our society over the last five decades," which had finally produced a "democracy oriented toward an unaffordable egalitarian sharing of production rather than equal opportunity."[10] To business leaders capital was in danger of becoming something like a municipal public utility—that is, investment was becoming harnessed less to private profit than to the public good. To save the free enterprise system, neoliberals called for the deregulation of business, the taming of militant unions, a shift of the burden of taxation away from the rich, cuts in entitlement expenditures, and a return to a reliance on the private market and the individual work ethic.

Though elite opinion in Washington and most of the media endorses this neoliberal view, polls show that the average American still supports the social democratic ethic in the form of Social Security, Medicare, Medicaid, universal health care, and a robust role for government in securing an economy close to full employment. But the turn in elite public opinion toward neoliberalism has seriously weakened the old consensus.

The results of forty years of neoliberal policies in the United States have been ambiguous. Neoliberals *were* able to implement large permanent income tax cuts favoring the rich (though the rich still pay most income taxes); deregulate key areas of the economy, including the financial sector; destroy or render impotent collective bargaining; and slow the creation of new federal spending programs. But they were not able to roll back federal spending, reduce the size of the federal government in relation to the economy, or decrease social welfare payments. Indeed, the percentage of transfer payments in relation to total personal income has actually risen, as the economy has been unable to provide an adequate number of jobs that pay above the poverty level.

The difficulty in enacting new federal spending programs has led much federal activity targeted toward reducing social inequality to be accomplished through the tax system. Tax deductions for health care, home ownership, and college attendance have already been mentioned. In addition, a major bipartisan effort to aid American working people occurred through the earned income tax credit enacted in 1975 as a way of offsetting the high burden of the payroll tax (the withholding of employee income to fund Social Security and Medicare) on low-income workers. By 2011, the program served twenty-two million Americans and could provide more than five thousand dollars each year to a married couple with two children. Most Americans do not realize the extent to which private-sector activity is being subsidized and redirected through the tax system, activity that includes both social welfare and an enormous array of tax breaks for the rich and large corporations. If tax expenditures are added to private and public welfare expenditures, the United States spends significantly more for social purposes than the average of other top-income countries (defined as the members of the Organisation for Economic Co-Operation and Development). On the other hand, tax expenditures are an inefficient way to deliver social services. If the US government spent directly on a service such as health care, it might save as much as 7.6 percent of GDP.[11]

The previously mentioned view of American politics and government contrasts with the typical view one often reads in the media and hears from some scholarly observers. That view contrasts the Republican Party, which is probusiness and antigovernment regulation and welfare spending, with the Democratic Party that seeks to expand government at the expense of profits and business autonomy. While there is some truth to that point of view, especially since 2010, any discussion of American democracy must define the common ground the two parties shared. Thus, despite differences, Democrats have not advocated removing from corporations the ability to set prices and allocate investment; nor have Republicans until very recently made a serious effort to end government provision of social benefits. Indeed, before the election of President Obama, the largest expansion of government welfare since the 1960s came in 2005 with Republican President George W. Bush's trillion-dollar prescription drug benefit plan. Despite occasional deviations from this consensus from the extremes and the overheated rhetoric of political campaigns, and whether for good or ill, the norm of corporate governance of the economy modified by government regulation and welfare spending has been America's political common ground.

# 4

# DEMOCRACY AND US FOREIGN POLICY

*We look forward to a world founded upon four essential human freedoms. The first is freedom of speech and expression—everywhere in the world. The second is freedom of every person to worship God in his own way. The third is freedom from want. . . . The fourth is freedom from fear.*

Franklin Delano Roosevelt declaring America's war aims in
World War II (1941)

When America entered World War I in 1917 on the side of the Allies against the Central Powers, President Woodrow Wilson told the nation that America's goal was to make the world "safe for democracy." Indeed, in all its major policy formulations and actions, the country's leaders have invoked democracy, freedom, and sometimes peace as their rationales. On the other hand, many observers have viewed such idealistic rhetoric as an alternative to or mask for America's more realistic and self-interested motives, such as the extension of overseas markets and profits or the maintenance of the balance of power in the world. Which of these alternatives best describes America's international relations? What role does democracy have in America's foreign policy?

We may begin by noting that institutionally, American foreign policy is conducted, with some notable recent exceptions, according to democratic procedures and norms. Due to the need to endow foreign policy with initiative, unity of will, and speediness of response, the Constitution allows the president to formulate foreign policy with the "advice and consent" from Congress and review by the Supreme Court. Thus, the president is commander in chief of the armed forces and, through his appointees, conducts diplomacy with other nations. But Congress must confirm the secretary of state and other cabinet members and ambassadors, must ratify treaties with at least a two-thirds vote in the Senate, and is endowed with the power to declare war. The Supreme Court may declare actions of the president null and void if they violate the Constitution. More generally, foreign policy is determined by the policies of the party in power, broader currents of public opinion, and the lobbying influence of organized groups and movements constituting civil society.

The content of American foreign policy, which is the topic of this chapter, has also had democratic features. But it is important to understand that democratic content is not necessarily in conflict with more self-interested and material objectives. Both idealist and realist motives have together constituted US foreign policy, though not without some conflict between these objectives when they have seemed irreconcilable.

## From Continental Settler Expansion to Global Market Expansion

The democratic aspects of American foreign policy have always been rooted in the nation's dominant socioeconomic arrangements. In the course of American history, there have been two stages or phases of foreign policy, one based on widely dispersed landed property and another based on the consolidation of property in the form of corporate capitalism. From the eighteenth through much of the nineteenth century, democratic citizenship was based on a producers' or self-employed economy. In that societal arrangement, white male citizens claimed independence and the ability to make political judgments through their ownership of private property in the form of family farms and artisan and mercantile proprietorships. In the southern part of the United States, property was based on slave labor, as well as self-employed labor, on a multitude of small farms and a smaller number of large plantations.

As an outgrowth of this intertwining of democratic development and agrarian property ownership, America's foreign policy was oriented toward expanding the amount of free land available for settlement and farming. A corollary of landed expansion was the goal of maintaining and expanding markets for farm output and other primary commodities, mainly lumber, ore, and fish. In doing so, America's leaders tried to keep foreign powers at arm's length, while the country expanded west. This was the gist of George Washington's policy of "no entangling alliances" enunciated in his 1796 Farewell Address. The United States would remain neutral in relation to great power conflicts. The other great pillar of early American foreign policy was the Monroe Doctrine articulated by President James Monroe's secretary of state, John Quincy Adams, in 1823. The goal was to wall off the entire Western Hemisphere from European colonialism. At the time the doctrine was issued, many Latin American countries were on the verge of becoming independent from Spain, and the United States wanted to prevent any European power from recolonizing them.

America's early foreign policy in the decades following independence centered on negotiating a favorable position within Britain's navigation system or trading empire without implicating it in great power conflicts. When the United States went to war with Britain in 1812, the immediate issue was neutral trading rights. But a coequal goal was landed expansion in the form of defeating an alliance between the British and the Indians intended to break off the western part of the United States. The United States also invaded Canada (then part of the British Empire) with the intent of adding that land to the United States.

The first great addition of land to the United States came with the Louisiana Purchase in 1803, negotiated fortuitously with the French emperor Napoleon, who needed cash for his upcoming invasion of Russia. The purchase doubled the landmass of the existing United States and led President Thomas Jefferson to comment that the purchase ensured countless generations of Americans access to land as yeomen farmers. Because Jefferson and his fellow founding fathers believed that being enmeshed in relations of dependence—as, for example, were slaves or wage laborers—made people unfit to be citizens, landed expansion was synonymous with the maintenance of democracy. In a common phrase of the day, America was a "republican empire." It was an empire because it was expansionist, but it was republican because the yeomen farmers who settled the new land would be free and equal to those citizens already in the country.

Americans again went to war to add land in the 1830s and 1840s. In the conflict over the independence of Texas in 1836 and the Mexican-American War of 1846–8, American leaders acted with expansionist purposes. As a result of the Mexican-American War, the United States added the land that now constitutes the states of California, Nevada, Utah, New Mexico, and large parts of Colorado and Texas. But, during the war, the consensus on landed expansion fell apart as a mass antislavery movement emerged in the northern states. When Abraham Lincoln was elected president in 1860 setting off the Civil War, the goal of the Republican Party he led was the reservation of land in the West to free white settlers only.

By the end of the 1860s, the number of wage laborers exceeded the number of small proprietors, an indication that capitalism had become the dominant socioeconomic arrangement in the United States. Under *corporate* capitalism, which emerged in the late nineteenth century, the overriding goal of foreign policy was not land but markets for commodities and outlets for capital investment.

But can corporate capitalism be said to be democratic in the way the small family farm was? As argued in chapter three, the large corporation is just as much a medium for public policy and for the diffusion of property as it is for wealth accumulation by the few. Its broad economic and social influence and its ability to pass on the costs of public regulation through the market both compel and enable government to use it as a vehicle for public goals—for example, the minimum wage, collective bargaining, health benefits, and environmental protection. Over time, the spread of stock ownership to larger and larger segments of the public has also made the corporation integral to retirement saving. For these and other reasons, beginning in the early twentieth century, the large majority of Americans has accepted the economic health of the corporate-run economy as a legitimate cornerstone of American foreign, as well as domestic policy.

## America's Open-Door (Post)imperialist Alternative

The turning point in the emergence of a new foreign policy came in the 1880s and 1890s. Before this time, the United States was a net importer of British and European manufactured goods and had a chronic balance-of-payments deficit. The desire to escape from this relationship by industrializing led the triumphant Republican Party in the Civil War to institute a protective tariff on imported goods. By the turn of the century, America's relationship with Europe had changed dramatically. The United States had become the world's largest industrial producer, no longer relied on foreign capital, and had consolidated its economy under the control of large corporations. These large corporations began competing with, and in many cases outcompeting, their European rivals both at home and abroad. When a deep depression hit the country in 1893, it also became clear to policy makers that the United States for the first time was producing more than it could profitably consume domestically.

Three important theorists helped Americans make sense of these new developments. Frederick Jackson Turner was a historian who delivered a famous address at the 1893 World's Fair in Chicago called "The Significance of the Frontier in American History." To Turner, America's unique brand of democracy flowed from the frontier of free land in the West. In the course of building new farms on the frontier, Americans shed European culture and generated a hardy individualism characterized by self-reliance. Turner looked at the US Census and found that the frontier of western lands available for settlement had come to an end. With the West settled, he predicted a coming crisis for American democracy when would-be farmers would be turned back to the cities, where they would bid down wage rates and create an impoverished proletariat seething with social discontent. The alternative, according to Turner in a later essay, was to create a new frontier overseas for our expansionist energies.

Another prophet of the new American expansionism was Brooks Adams, grandson of President John Quincy Adams. In *The Law of Civilization and Its Decay,* Adams argued that all history consisted of cycles in which empires rose and then declined. In this process, empires moved from east to west: from the Chinese to the Middle East empires, to the Greeks, then Carthage, then Rome, followed by the European-based Holy Roman Empire, then the British Empire. Adams argued that America was destined to become the next great empire.

The third great theorist of empire was Charles Arthur Conant. Conant was an advisor closely connected to America's leading investment banking firm, J. P. Morgan, which was marketing the securities of America's new corporations. Conant understood that the overproduction, which caused the 1890s' depression, stemmed from something deeper: a surplus of savings invested in domestic production. Building on this proto-Keynesian analysis, Conant argued that somehow new outlets for this surplus of capital must be found. One solution was tax it away for the public good; still another solution was to have the big corporations monopolize production. The first solution meant socialism, which Conant viewed as destructive of American individualism and innovation; the second solution would not be enough to mitigate overproduction. Conant's major solution was to export this surplus overseas. Such a solution would be in the interest not only of Americans but also of underdeveloped countries. The alternative would be to risk frequent depression, which would destabilize American class relations in the form of unemployment, strikes, agrarian unrest, and political radicalism.[1]

Conant called for America to reorient its foreign policy toward Asia. China then had a population of four hundred million people, a market potentially larger than that of Europe. In addition, China was still outside the control of the European and Japanese colonial powers. China, thought Conant (along with Brooks Adams), was the key to America's destiny. By fostering the independence of China, but at the same time promoting its development, the United States would be setting a precedent for an alternative world order.

There were only two problems. One was that the Chinese might not want to be part of America's future. But Conant, along with other Western leaders and thinkers, believed that the European peoples and others, such as the Japanese, who adopted a developmental framework, were the trustees for the rest of humanity. Neither the Chinese government nor other less developed countries states had the right to sit on resources, including human labor, without exploiting them for the sake of progress. Indeed, this had been America's justification for driving the American Indians off their land in the nineteenth century: the Indians had no concept of private property and were not developing their resources. In contrast to the Europeans or the Japanese, American leaders thought they would be better trustees. As a democratic country, we stood not for selfish interests but for equality of opportunity in the market, a principle that we could then elevate to the world level. So by helping preserve our own unique synthesis of democracy and capitalism from the threat of depression and social disorder, we would be exporting that synthesis abroad to help others.

The other problem was that it seemed that the great colonial powers, which now included Japan, had beaten America to the punch. Following the surprisingly easy defeat of China by Japan in 1894–5, all indications were that the ancient empire was ripe for the plucking. The European powers descended upon China like a pack of hungry sharks, demanding a host of special concessions and spheres of influence. Into this situation stepped American Secretary of State John Hay, who attempted to preserve Chinese sovereignty and the integrity of its market for *all* the great powers. In 1899, he delivered the "Open Door Notes," the first great formulation of America's new foreign policy. The notes called for protection of Chinese administrative and territorial sovereignty and championed equal opportunity for all the great powers, including the United States, to trade with and invest in China. Following the nationalist Boxer Rebellion, which the Europeans put down with the cooperation of the United States, the Europeans launched a whole new round of trade demands on China. It was clear to US leaders that only if the United States could project power into the Asian theater could it hope to implement its open-door policy. But how could this be done?

The answer came from a different part of the world. US expansionists received a heaven-sent opportunity when the Cubans began a revolt against the Spanish Empire. Eventually, the United States would go to war with Spain ostensibly over Cuba. A clue as to the broader goals of the war came at the start. The United States ordered its navy under Commodore George Dewey not to Cuba but to the Philippines. At the war's end, the United States granted Cuba its conditional independence but annexed the Philippines so that it could have a naval base to project its power into Asia. It also annexed Hawaii (in part) as a base and Guam as a coaling station in the Pacific. In the Caribbean, the United States claimed a naval base in Cuba—Guantanamo—to guard the approach to the Isthmian Canal to connect the Atlantic with the Pacific oceans it planned on building; it also annexed the small island of Puerto Rico.

Was the United States now an imperial power in the mold of the great European powers and the Japanese? Yes and no. The United States was an imperial power in terms of its willingness to govern other peoples without granting them the same freedom and equality its own citizens enjoyed. But the real significance of the war's outcome was strategic: the United States had needed to put muscle behind its open-door foreign policy in Asia. The long-term US foreign policy goal was a concert of the great powers, with the less developed world gradually joining based on equal access to an integrated world market—a kind of self-liquidating imperialism. That would make violent conflict between the great powers unnecessary, as predicted by some theorists, notably V. I. Lenin, and maximize economic growth by keeping tariff and other economic barriers equitable and on the level of the "most favored nation." It would also, according to US leaders, obviate centralized, militaristic dictatorships and fuel an evolution toward worldwide democratization, as economic development created a prosperous middle class in place of a mass of impoverished peasants. To Marxists like Karl Kautsky, the proposed system was a form of cooperative imperialism—otherwise termed "ultra-imperialism," "super-imperialism," or "post-imperialism." To Americans, however, this alternative to colonial empire would fashion a world of peace, prosperity, and freedom.[2]

The American approach was not without its inconsistencies—sometimes only apparent, sometimes very real. Throughout much of the twentieth century, the United States routinely intervened militarily in Central American and Caribbean nations to secure American economic or strategic interests. The idea that these weak nations to America's south could be a US "sphere of influence" was imperialistic and contradicted the goal of an integrated world market. There would be other imperialist interventions that seemed to the world—and many Americans—to contradict the US ideal of an open global market: for example, covert support for a military coup d'etat in Chile in 1973 and the unprovoked invasion of Iraq in 2003. American foreign policy has been a mix of imperialist and postimperialist elements, though the open door would become the most basic framework and strategy of US foreign policy for dealing with other great powers.

In the early twentieth century, as the European powers fashioned alliances to protect their empires (the British, French, and Russians) or redivide them (the Germans and Austro-Hungarians), Americans tried to diplomatically mediate disputes on the basis of the open door. Recognizing this, President Woodrow Wilson stated that "the seed of war in the modern world is industrial and commercial rivalry." When the Great War broke out in August 1914, Americans reverted to the same neutrality they had claimed a hundred years earlier. But it was a neutrality that favored the British, as Americans complained only about German submarine warfare and not about the British blockade. Moreover, the United States supplied the British with munitions, food, and private bank loans. The reason for this biased neutrality was that the United States perceived the Germans as a much more potent threat to the open door than the British and French. The Germans were ruled by a militaristic authoritarian regime, which was willing in both world wars to employ force to unite Europe.

When it seemed the Germans were about to win the war, the United States openly chose sides with the Allies (the British and French) in 1917. Wilson then declared to the world America's war objectives in his Fourteen Points. They were not the spoils of empire, but a new world order based on national self-determination, governance of Germany's former colonies on the basis of the open door, removal of trade barriers, freedom of the seas, and a system of collective security. American troops arrived in Europe in time to turn the tide, and in 1918, the Germans were defeated.

A military victory, however, could not be translated into a political one. The Europeans resisted Wilson's Fourteen Points. Though they did finally concede a League of Nations to Wilson, the US Senate refused to ratify the resulting Treaty of Versailles. However, it would be wrong to think that the United States retreated into isolationism in the 1920s and 1930s. US firms continued to invest and trade abroad, and American leaders negotiated two massive loans to Germany so that the Germans could pay their reparations to Europe, which in turn would grease the wheels of world trade. In 1921 and 1922, and United States also hosted a nine-power naval disarmament conference, which reaffirmed the open door in China. Still, whatever the far-flung commitments and aspirations of US foreign policy leaders, most of the American public was determined not to be involved in another European war. Nonetheless, that was precisely what happened.

In 1933, two new leaders took office who would present stark contrasts with each other, and face off in the next world war. The United States elected Franklin Delano Roosevelt, and Germany elected Nazi Party leader Adolph Hitler. By the end of the decade, it appeared that the major threat to the open door came from the Axis powers—Nazi Germany, Fascist Italy, and Imperial Japan—all three expansionist empires with a collective goal of creating a fascistic world order. In 1938,

Germany swallowed up Austria and Czechoslovakia, and in 1939 Poland (with the military cooperation of the Soviet Union), setting off another European war.

In Asia, Japan had invaded Northeastern China in 1931 and established the puppet state of Manchukuo. Then, in 1937, Japan launched a full-scale invasion of China, seeking to control its raw materials, food, and labor. The Sino-Japanese War, which was the largest Asian war of the twentieth century, contributed more than half of all casualties in the Pacific (if 1937 is taken as starting date). Chinese civilians suffered horrendous losses. In the Nanjing Massacre, the Japanese Imperial army slaughtered hundreds of thousands of Chinese civilians and raped tens of thousands of Chinese women. The Japanese also used Chinese civilians for experiments in germ warfare, killing more than half a million innocent people.

The US government, backed by an American public outraged at the Nanjing Massacre, condemned the Japanese invasion. Yet fear of involvement in another world war kept the United States from taking a strong stand. Then, in 1941, after Japan signed a defense pact with Nazi Germany and the Japanese moved into French Indochina and the mineral-rich East Indies, the United States cut off all trade with Japan and ceased supplying it with oil. Heavily dependent on oil imports, fascist Japan now viewed the United States as its chief enemy. On December 7, 1941, Japan launched a surprise attack on the US fleet at Pearl Harbor, Hawaii, pulling the United States into a world war against the Axis powers.

Even before Pearl Harbor, President Roosevelt had met with British Prime Minister Winston Churchill to issue the Atlantic Charter, which declared the goal of the United States and Britain to be "the four freedoms": freedom of speech and expression, freedom of religion, freedom from want (the elimination of poverty), and freedom from fear (a reduction in armaments and a system to prevent aggression). Entrance into the war was a turning point in US foreign policy history because the American public abandoned for good an older politics of "no entangling alliances" and accepted a new dictum: if they were to make their democracy and open-market system viable, it was necessary to internationalize it. The corollary of this was that the expansion of antidemocratic, closed-market forces abroad would be seen as a threat to American democratic capitalism at home.

During World War II, the United States forged a military alliance with Great Britain, the Soviet Union, and China. The United States had important ideological differences with each of them. Though Britain was democratic, it was also a colonial power. The Soviet Union was an authoritarian communist regime, which also desired expansion. Finally, the Kuomintang Party, ruler of China, was another authoritarian regime with marked similarities to European fascism. However, given the overriding need of defeating Germany and Japan, the United States offered significant material and military assistance to the British, Russian, and Chinese governments.

At the end of the war, the United States occupied both Japan and Germany (its western part) until 1952 and 1955, respectively. The United States prosecuted top leaders for war crimes and demilitarized and democratized these once authoritarian and expansionist countries. In Japan, the United States redistributed land from wealthy landlords to farmers, legalized trade unions, abolished Shinto as the state religion, and prohibited the teaching of its military code. Under American tutelage, the Japanese adopted a constitution that transferred sovereignty from the emperor to the people, established parliament as the country's supreme institution, enfranchised women, weakened the power of the police, and guaranteed human rights. The same constitution also outlawed war as an instrument of state policy and limited military expenditures to 1 percent of the national budget. Even today, small contingents of US troops remain in Germany and Japan as a token of America's commitment to undertake their national defense and assure neighbors that a resurgence of militarism will not occur.

The triumph of the United States and its allies in the war against the Axis powers ushered in a new era in international relations. The European powers were too devastated and economically weak to retain their empires or to resist the introduction of American open door principles internationally. In the decade following World War II, a host of new nations emerged from the formerly colonized areas of the world, particularly in Asia and Africa. Under American leadership, an array of international institutions was created: the United Nations (UN), the General Agreement on Tariffs and Trade (GATT), the International Monetary Fund (IMF), and the World Bank (WB). These institutions created a forum to settle international disputes and mobilize world opinion against aggression (UN), construct and maintain an integrated world market (GATT, superseded in 1995 by the World Trade Organization), prevent global deflation and depression (IMF), and fund development (WB). For the first time since the original American vision of the open door, truly effective international institutions existed to construct an open global economy.

## Democracy and the Cold War

But the defeat of the Axis powers and the advent of these new institutions were not enough to usher in a new era of global markets. Barely a year after the Japanese surrender, a new conflict emerged that divided most of the world for the next forty-five years: the ongoing conflict between the Communist and the non-Communist worlds, beginning with the fallout between the two former wartime allies—the United States and the Soviet Union.

Three critical events ignited what became known as the Cold War. At the Yalta summit in February 1945, while the war was still in progress, the Americans, British, and Soviets confronted the future of Eastern Europe. Though the United States recognized the need of the Soviet Union for a friendly government on its Polish border, it hoped for the inclusion of non-Communist elements in the Polish government. In return for this and other concessions, the Soviet Union agreed to support the UN and enter the war against Japan, the invasion of which was expected to cost half a million American casualties. When the Soviets established a Communist government in Poland, the United States protested. To Stalin this was merely a defensive move for Russia to establish and protect its traditional sphere of influence. But to the new American president Harry S. Truman, this was a betrayal of the Yalta agreement and a violation of the American commitment to the open door.

A second and related event was the US refusal of any reconstruction aid to the Soviet Union until it would pledge "non-discrimination in international commerce" in its spheres of influence. The Soviets refused.

The third event that led to the Cold War was the Potsdam conference. If the Soviet Union was not going to get a reconstruction loan from the United States, it wanted to take reparations from the defeated Germans. The United States and other Western leaders thought that high reparations, which the Versailles Treaty exacted from the Germans after World War I, was a direct cause of the economic and social instability in Germany that produced Nazism and Hitler. They opposed any reparations, especially if it required US loans to Germany that would be immediately transferred to the Soviet Union in the form of German reparations. The two sides finally agreed to allow the Soviet Union to strip the eastern half of Germany of its industrial equipment, but this meant that Germany had to be divided into western and eastern parts.

These three lesser known events set the stage for the more well-known events that followed—the 1947 coup d'etat by Communist forces in Czechoslovakia, the US Marshall Plan to reconstruct Western Europe, the 1948 Berlin blockade and airlift, the 1949 Chinese Revolution, the 1950–3 Korean War, and the ensuing military standoff in Europe between the US-led North Atlantic Treaty Organization (NATO) alliance and the Soviet-led Warsaw Pact alliance—which institutionalized the long Cold War.

In 1947, President Truman enunciated America's Cold War doctrine in two seminal speeches. In a speech justifying US foreign aid to Greece and Turkey, he compared the Soviet Union to Nazi Germany and asserted what became known as the Truman Doctrine: support for non-Communist governments was necessary to prevent the takeover of Europe by the Soviet Union and its allies. In another speech, Truman blamed the depression and political conflict on trade wars and pledged that the United States would take the lead in reducing trade barriers.

In retrospect, the US conflict with Communism during the Cold War can be understood as an outgrowth of the long-standing American opposition to closed markets and spheres of influence, an opposition to closed political systems dominated by a monarch or single political party, and an opposition to Communist-led national liberation movements in less developed countries. Americans' support for open markets, capitalism, civil freedoms, and democracy worldwide was closely connected to its commitment to these institutions at home. The underlying premise of America's commitment to the containment of Communism was the belief that the country's domestic institutions could not survive without a hospitable world order. Ironically, this was a belief that Communist leaders shared about their own institutions.

Though the United States had superseded the war-devastated European powers as the leader of the West, its ongoing conflict with the Communist world kept its foreign policy in severe constraints. With the advent of the Cold War, a bipolar world order emerged with a balance of power resting on competition in nuclear arms. Each side relied on a strategy of mutually assured destruction, which required a massive buildup of nuclear weapons. Each side feared a preemptive war by the other, and both sides retained arsenals capable of destroying the other and much of the planet. One result of this nuclear standoff was the shift of political rivalry to the peripheries of the international system in the form of proxy wars, which were limited in scope. Each side avoided direct confrontations that could escalate into total war as almost happened during the Cuban Missile Crisis in October of 1962.

As during World War II, the United States took the position that the enemy of my enemy is a friend. Thus, US foreign policy supported authoritarian regimes as long as they could be trusted to be effective bulwarks against Communist revolution and Communist intervention from abroad and were friendly to Western business interests. The commitment to democracy and human rights—evident in the four freedoms of World War II and the reconstruction of Germany and Japan—often took a back seat to strategic considerations. Thus, the United States supported the fascist Francisco Franco regime in Spain, General Suharto in Indonesia, Chung Hee Park of South Korea, Ferdinand Marcos in the Philippines, P. W. Botha of South Africa, the Al Saud dynasty in Saudi Arabia, and the Shah Mohammed Reza Pahlevi in Iran. The United States also undertook military interventions—for example, in Guatemala and Iran—to preserve anti-Communist, probusiness governments against more popular and democratic forces. The so-called domino theory dominated American strategic thinking. According to this view, a change in the balance of power would result from the toppling of a pro-Western government by anti-Western forces possibly friendly to the Soviet Union or Communist China. The fall of one domino would weaken the resolve of friendly pro-Western governments, embolden anti-Western forces, and provoke miscalculations from each side, thus making nuclear conflict more likely. The most glaring example of this policy occurred in Vietnam.

Vietnam was a former French colony conquered by the Japanese during World War II. Immediately following the war, the leader of the Communist insurgency, Ho Chi Minh, asked for American support for the Vietnamese independence movement. Despite the long-standing American commitment to national self-determination, the United States refused on the grounds that French support was needed to stabilize Western Europe against internal or external Communist threats. Ho nonetheless declared independence and, using a peasant guerilla army, defeated the French military expedition, which had been wholly bankrolled by the United States.

The 1954 Geneva Accords temporarily divided Vietnam into North and South, the North Communist, the South non-Communist, but mandated elections in 1956 to reunify the country. The United States backed Ngo Dinh Diem, an anti-Communist nationalist authoritarian ruler. Socially, Diem represented the minority of French-speaking Catholic Vietnamese who controlled the country's government and economy. In 1956, Diem cancelled elections and consolidated his authoritarian rule, setting off a revolt in the south. Over the next eight years, the military situation of the pro-American regime deteriorated to the point that South Vietnam's rural areas, where most of its population resided, came under the control of Communist insurgents (also known as the Vietcong) in the National Liberation Front (NLF). In 1965, US president Lyndon Johnson introduced American ground troops into Vietnam. Johnson argued that Americans were in Vietnam to contain the spread of Communism and the influence in Asia of Chinese Communism. By the end of 1967, approximately half a million US troops were engaged in a military struggle with the NLF, which was supplied by the Soviet Union and China.

Despite the fact that the United States was the most advanced military power on the globe and had more than five times Vietnam's population, the war went badly for American troops and their South Vietnamese allies. The conflict was not a conventional one as in World War II or Korea, but a guerilla war or what Mao Zedong termed a "People's War." To prevail, Americans had to win the "hearts and minds" of Vietnamese peasants, and as foreigners, this was extremely difficult. Making matters worse, the United States engaged in indiscriminate bombing, which by the end of the war had killed hundreds of thousands of civilians.

The carnage among innocent Vietnamese villagers and the growing number of American casualties sparked a large domestic antiwar movement. By the end of the 1960s, the insurgency embraced millions and had become the largest movement in American history. College students, professionals, housewives, prominent businesspeople, ordinary working people, and even members of Congress marched and protested against the war. Still, most Americans supported the Vietnam War on the strength of the Cold War consensus that the United States must act to contain Communism at all costs. Then came the spectacular Vietcong offensive in 1968, which undermined the American public's support for the war.

With a new president, Richard Nixon, at the helm, American foreign policy after 1968 focused on extricating the United States from the mess in Vietnam. But because the goal remained the maintenance of the anti-Communist government in the south, the war dragged on for another four years. When the United States finally withdrew in 1973, it had suffered fifty-eight thousand dead and another three hundred thousand wounded. An estimated 1.5 million Vietnamese lost their lives, and the war created ten million Southeast Asian refugees. In 1975, the anti-Communist South Vietnamese government fell when the Communist North invaded the South.

The Vietnam War and its stunning outcome shook American foreign policy almost to its foundations. Domestically, foreign policy became much more subject to public opinion and party differences. Up until this time, Americans through their Congress had largely deferred to the president in the making of foreign policy. Some critics even talked about an "imperial presidency" based on the fact that during the Cold War the president had committed troops abroad without a Congressional declaration of war and conducted his foreign policy through new agencies—for example, the National Security Agency—that were not accountable to Congress.

The old consensus that party conflict should stop at the nation's shores was shattered by the Vietnam War. Republican Party conservatives, starting from the premise that world was inherently conflictual and dangerous, tended to rely on American military power and other forms of coercion, and as a result they were often unilateralist. Democratic Party liberals, believing that the world could be made orderly and democratic, relied more on international institutions and tended to be wary of military interventions; as a result they were usually multilateral in decision making. In practice, foreign policy was normally a blend of the two political tendencies.

The democratization of foreign policy has gone further. The strength of the antiwar movement led President Nixon to replace the draft with the volunteer army and to gradually withdraw US troops. In 1973, under the influence of anti-Vietnam War sentiment, Congress passed the War Powers Joint Resolution, which attempted to take back from the president the power to declare war. Since that time, social movements have often had an important impact on US foreign policy. The nuclear-freeze movement of the 1980s helped push the Reagan administration toward a more moderate policy with the Soviet Union. A campaign to stop American corporations from investing in South Africa because of its apartheid policies led to a congressional ban on all US investment in that country. Congress overrode President Reagan's veto of the law, which soon led the South African regime to release Nelson Mandela from prison, negotiate with the African National Congress, and ultimately dismantle apartheid.

The more lasting influence of the new phase of democratization of foreign policy making lay in the public's great reluctance, for the first time since World War II, to support the deployment of American military power abroad—the so-called Vietnam Syndrome. In a major modification of the Truman Doctrine, the United States began to resort to new diplomatic options to contain the spread of Communism. The United States relied more heavily on regional allies to police the non-Communist world, such as Brazil in Latin America, Israel in the Middle East, and its European allies in Africa. The United States also turned to new tactics, notably covert operations, to counter Communist expansion. The US support for the contras in Nicaragua, the mujahideen in the conflict over Afghanistan, and Joseph Namibi in the Angolan civil war exemplified tactics that seemingly would require less blood and treasure from the American public.

A second major innovation in US foreign policy following the Vietnam War was the new attitude toward support for democracy internationally. The old idea had been that support for worldwide democracy played into the hands of the Communists and was an unrealistic option for most of the world. The antiwar civil rights leader Martin Luther King Jr. famously condemned this policy when he said, "It is a sad fact that, because of comfort, complacency, a morbid fear of communism, and our proneness to adjust to injustice, the Western nations that initiated so much of the revolutionary spirit of the modern world have now become the arch anti-revolutionaries."[3] Even though American foreign policy elites were split, President Jimmy Carter launched a renewed emphasis on human rights in American foreign policy. Indeed, Carter's pressure on the Shah of Iran to release political prisoners, end military tribunals, and permit free public assemblies is widely believed to have undermined the Shah's rule and inadvertently opened the way for the Islamic fundamentalist Iranian revolution of 1979. Carter's successor, Ronald Reagan, though he was a conservative, eventually endorsed and expanded Carter's policy. The revised idea was that support for democracy might help legitimize America's open-market principles and serve as a bulwark against Communism.

The new thrust of American foreign policy helped launch the third wave of global democratization. The tide began in Europe in 1974 in Portugal, Greece, and Spain and then moved on to Latin America, with notable successes in Brazil and Argentina, as the military withdrew from politics. In 1974, eight of ten South American countries were undemocratic, but by 1990, nine of ten were democratic. The Philippines, Turkey, and South Korea also returned to and consolidated their democracies. By the end of the 1980s, the democratic wave engulfed the Communist world, first in the Soviet Union's sphere of influence in Eastern Europe and then in the Communist behemoth itself. Though the third wave was truly a global development, there was only limited movement toward democracy in Africa and the Middle East.

Still, democracy had become the world's new common sense in governance. According to Nobel prize–winning economist Amartya Sen,

> In any age and social climate, there are some sweeping beliefs that seem to command respect as a kind of general rule—like a "default" setting in a computer program; they are considered right *unless* their claim is somehow precisely negated. While democracy is not yet universally practiced, nor indeed uniformly accepted, in the general climate of world opinion, democratic governance has now achieved the status of being taken to be generally right.[4]

What explains the renewed impetus to democracy in recent times? One major reason was the new pro-human rights attitude of the Catholic Church since Vatican II, which undermined the legitimacy of traditional authoritarian rulers. The third wave was overwhelmingly based in countries with large Catholic populations, especially in Latin America.

Another reason was the prodemocratic influence of global powers. Not only the United States and the Vatican but also the Soviet Union under Mikhail Gorbachev, who ascended to power in 1985, paved the path away from authoritarian rule. Gorbachev's policy of glasnost (openness) in the Soviet Union and his renunciation of the Brezhnev doctrine (the pledge that the Soviet Union would militarily intervene in other Communist countries to maintain their form of government) encouraged dissidents in Eastern Europe. In 1989, the Communist governments in Eastern Europe came tumbling down: Poland, East Germany, Hungary, Czechoslovakia, Romania, Bulgaria, Albania, and Yugoslavia. Two years later, the Soviet Union dissolved as well. The USSR transformed itself into a fragile democracy in Russia under the leadership of Boris Yeltsin and enabled the formation of fourteen new democratic states, which had been part of the old Soviet Union. With these sudden, stunning, and unexpected events, the Cold War was over.

Only the People's Republic of China remained a large Communist state. But China was not immune from the time's democratic tendencies. In 1978, Deng Xiaoping had initiated reforms that led to the growth of a market economy in China and the relaxation of strict party controls. In 1989, sparked by the funeral of prodemocracy official Hu Yaobang, one hundred thousand prodemocracy students and intellectuals gathered in Tiananmen Square. Over the next seven weeks, the movement spread to other Chinese cities. But the government cracked down severely on the protests and the Communist Party remained firmly in control of China.

There was another, stronger reason that explains the shift of American foreign policy to support for democracy abroad. Democracy is closely correlated to economic and social development. Democracies were very rare before the Industrial Revolution; conversely, none of the wealthy democracies have ever degenerated into authoritarianism. The states that democratized in the third wave were overwhelmingly those in the World Bank's middle- to upper-middle-income category. The process seems to work this way: when development has created a large enough middle class—businesspeople and managers, professionals, relatively prosperous workers and farmers, and intellectuals—they become confident enough to demand a say in how government is run. In part, this is because a modernizing economy generates diverse forms of property and social and economic organizations outside the state, which are difficult to control efficiently from a central location. Development also presupposes participation in the market and higher educational levels, which engender greater interpersonal trust, personal autonomy, and competency. The demand for a government based on consent—the core of democracy—was also promoted by the spread of democratic and liberal ideas from abroad through television, literature, radio, and now the Internet.

Many observers used to think that a form of government called "bureaucratic authoritarianism," mainly in Asia with its Confucian and sometimes Islamic heritage and Latin America with its traditional Catholicism, was more conducive to development than democracy. But with industrialized Latin American and Asian countries such as Brazil, Chile, Mexico, South Korea, Taiwan, Singapore, Indonesia, and others embracing democracy, social scientists now believe that democracy is a powerful worldwide tendency at middling and higher ranges of development.

One large region of the world that was impervious to democratization during the third wave was the Middle East. Unlike the countries that democratized in the 1970s and 1980s, most Middle Eastern despots had the support of a powerful outside actor: the United States. Moreover, the oil wealth many of these regimes controlled afforded them relative immunity from having to satisfy the material demands of their populations. It took until 2010 for the Arab Spring to emerge, a wave of democratization from below that erupted in Tunisia and swept through Egypt, Libya, and Bahrain and has led to ongoing insurgencies in other Arab countries, including Syria. As with previous democratic transitions, it was the urban middle class with crucial support from youth, feminists, and Muslim fundamentalists that propelled the uprising. It is too early to predict if the new regimes can reconcile with local bourgeoisies and satisfy the demands of the religious-minded lower classes. Whatever the result, the Arab Spring has bolstered confidence that democracy remains a growing global trend.

## Neoliberalism and the New Wave of Globalization

The era of the 1970s witnessed another major international development in which the United States played a critical role: globalization. What is normally referred to as globalization—the heightened movement of commodities (exports and imports), capital (overseas investment), and population (out-migration and in-migration) across national boundaries—is not new. In the modern era, an earlier period of globalization based on the international gold standard prevailed during the nineteenth century and was only halted and reversed with World War I and start of the Great Depression of the 1930s.

The present wave of globalization originated in the United States and United Kingdom in the 1970s as a response to three major internal developments. First, the stagnation in growth, incomes, and asset prices combined with inflation created an occurrence unique in economic theory: stagflation. It seemed to discredit Keynesian economics, which had justified government spending in excess of tax revenue to combat unemployment, stimulate economic growth, and reduce social and economic inequalities.

During the period of retrenchment from the earlier phase of globalization—the 1930s to 1970s—the United States had developed a robust social contract based on the strength of the labor movement and a consensus that government should be used to regulate the activities of big business and minimize extreme inequalities with social welfare spending. The forty-year period beginning in the 1930s saw the advent of government support for the right of workers to unionize, the passage of Social Security (old-age pension and disability benefits), strict regulation of financial institutions, enforcement of civil liberties for minorities and women, the war on poverty, medical insurance for senior citizens and the poor, and, not least, a raft of legislation to protect the environment. The 1960s and early 1970s was the high point for this social contract. The percent of income accruing to the top 1 percent fell from 20 percent in 1927 to an all-time low of 8 percent in the late 1970s.

The decade of the 1970s would prove to be an important turning point. The value of stocks, bonds, and other forms of property plunged, while the regulatory burdens felt by large business became significantly heavier. Many corporate leaders feared that a long slide from capitalism toward socialism would culminate in corporations being viewed as public utilities (wealth-making institutions to be exploited for the public good) rather than engines for profit. In response to stagflation and the limitations on property accumulation and profit-seeking activities, these leaders rejected the old social contract and shifted toward what became known as neoliberalism.

Neoliberalism, the second development, was the ideology that emphasized the market values of personal responsibility, competition, and entrepreneurialism over social responsibility, social cooperation, and social-welfare spending by government. It called for deregulation of business to stimulate investment, opposed unions and collective bargaining, advocated cutbacks in social spending, and justified the growth of inequality as the price to be paid for innovation and growth. The prime purpose of government was not to ameliorate inequalities and minimize unemployment but to promote investor confidence by reining in inflation, protecting profits from high taxation, and shielding corporate property from excessive regulation.

After neoliberalism triumphed in the United States and the United Kingdom, it spread throughout the world in the form of the 1990s "Washington Consensus." The consensus, which penetrated Latin American countries and then many Asian and African countries, promoted reliance on markets rather than government, free trade, and human rights and democracy. American leaders used their power and leverage to promote new policies for less developed countries. These policies aimed to *downsize* government, *deregulate* business, *privatize* state-owned industries, and create *fiscal austerity* (eliminate government budget deficits and money creation in order to stabilize prices to encourage foreign investment). The fundamental character of the post-1970s phase of globalization has been largely shaped by neoliberal policies.

In addition to stagflation and the neoliberal doctrine, there was a third factor opening the way to a new commitment to globalization on the part of US political and economic leaders. The sudden run-up in oil prices by the Organization of Petroleum Exporting Countries (OPEC) created an acute financial shock for Western consumers of oil. The outflow of billions of petrodollars, along with stagflation, threatened to stifle economic growth in the United States. Under great pressure from Western powers, Saudi Arabia, the principal Middle Eastern oil producer, agreed to recycle its petroleum earnings through Western banks. Awash in funds available for loans, the banks, backed by the US government, began to push less developed countries to jettison capital controls and open their economies to foreign lending. Over time, the push for the free flow of capital across borders largely succeeded. Within the American economy, the major financial institutions greatly increased their share of domestic profits from less than 16 percent in the early 1980s to a high of 45 percent in the 2001. In short, the US economy became heavily dependent on the new globalization just as many less developed economies became heavily dependent on foreign loans.

Along with neoliberal policy doctrine and the enhanced role of large banks, the multinational (also termed "global" or "transnational") corporation has become a central institution of globalization. Since 1900, large American corporations have sold their products abroad and established production facilities overseas. What is new is the degree to which these firms have become globally integrated and able to locate subsidiaries and contracted services anywhere in the world. According to UN data, some thirty-five thousand firms have direct investment in foreign countries, and the largest one hundred of them control about 40 percent of world trade. For example, Walmart, the largest corporation in the United States and the third largest in the world, is the largest American importer of goods produced overseas, and the majority of its private-label clothing is manufactured in at least forty-eight countries around the world—and almost none in the United States. Walmart's biggest trading partner is China, and Walmart imports *nearly 10 percent of all Chinese goods sold in the United States.*

The term *American imperialism* does not come close to capturing the new globalization. One reason is that the central institutions of globalization are truly multinational and not national. Global corporations not only exercise great influence on national governments in regulating the world economy but also are no longer centers of national competition. Increasingly, they are owned internationally and operated according to global standards. More important, they do not necessarily subjugate or limit the development of less developed societies. Using foreign capital, a significant number of less developed countries—collectively known as the newly industrialized countries (NICs)—have entered the ranks of the developed. The largest include Brazil, Mexico, South Africa, Turkey, the Philippines, Malaysia, Thailand, and most recently the giants, China and India. One measure of this change is the establishment in 1999 of the G20, which includes all the NICs, to discuss key issues in the global economy. In this sense, the open-door system promulgated by the United States for over a hundred years and now taking the shape of a global postimperialism has proved to be a partially self-liquidating imperialism and compatible under the right circumstances with development, nation building, and democracy.

The lynchpin of the global system has been the open US market. While supplying the capital needs of the NICs, the US economy has served as the market for the exports from less developed countries. This has been particularly true of the Asian NICs, which have pursued an export-led model of economic development, following Japan's success after World War II. The United States has accommodated the Asian exports along with those of the Japanese and Germans, who have also continued to rely on export-led growth. As a result, the United States has run an ever-growing trade and balance-of-payments deficit with the rest of the world since the late 1970s. That is, US consumers and producers increasingly import more than they export. But beginning in the late 1990s, this relationship turned dysfunctional.

The free flow of capital around the global economy, much of it speculative in nature, has resulted in a series of financial panics. Speculative investors have created financial bubbles by pouring loan capital into countries on favorable terms and then suddenly pulling out their funds when high returns appeared to be threatened. Financial bubbles burst in Mexico (1995), Russia (1998), Argentina (1998 and 2001), and in East Asia (1997–8). Following the latter crisis, East Asian countries began to accumulate foreign exchange surpluses to guard against another flight of foreign capital. To accumulate these surpluses, as well as maintain their export-led growth, they needed to undervalue their currencies against the dollar. To keep the value of their currencies low relative to the dollar, they needed to bolster the dollar's strength by investing their surpluses in the United States rather than at home. Coincidentally, at this moment the global economy had entered a period of surplus capacity to produce. There were simply not enough investment outlets that offered profitable returns. Thus, Asian, particularly Chinese, savings tended to go into unproductive outlets. In particular, these savings financed the consumer debt that allowed American workers to live far beyond their stagnating incomes; it financed the housing bubble in the United States; and it financed the US wars in Afghanistan and Iraq, all through the purchase of US treasury bonds.

A truly productive investment outlet would have been raising the standard of living of the Chinese and Asian people, which would have also aided Western producers by providing an export market for them. But this did not fit the export-focused policies of Asian governments or the role of the United States as lynchpin of the global economy and policeman of the world.

The relationship was truly unsustainable because the Chinese could not continue to save 50 percent of their incomes; nor could Americans continue indefinitely piling up debts that were used for non-income producing activities. The bursting of the US housing bubble in 2007 exposed this relationship and plunged the world into the worst business downturn since the Great Depression of the 1930s.

Even before the Great Recession that so profoundly rocked the world economy, American world leadership had come up against its limits in the Iraq War. Prior to that conflict, American foreign policy had undergone a radical shift in response to a unique unipolar moment. As the only remaining superpower following the fall of the Soviet Union and the end of the Cold War in 1991 and with the absence of a rival power with an alternative grand plan for organizing the world, American foreign policy leaders briefly seemed to abandon the policy goal of postimperialism. America's post-World War II strategy was based on cooperation, or at least a balance of power, among the great powers. According to the new strategy of right wing neoconservatives, America would disentangle itself from its multiple commitments to international cooperation and use its overwhelming military superiority to cow other nations' opposition to the project of aggressively spreading freedom (read, the spread of global market relationships and basic civil liberties) throughout the world, starting in the Middle East.

The September 11, 2001, terror attacks on New York City's World Trade Center and the Pentagon in Washington, D.C., became the occasion for the unfolding of this doctrine before the American public. According to the neoconservatives and President Bush, the existence of weapons of mass destruction and the presence of terrorists willing to use them made necessary the doctrine of preemption, under which the United States was justified in attacking other countries first if the United States thought other countries would attack them. The Bush strategy circumvented democratic constraints in that it allowed the president to bypass the Constitution and suspend civil liberties for Americans in wartime, which, under the newly proclaimed War on Terror, could last indefinitely.

In 2003, US military forces attacked the country of Iraq led by a brutal dictator, Saddam Hussein. There was no imminent threat to the United States or its allies, nor did the United States gain support from the UN Security Council despite the fact that Iraq had not cooperated fully with weapons inspectors. In contrast to the Gulf War of 1991 when the world's great powers, including Russia, had united to defeat Iraq's military takeover of its neighbor Kuwait, the 2003 invasion had no support from great powers except from the United Kingdom.

The US invasion with its reliance on shock and awe was at first stunningly successful in toppling the Hussein regime. But after an initial euphoria, the invasion ran into problems. The Iraqi Army, which might have been used to keep order in the streets, was disbanded, and with only a moderate-sized American invasion force, the country descended into chaos, regularly punctuated with suicide bombings. Meanwhile, American forces could find no weapons of mass destruction, the initial justification for this preemptive war, which undermined American domestic support. Even worse, an armed insurgency of Sunni tribesmen—an ethno-religious faction that lost power when Hussein was overthrown—engulfed the country.

In 2007, with the American-backed government on the verge of failure, President George W. Bush dispatched a new general with a new strategy. Though it included a small surge in troops, the thrust of General David Petraeus's approach was to negotiate with or buy off the insurgents and pull back from direct military confrontation. The new military strategy was a turning point in the return of American foreign policy to its roots during Bush's second term. With the neoconservatives repudiated in public opinion, newly elected President Barack Obama abandoned the doctrine of preemption, the emphasis on military solutions, and the commitment to a War on Terror, which would forbid the United States from talking to its enemies. Even as the sole remaining superpower, the United States could not lead mainly through military power. After all, one of the central ideas of postimperialism was to make military solutions to economic and geopolitical conflicts unnecessary.

There were other problems, flaws, or imbalances in the new global economy and postimperial international order. Each of them has served to remind Americans of something they learned during World War II: American prosperity and security are intertwined with global prosperity and security.

Notable among these problems are the following:

- *Nuclear proliferation.* Since the 1970 nuclear nonproliferation treaty was signed, the United States has endeavored to prevent the spread of nuclear technology, fissile materials, and nuclear weapons beyond the original five possessors of the bomb (the United States, Russia, China, the United Kingdom, and France). With the spread of the bomb to other regional powers—Pakistan, India, Israel, and most recently North Korea and Iran (expected soon)—the probability that a bomb will be used has risen appreciably. This is particularly true in the Middle East.

- *Global terror.* Beginning with the attacks on the US World Trade Center on September 11, 2001, and the similar attacks in London, Madrid, and Casablanca, the problem of terror attacks on the United States or its allies and the use of terror to destabilize emerging economies has become one that requires global cooperation. The possibility that terrorists could acquire nuclear weapons from an unstable state is frightening to all the world's nations. Within the United States, the War on Terror has led to renewed debates about the proper balance between civil liberties to security.

- *Failed states.* States that are unable to exercise authority over their territory and the people residing there have become a growing global problem. International terrorist networks and drug traffickers can use these countries as bases of operations, infectious diseases and civil violence can spill over into their neighbors' lands, and failed states are powerless to prevent environmental destruction and other more immediate threats to their populations. Currently, there are over thirty states that fit the category and many more on the danger list. They include Somalia, Sudan, Zimbabwe, Afghanistan, Pakistan, and Iraq.

- *Energy and food security.* Many countries rely almost entirely on imports of increasingly expensive fossil fuels, lack arable land to grow enough food for their populations, and lack adequate water resources. Hunger, reflected in rising grain prices, is a growing problem throughout the world. When food-exporting countries take unilateral actions, such as converting grain to biofuel as the United States has done or stopping exports altogether, a crisis is created in importing countries, and they too resort to unilateral actions, threatening global cooperation.

- *Inequality and global poverty.* While industrialization has pulled tens of millions of people out of extreme poverty, inequality has risen, both within countries and between the more successful ones and least successful ones, particularly those in Africa and the Middle East. According to the UN Human Development Report, in 2005 only nine countries (4 percent of the world's population) have reduced the wealth gap between rich and poor, while 80 percent of the world's population has experienced an increase in wealth inequality. The report states that

> the richest 50 individuals in the world have a combined income greater than that of the poorest 416 million. The 2.5 billion people living on less than $2 a day—40% of the world's population—receive only 5% of global income, while 54% of global income goes to the richest 10% of the world's population.[5]

- Growing inequality makes it difficult to address a host of dysfunctional social practices, such as overuse of scarce resources, overpopulation, civil violence, violation of human rights, and authoritarian rule.
- *Global climate change.* Looming over all other problems is the increasingly inescapable one of climate change created by man-made global warming. Global climate change promises to create disasters that would make a mockery of the highest hopes for globalization, development, and democracy. For example, the disappearance of glaciers that feed rivers and fertilize agricultural areas could cause mass starvation in central Asia, India, and Tanzania. In the United States, the melting of the Sierra Nevada ice packs would cripple agriculture in the Central Valley. The melting of the glaciers elsewhere could cause a catastrophic rise in sea levels that would doom hundreds of millions of people to refugee status. A struggle for increasingly scarce resources could develop that would unleash wars, famines, destabilizing population movements, and undermine global cooperation.

Global climate change is a classic example of actions taken in the immediate national interest, narrowly conceived, increasing the long-term prospect for world catastrophe. The United States, with 4.5 percent of the world's population, emits one-fifth of the world's greenhouse gases. Yet American business leaders and American voters have thus far refused to take into account the long-term social and economic costs of climate change, many of which will have to be borne by other peoples or future generations. Unfortunately, the same shortsighted view characterizes the large majority of the world's population.

Addressing these and other problems will be the crucial test of a postimperial global order. In such an order, development through the spread of capital and technology is not the jealously guarded property of the advanced nations but is shared with the emergent and recently developed nations. Nations and the world's peoples are increasingly knit together by the supply chains and consumer markets for multinational corporations; dense communications links, notably the Internet; an international popular culture; and an increasingly shared commitment to democratic values. Finally, economic and political disputes are settled mainly through multilateral rather than unilateral decision making, and the resort to coercion and military force becomes increasingly rare.

There is no inevitability to this previously mentioned trend. The main alternative to postimperial solutions comes from the vestiges of imperial thinking. When nations seek to lock up natural resources, notably oil, for their exclusive use; when they use intimidation and outright military action to invade weaker neighbors or establish spheres of influence; and when they erect obstacles to open trade—for example, devaluing their currency to maintain competitive trade advantage—they revert to the older strategies of empire. If that happens, the world may become divided into regional trading and security blocs, states will become more militarized, nuclear weaponry will spread, and democratic norms will weaken. Whether the world reverts to imperial rivalry or chooses to expand and democratize, the global order will depend on whether and how the previously mentioned challenges are resolved.

# 5

# THE NEOLIBERAL ERA

## Postindustrial Society in a New Gilded Age

*It is time to check and reverse the growth of government, which shows signs of having grown beyond the consent of the governed. . . . [O]ur present troubles parallel and are proportionate to the intervention and intrusion in our lives that result from unnecessary and excessive growth of government.*

Ronald Reagan, First Inaugural Address (1981)

*We the people declare today that the most evident of truths—that all of us are created equal—is the star that guides us still; just as it guided our forebears through Seneca Falls and Selma and Stonewall; just as it guided all those men and women, sung and unsung, who left footprints along this great mall, to hear a preacher say that we cannot walk alone; to hear a King proclaim that our individual freedom is inextricably bound to the freedom of every soul on Earth. . . . Our journey is not complete until our gay brothers and sisters are treated like anyone else under the law—for if we are truly created equal, then surely the love we commit to one another must be equal as well.*

Barack Obama, Second Inaugural Address (2013)

With the perspective drawn from hindsight, the period from the mid-1970s through the first decade of the twenty-first century now appears to many observers to be a second Gilded Age. The term is used because the period resembles in important ways the first Gilded Age during the late nineteenth century. During that time, great fortunes were built by leading industrialists and bankers, dwarfing previous ones accumulated by merchants and slave owners. The economy was marked by frequent financial panics and intense competition among businesses and workers to lower labor cost, and globalization undercut the wages and working conditions of native-born skilled workers. Meanwhile, government officials

**109**

shamelessly accepted bribes and campaign contributions from wealthy entrepreneurs, allowing them to gain special favors from government, and the Supreme Court routinely struck down legislation protecting the interests of workers and consumers and regulating the behavior of business. Political discourse was dominated by the upper class fear that government would redistribute wealth downward toward the working class.

There is another similarity between the late nineteenth-century Gilded Age and the present period. Though the first Gilded Age was a complex and often-contradictory mix of trends, it launched an antidemocratic wave, countering (though not eliminating) the democratic trends that marked the Civil War and Reconstruction, including the expansion of the public sector and the policies that led to civil equality and the public participation of the freed slaves. The *second* Gilded Age inaugurated a reaction against the wave of economic democracy that culminated in the 1960s. That wave took the form of expanded public-sector social spending (pejoratively termed "entitlements"), new regulation of corporate abuses, the granting of civil rights and voting rights to African Americans, and the inclusion in society and culture of women and minorities on an equal basis.

## Neoliberalism, Postindustrialism, and the Watershed of the 1970s

The 1970s turn against the second democratic wave resurrected the old economic doctrine that dominated the thinking of late nineteenth-century civic leaders: classical liberalism (not to be confused with New Deal liberalism). That older doctrine taught that reliance on the hidden hand of market competition was sufficient to attain the public good. The corollary of this dogma was the belief that government intervention in economy and society was counterproductive because it distorted the optimal allocation of resources provided by the market. Such intervention was also immoral because it distorted the market's just rewards for productive labor and undermined the ethic of personal responsibility. In classical liberalism, the realm of the market was the arena of freedom where natural laws operated. Control of market activities by associations of workers and capitalists or by government was unnatural and risked tyranny.

This theory contradicted actual government practice in the late nineteenth century. The federal government in that era used a protective tariff to shift income to business interests, and it funded a massive pension system for soldiers and their relations. Nonetheless, newspaper editors and leading public figures unceasingly espoused classical liberal ideas.

In the present era, what has been called "neoliberalism" has resurrected this dogma, once thought by Americans to be unworkable and antiquated. Prior to this period and throughout the twentieth century, Americans affirmed the necessity for an open market but at the same time have understood that it had many flaws. The unrestricted working of market competition allows employers to take advantage of dependent employees, pushes business rivals to combine to limit competition, and results in recurring financial panics and depressions. More recently, it is widely understood that the market does not adequately price the costs created by the destruction of the natural environment. For these and other reasons, Americans of all classes during the twentieth century supported the widespread regulation of market activity for the common good. Philosophically, they understood the need to supplement negative liberty, the absence of external constraint with positive liberty, the provision by associations within the market and by government of the means to take advantage of market opportunities.

The return to the older faith in the market, now called neoliberalism, has been the major justification for the reaction against the democratic wave of the 1960s and 1970s. Philosophically, neoliberalism tends to limit and undermine democracy because it denies the synthesis of negative and positive liberty and instead values only negative liberty. Politically, by supporting policies that destroy or hamper union power, lower taxes, reduce the size of government, lower public spending, deregulate business activities, and privatize government services, neoliberal policies end up eliminating or circumscribing those realms where public participation and the voice of the average American has been the greatest. By returning services and activities that were once public to the world of the deregulated large corporation, neoliberalism promotes relations of authority that are little subject to democratic accountability. Neoliberalism maintains a continuous drumbeat of attacks against government at all levels and of the taxes needed to support government. In doing so, neoliberalism delegitimizes and stigmatizes the basic principle of democracy: public deliberation to achieve the common good.

In addition to the commonalities between the first Gilded Age and the second Gilded Age, a critical difference must be taken into account. In the original Gilded Age, America was making a transition from an agricultural to an industrial economy, while today it is in the midst of a transition from an industrial to a postindustrial, or a knowledge and information, society. In our present postindustrial era, consumer spending and knowledge creation, rather than investment in physical plant and equipment, have become the driving forces for economic growth. The fact that industrial output can be increased with no additional workers or new investment and relies more on knowledge than plant and equipment opens up a liberating social prospect. It is possible that the amount of time necessary for work can be reduced and the amount available for leisure, creativity, and nonprofitable activities can expand correspondingly.

A wide array of developments can be explained by the postindustrial prospect. During this new era, millions of Americans have taken advantage of the benefits of private and public social insurance, from claiming disability, to taking advantage of early retirement, while the leisure and recreation industries, as well as employment in the not-for-profit sector, have expanded enormously. Concurrently, the economy has also seen a steady decline in manufacturing and industrial employment on top of the earlier decline in agricultural employment. Women have moved out of the home and into the workplace in education, health and human services, and sales work. A new class of college-educated knowledge workers—doctors, nurses and other health workers, teachers, professors, other employees of higher education, engineers, software and web developers, financial analysts, and the like—has overtaken the shrinking industrial working class.

But in other ways, the governance of postindustrialism by the leaders of corporations and government has stifled the potentialities of democratic individuality. The widely trumpeted promise that postindustrialism would create a new and expanded middle class based on education has not come to pass. The bulk of the new service jobs created since the 1980s have been low-wage jobs with few or no benefits and requiring little or no education beyond high school, thus contributing to inequality. The decline of necessary labor in the expansion of the economy has also created an ongoing problem for America's investment-for-profit system. It has shrunk the outlets for profitable investment, creating a more-or-less permanent tendency for the economy to stagnate without new ones. Much of the politics in the New Gilded Age has revolved around creating new investment opportunities for surplus capital. This has occurred through increasing overseas investment, expanding domestic demand through government deficit spending and consumer borrowing, and engaging in speculative financial activities, which have created dangerous bubbles.

The new knowledge economy, in short, has not lived up to its billing and has created as many difficulties as it has benefits and opportunities. Except in the dynamic realm of postmaterial culture (discussed in chapters one and two), American leaders have not embraced the egalitarian, democratic possibilities of postindustrialism. That resistance has led Americans into a second Gilded Age. How and why the country attempted to recreate a new Gilded Age leads us to the events of the 1970s, when the forces opposed to economic democracy successfully mobilized.

Two things happened to stymie, slow, and in some cases reverse the gains of the New Deal and Great Society. The first development occurred among business leaders; the second among American workers. In the 1970s, the American economy was beset by stagflation, a peculiar combination of high inflation and low economic growth. Stagflation provided the political opportunity for the return of market thinking in the form of neoliberalism among America's corporate elite and neoconservatives. These two groups argued that government interference in the workings of business and the high wages won by unions were the underlying causes of stagflation.

That argument provided the traction for the belief among articulate corporate leaders during the 1960s that a creeping socialism had become a galloping socialism. In the postindustrial era, when economic growth is possible with fewer and fewer inputs of capital, the institutions of private profit and investment are under constant threat. Postindustrialism raised the real possibility that the industrial system could be operated as a public utility—a social service for the good of all—and that capitalism and profits are not ends in themselves but means toward the end of the public good. If profits are less and less necessary for growth, why could not the idle social surplus be used to end poverty and for other public purposes? The expansion of social insurance promised as much. If one lumped Social Security—old age, disability, and aid to dependent children—together with Medicare and Medicaid, food stamps, unemployment compensation, income maintenance payments, and veterans' benefits, these forms of government-supplied income were growing faster than market-derived income. In the ten years from 1965 to 1975, transfer payments doubled as a share of total personal income from 6.5 percent to 13 percent. The neoliberal political scientist Samuel P. Huntington referred to this "welfare shift" as a "democratic distemper."[1]

Corporate leaders and neoconservatives also pointed to the hemming in of corporate decision making by regulations and the enormous costs that they added to investment. Some of the regulations mentioned included the Occupational Safety and Health Act, environmental legislation, consumer protection, and restrictions on oil and gas exploration. Together, such laws were said to require tens of billions of dollars in increased business costs to protect the well-being of workers and the public at large from industrial pollution into the air, water, and ground.

Henry B. Kaufman, a Salomon Brothers partner and one of the most influential Wall Street analysts of the 1970s, gave a widely quoted speech at the New York Economic Club in May 1980. "Fundamental change," he said, "has been taking place in our society over the last five decades," which had finally produced a "democracy oriented toward an unaffordable egalitarian sharing of production rather than equal opportunity."[2] Something very similar was being said in another influential document: the 1971 memo of Lewis F. Powell Jr., a leading corporate lawyer. Powell argued that American capitalism was under "broad attack" not only from radicals but also from respectable elements of American culture, including the media. "The overriding first need," wrote Powell, "is for businessmen to recognize that the ultimate issue may be survival—survival of what we call the free enterprise system, and all that this means for the strength and prosperity of America and the freedom of our people." Powell counseled business leaders to mount a broad ideological countermovement.[3]

The first response to this widely shared perception among corporate leaders came with the founding in 1972 of the Business Roundtable by the CEOs of ALCOA Aluminum and General Electric. The Business Roundtable, which included one hundred of the nation's largest corporations, successfully lobbied to defeat a proposed consumer protection agency, antitrust legislation, and labor law reform that would have strengthened construction unions. Later, the roundtable would lead the fight for free-trade legislation, a key feature of globalization. During this time, the US Chamber of Commerce also greatly expanded its base and lobbying operations. The impact on Congress was a historic turnaround. In 1968, there were more labor staffers in Congress than business ones, but by 1978, the numbers were reversed.[4]

Meanwhile, corporate leaders played a critical role in a revival of the conservative movement by founding and funding new procapitalist think tanks such as the Heritage Foundation and Cato Institute and a new cadre of conservative writers and activists to counter what Huntington called "an excess of democracy."

The old framework of economic democracy was not only threatened by the counter mobilization by business leaders. It was also undermined by developments in America's working class. American workers have always faced divisions based on immigrant status, ethnicity, race, gender, and region. But during the 1930s and 1940s and into the 1970s, the labor movement was able to overcome these divisions as they organized unions in large-scale corporate industry. During the thirty years following World War II, organized labor in the American Federation of Labor-Congress of Industrial Organizations AFL-CIO had enrolled between a quarter and a third of all American employees. Unions didn't just benefit their members. They helped raise the pay and standards for all workers because nonunion employers kept their standards competitive with unionized employers' standards. As a result, organized labor served as a force for greater equality far beyond its own sphere by setting the employment norms for the country. For that reason, it could make a politically credible claim to speak for the majority of American workers. The Democratic Party could also count on these unionized workers to vote with them. This all changed in the 1960s and 1970s with the civil rights and Black Power movements. Attempts to desegregate schools, other public facilities, and residential neighborhoods; to extend the vote to African Americans in the South; and to use court-ordered affirmative action to increase the number of black employees evoked fierce white resistance. The always-simmering issue of race exploded into public life and badly divided America's workers.

Workers were also divided by the spread of postmaterial values characteristic of postindustrial society. The postwar prosperity had enabled millions of white workers who had lived from paycheck to paycheck to afford middle-class living standards. Abraham Maslow's "hierarchy of needs" posited that the more basic material needs of food, clothing, shelter, health, and employment must be met before the secondary or higher-level needs of love and belonging, self-esteem, self-actualization, and self-transcendence can become the focus of individuals in society. The 1960s movements asserted these higher needs as it fought for women's equality, environmentalism, and the inclusion of gays and other minorities on a position of equality in public life. The counterculture, which criticized the country's focus on a soulless accumulation of wealth, its divorce from nature, and its lack of a spiritual core, also diffused into everyday life. It contributed to a new political agenda for the expressive individualism discussed in chapter two.

In the face of rapid cultural change, many working-class white males were resentful and often angry over perceived threats to their newly won and still tenuous middle-class way of life. At the very moment that they had achieved what had long been denied them, it seemed that much of society had moved on to new values. Issues such as affirmative action, sexual harassment in the workplace, abortion, and later gay marriage became flashpoints for these cultural resentments. As the only party hospitable to postmaterial values, while also being the party of working-class unity, the Democratic Party tried to reconcile or paper over the tensions and divisions occurring within its labor constituency over these matters. It could not.

Between the late 1960s and late 1970s, it still seemed possible that working people could renovate their class identity. The antiauthoritarianism and assertiveness of the 1960s upheaval had diffused into the rank and file of the labor movement, and a series of rank-and-file revolts among union coalminers, truckers, and autoworkers demanding union democracy shook labor's leadership. But it would take another generation for these reform forces to ascend to power in the AFL-CIO, and by then, it was too late.

Segments of the counterculture sought to extend their quest for personal authenticity and emancipation to the broader democratic community. One of these was the rocker Bruce Springsteen, who wrote songs sympathetically portraying working-class life. However, these songs did not celebrate an existing genuine community, but rather escape from the death trap of decaying industrial towns. Something similar could be said about the disco craze that swept American popular culture from the 1970s into the 1980s. Disco was joyous dance music with a feminine lushness, starring black female disco divas. It had emerged from the newly liberated gay, black, and Latino working-class ghettoes. But it didn't connect with the suffering and pain of working-class life as did older genres: country music for whites or the blues for blacks. Materially, disco offered as an alternative only escape into a middle-class lifestyle as in the ending of the movie *Saturday Night Fever*. In reaction, young white workers launched a "Disco Sucks" movement, which rejected the cultural integration of the 1960s. A popular radio DJ organized a spectacular bonfire of disco records in Chicago's White Sox baseball stadium in 1979. In the words of historian Jefferson Cowie, it was the Beer Hall Putsch to disco's Weimar.[5]

As hope faded for an integrated working-class public identity that might unite white and minority, male and female, material and postmaterial workers, many white workers looked for a new identity. During the 1930s and 1940s, labor organizers and Democratic politicians had constructed a patriotic American identity that harnessed workers' aspirations for social change to reforms sponsored by the federal government and the labor movement. But the Vietnam War debacle, the 1960s movements, and Nixon's Watergate scandal splintered and delegitimized that identity. In its place, minority groups and middle-class women found pride in their own ethnic, racial, sexual, and gender heritages. African Americans led the charge when they refused any longer to be called "colored people" or "Negroes," and embraced the term "black," which reversed the old stigma of having black skin. Something similar was going on among Mexican Americans, women, gays, and Native Americans. Many young third-generation ethnics followed suit, rediscovering their European national traditions. What proud heritage could Southern whites and Northern rural whites claim now that a working-class identity was no longer viable? That space or vacuum would be filled by the Populist heritage. We are "the real people," the "real Americans," they claimed, America's bone and sinew.

Born in the age of Andrew Jackson and flowering in the late nineteenth-century South and Midwest, Populism represented the interests of a purportedly virtuous, hardworking middling element known as "the people" beset by powerful enemies from above and below. Above them were the arrogant and effete elites, while below them were the slothful, undeserving poor. Populism, however, should not be confused with democracy. First, it rests on a fiction that the middling element of the population can stand in for the whole people, because they are more real or true. Democracy, however, requires the participation and representation of all elements of society in the spheres of government, the economy, and culture. Second, Populism favors direct rule, sometimes by referendum and sometimes by resort to a powerful leader, bypassing the institutions of democracy that represent, balance, and reconcile diverse interests in public opinion: institutions such as civil society and political parties, along with civil liberties to protect minorities and the checks and balances of government.

While Populism can and has been an ideology and a language fueling a prodemocratic social movement, it has never been able to develop an alternative governing philosophy in the United States, though it has done so in Latin America and other undeveloped countries. Instead, American Populism has served as an ally to other more viable governing philosophies: modern New Deal and Great Society liberalism and, more recently, neoliberal conservatism.

The decisive shift of Populism from its alliance with liberals to alliance with conservatives occurred in the period following the 1960s upheavals. Alabama governor and presidential candidate George Wallace led the way in translating a class into a Populist identity for many white working people. Wallace started his political career as a mainstream liberal and a moderate on racial issues. In his first unsuccessful run for governor he was endorsed by the National Association for the Advancement of Colored People (NAACP) but was defeated by a candidate endorsed by the Ku Klux Klan. Determined to win at any cost, he became a hard-line segregationist and was elected Alabama's governor in 1962. At his inauguration he famously declared, "I say segregation now, segregation tomorrow, segregation forever."

But when he campaigned throughout the country for the presidential nomination in the Democratic primaries in 1968 and again in 1972, Wallace did not resort to his usual race-baiting. Instead of directly attacking blacks and defending segregation, he portrayed the civil rights movement as an imposition on white working people by arrogant liberal elitists using the power of the federal government. The popularity of his attack on the Democratic Party establishment and Washington bureaucrats forged a new political language that was soon appropriated by

Republican candidate Richard Nixon and subsequent Republicans up through the Tea Party. The new Populism allowed Nixon to formally accept the country's hard-won national commitment to racial equality while informally appealing to white working-class Democrats who were resentful over measures that seemed to help blacks at their expense: busing of African American students into white neighborhood schools, antipoverty and welfare spending, and affirmative action in hiring.

## New Wine in Old Bottles: The Parties in the Second Gilded Age

Nixon's renovated Republican Party bore little resemblance to the Republican Party of the previous century. That party had had powerful isolationist tendencies as evidenced by its divisions over entering World War II, was dedicated to fiscal orthodoxy as evidenced by Herbert Hoover's disastrous attempt to balance the budget during the Great Depression, and was economically libertarian in the sense that it favored self-government in business and was suspicious of, though not entirely opposed to, government regulation. The old Republican Party also was mildly pro-civil rights for African Americans and advancement for women, a legacy of its Civil War-Reconstruction heritage.

By contrast, the new party was largely composed of the Southern and Western wings of the Democratic Party of the New Deal and Great Society era. It was more internationalist and favored military interventionism, it was comfortable with deficit-financed military spending to stimulate the economy as had been done by Franklin Delano Roosevelt and Harry Truman, and it opposed the expansion of the federal regulatory apparatus, though mainly because it limited the ability of Southern states to maintain the secondary status of racial minorities. In one respect, the new Republican Party remained true to its heritage: it continued to be the home of the nation's wealthy classes and the corporate managerial elites.

After the departure of its Southern wing, the Democratic party was left with liberal advocates of economic democracy and social justice, the dwindling labor movement, the postmaterial middle class, and racial minorities, including Jews, African Americans, Latinos, and more recently, Asians. As it became clear that the old Republican Party existed only in name, its once powerful New England and urban Midwest elements drifted into the arms of the Democrats. These new Democrats brought with them a historic support for civil rights, an assent to mild forms of business regulation, and a priority on good governance and fiscal orthodoxy. The reliance of Democrats on these former Republicans to make up for its loss of Southern whites greatly diluted the party's old commitment to labor liberalism.

The two parties were new, though they kept the same names. In effect, the old Republican Party had gone out of existence, while the pre-1968 Democratic Party had split into two new mainstream parties. This shift in American politics has parallels in its past. The old Federalist Party went out of existence in the early nineteenth century and was replaced by the Democratic Republican Party as the nation's dominant party. But by the 1820s, that dominance had given way to two competing parties in the form of the two former wings of the Democratic Republicans. These wings became the Democrats and the Whigs.

The pouring of new wine into old bottles, as it were, and the attempt to mask it posed enormous problems for party leaders and led to a radical disjuncture in rhetoric and political practice, which has characterized this era. Ronald Reagan, the first Republican president who was openly from the right wing of the party (Nixon was a moderate and governed in large part as a liberal), demonstrated that gap in his signature rhetoric. In his inaugural address, Reagan said famously that:

> In this present crisis, government is not the solution to our problem. From time to time we have been tempted to believe that society has become too complex to rule, that government by an elite group is superior to government for, by, and of the people. . . . We are a nation that has a government—not the other way around. And this makes us special among the nations of the Earth. Our government has no power except that granted it by the people. It is time to check and reverse the growth of government, which shows signs of having grown beyond the consent of the governed. . . . [O]ur present troubles parallel and are proportionate to the intervention and intrusion in our lives that result from unnecessary and excessive growth of government.

Reagan was appealing to an old principle of American democracy—that society should remain superior to the state and that the state should serve society. How much government intervention in society to rectify social imbalances and injustices could be tolerated without violating that principle? Americans, of course, differed and still differ in their answers to that question. The rise of Reagan and his fellow Republicans gained its great force because it seemed to give substance to that early nineteenth-century principle in a time of crisis. In different words, a reviving of the spirit of capitalism in the form of market competition and entrepreneurialism had become in the 1980s the means of reviving the spirit of the country.

The policy that seemed to give substance to this return to first principles was supply-side economics, which arose as a cure for the stagflation of the 1970s. The new economics argued, contrary to Keynesian economics, that the economy suffered not from a surplus of capital or savings but from a lack of it. Supply-side thinking also said that the government should focus on inflation rather than unemployment as the major economic problem and that monetary (Federal Reserve) polices rather than Keynesian fiscal (federal budget) policies should be used to combat it. In policy, supply-side economics argued for a return to the wealthy of a large portion of the federal income taxes they paid. They would presumably invest it, and businesses would use the additional funds to create jobs.

The theory was utterly mistaken. The American economy suffers from insufficient markets for its surplus capital rather than a lack of capital as it had in the nineteenth century. Consumer demand rather than investment demand drives the postindustrial economy, and federal fiscal policy is a critical tool in avoiding and recovering from depressions. Regardless of the accuracy of supply-side theory, the practice under Reagan and other Republicans was largely Keynesian in its support for fiscal stimulus. Thus, Reagan's budget decreased by 25 percent individual income taxes over three years, it cut business and inheritance taxes, and the government dropped suits against large corporations. At the same time, Reagan pushed through Congress an enormous increase—1.2 trillion dollars—in military spending. The cuts in federal revenue combined with the massive increase in spending produced huge budget deficits that continued throughout the Second Gilded Age.

High federal debt levels constituted a major addition to demand for surplus capital and had a stimulating impact on the economy, but it was not for the reasons given by supply-siders. By running a massive deficit and resorting to debt to fund a large increase in government spending, Reagan's, and later George W. Bush's (2001–9), administration recreated the military version of Keynesian economics—a great increase in deficit-financed military spending that explains how World War II ended the 1930s Great Depression. What was new about supply-side economics was not reliance on deficit spending but the use of tax cuts to subsidize consumption primarily by the wealthy—for example, multiple luxury cars, mansions, and yachts.

Even the notion of using tax cuts to stimulate the economy was a Keynesian device. It had been first proposed by President Kennedy's Keynesian advisors and became law in 1964. The difference is that Kennedy's tax cuts were targeted at average Americans, while Reagan's and Bush's were targeted at the wealthy with the result that income inequality was exacerbated. Supply-side economics predicted that economic growth would be driven by a rise in investment, but that didn't happen. In fact, under Reagan and his successors, the share of consumption in gross domestic product (GDP) has increased, while investment has declined.

This is not surprising. Net investment—the new investment beyond that being invested from depreciation funds (yearly savings to replace existing plants and equipment)—has been declining steadily since the mid-nineteenth-century era of intensive industrialization. One estimate is that it had declined by half in the hundred years since the Civil War. In a postindustrial economy, net investment is normally near zero. In different words, the aggregate investment needed for economic growth is mainly derived from the funds used by business to replace old plants and equipment and does not require funds derived from profits.[6] As a result, to the extent that it worked, supply-side economics was effective not because it stimulated new investment—supply—but because it stimulated demand in the form of upper-class consumption.

The old constituencies of the Republican Party—Northern middle-class conservatives and business leaders—were fiscal conservatives. These advocates of a balanced budget would have never tolerated huge deficits in peacetime. But ex-Southern Democrats would, especially if in the service of the military. Republican business leaders were brought on board the deficit wagon by the fact that they benefitted disproportionately from tax cuts and from the attempts by Republicans to deregulate the economy. To many in the general public, the tax cuts and deregulation seemed to give substance to the rhetorical goal of "getting government off the backs" of the people and restoring the country's founding principles.

Ironically, despite the ubiquity of its campaign rhetoric, the Republican Party was the preeminent party of big government, though the party's preferred mode of spending increase was for military rather than social purposes. Republicans routinely increased federal government spending at higher rates than Democrats. In the three decades from 1980 to 2012, annualized growth in inflation-adjusted federal government spending increased more than twice as much under Republicans as under Democrats. For example, in President Reagan's first term (1981–5) spending increased at an annualized growth rate of 8.7 percent, while under President Obama (2009–13), the growth was 1.4 percent.[7]

Moreover, despite their rhetoric, the Republicans did little to decrease welfare spending. Indeed, the largest addition to social welfare programs since the 1960s (before President Obama's health care enactment) was George W. Bush's prescription drug benefit plan. On the other hand, the major *cut* in a social spending program came under Democratic president Bill Clinton, who replaced Aid to Families with Dependent Children with a temporary assistance program funded by block grants to the states and designed by them as well. With its sixty-month limit and often-strict state eligibility standards, the number of families on welfare has decreased by more than 60 percent between 1996 and 2004.[8]

Notwithstanding Republicans' rhetorical support for the traditional Southern position of states' rights, the most centralizing reform, one that largely federalized what was once a state prerogative, was proposed and signed by a Republican president, though it passed Congress with bipartisan support. No Child Left Behind required all state-run schools to administer standardized tests yearly. Unless a school makes adequate yearly progress in raising the scores of its fifth graders, the school's teachers could be fired, the school could be turned into a semiprivate charter school, privatized, or closed altogether.

The Democratic Party exhibited a similar disjuncture between rhetoric and policy. Democrats appeared before the public in the guise of compassionate liberals defending the programs of the New Deal and Great Society. They campaigned nationally on a platform of defending civil rights for minorities and women, antipoverty programs, an expansion of government health care guarantees, environmental protection, and support for labor unions. Yet in power under presidents

Carter and Clinton, they did little to advance that agenda. In truth, they shared a new common ground with Republicans. Notwithstanding the latter's right-wing Populism and the former's ostensible prolabor liberalism, both supported the new reliance on market forces and for-profit business investment as a substitute for government services, social spending, and private-sector collective bargaining. Neoliberals viewed these new approaches as a way to spur innovation, to make business more flexible and adaptable to market demands, and to recharge economic growth following a decade of stagflation.

In policy terms, neoliberalism meant the privatization of government assets such as roads and public utilities; the outsourcing of social services, such as prisons and K–12 education; the deregulation of business, particularly where it had been closely monitored; the downsizing of government at all levels (cutting employees); free-trade agreements internationally; and fiscal austerity, which meant declining or low taxes and reduced government spending. Though the new political consensus was often limited in its ability to repeal popular government programs such as Social Security or environmental regulations, it constituted the guiding principle behind much public policy, for it promised to maintain an older commitment to public welfare while relying on the market and business investment to deliver these services.

Democratic president Jimmy Carter (1977–81) first promulgated neoliberal policies when he worked with Congress to deregulate the airline, trucking, and railroad industries, allowing prices and the allocation of resources to be determined solely by market forces in the expectation that it would result in lower consumer prices. The Ronald Reagan administration (1981–9) expanded those policies. Reagan used his executive powers to appoint cabinet officers who would not enforce existing environmental laws and would distribute public lands freely to oil, gas, timber, and ranching interests. Reagan also set a new direction for the country when he was faced with a walkout by twelve thousand air traffic controllers during his first year in office. Following in the footsteps of his antiunion counterpart across the Atlantic, Britain's Margaret Thatcher, Reagan fired every striker for violating federal law and hired permanent replacements. Television cameras pictured the leader of the union being led away to jail in chains. It was a stark reversal of the twentieth-century policy of accepting the legitimacy of labor organizations and union strikes and a return to the policy of the first Gilded Age, when President Grover Cleveland had used ten thousand federal troops to break the Pullman Strike, and a federal judge sentenced Eugene V. Debs to prison.

Reagan's handling of the strike signaled open season in the private sector on union workers engaging in strikes. Major work stoppages fell continuously from four hundred per year in 1974 to about fifty in 1985. At the same time, Reagan and his Republican successors appointed antilabor members to the National Labor Relations Board, which eroded legal protections for workers to organize unions. With unionists fearing replacement by strikebreakers and lacking legal protection, corporate management was able to successfully impose concessions in nearly every industry.

The new policy orientation was not always successful or fully shared, but it constituted the central tendency. With regard to public education, Democrats and Republicans differed, but not fundamentally. While Republicans championed school vouchers, which would channel public monies to private schools, including those affiliated with churches, Democrats responded by championing nonunion, privately run charter schools as a way of introducing choice and competition into education.

Democrats also assented to the Republican-led War on Drugs inaugurated under President Nixon. With strict sentencing guidelines, the criminal justice system incarcerated over one million Americans, overwhelmingly the young and minorities, simply for possessing illegal drugs. Though the United States has only 5 percent of the world's population, by 2008, it had 25 percent of the world's prisoners—more than any other country on a per capita basis. As in the Gilded Age, a large and growing slice of these prisoners—128,000 in 2010—are being managed by private companies.

President George W. Bush's (2001–9) ownership society as an alternative to public programs such as Medicare and Social Security was another example of using public programs as a new outlet for profitable investment. As with school vouchers, the ownership society would privatize public-benefit programs by granting individuals public monies through vouchers or tax deductions to spend on private-sector providers. Bush's solutions were never enacted except with his prescription drug benefit program.

The neoliberal policies from supply-side economics to strikebreaking contributed to a major increase in social inequality in the United States. It would be a mistake, however, to think that neoliberal government policies led the way or were mainly responsible; rather, it was corporate management's new norms and practices. Fearful of domestic socialism, and under pressure from intensifying domestic and international competition, American business adopted the Walmart model, characterized by the relentless cutting of labor costs to allow for low prices. Managers shifted risk from the firm to the individual worker and kept wages from rising in tandem with productivity as had been the case previously. For example, employers stopped offering defined-benefit pensions and shifted to making contributions to individually controlled funds (individual retirement accounts) that could be invested in the stock market. The returns from these accounts often varied wildly in contrast to the old guaranteed benefits. Managers also stopped giving annual wage increases and shifted income toward profits. At the same time, full-time, ongoing employment accompanied by health care, pension, and other benefits dwindled, while contingent or temporary employment, whether part time or full time, grew. The new jobs not only were nonunion and likely to lack employer benefits but also were not covered by basic federal labor protections, such as minimum wage, overtime, and health and safety standards.

## The Return of Inequality

During the period from America's New Deal in the 1930s through the mid-1970s, the disparity in incomes of Americans *decreased* markedly. Since then, they have become more unequal, recently returning to their pre-New Deal level. Between 1974 and 2006, the income of the middle class grew 21 percent, while that of poor Americans grew by only 11 percent. The incomes of the 1 percent of the richest grew by 256 percent, over ten times those of the middle class, and almost tripled its share in total income of the country to 23 percent, the highest level since 1928—the eve of the Great Depression.[9]

Not surprisingly, the US inequality index or Gini coefficient (where zero is perfect equality and 1 is perfect inequality) has risen from 0.39 in 1970 to 0.47 in 2011, making the United States more unequal than India or any European country; the United States is now on par with China in terms of inequality. Of large countries, only Mexico and Brazil are more unequal than American society.[10]

Americans have been proud of their country's reputation for being the land of opportunity. Intergenerational social mobility—the movement of individuals or families up (or down) the income scale as compared to their parents—has normally been relatively high in America. High upward social mobility has somewhat compensated for income inequality and has been used by some as justification for it. But social mobility, defined as the percentage of those who have moved out of their parent's income bracket, has declined markedly since the 1980s. According to at least five large studies, social mobility is now lower in the United States than in Canada and much of Western Europe.[11]

College, once the springboard to rising on the social ladder, now reinforces rather than undermines class. According to the US Department of Education, even those students from a low socioeconomic background who had the *highest* eighth grade test scores had the same chance of finishing college as those from a high socioeconomic status with the *lowest* test scores.

Many Americans wonder why the growth of inequality and declining social mobility matters for democracy. According to polls, a majority of Americans believe that as long as wealth is fairly earned in the course of market activity, government should not interfere. But growing disparities in wealth have grave implications for democracy. Americans in the country's early years believed that a republic (the Latin translation of the Greek word *democracy*) required a balanced, though not equal, distribution of wealth. Americans at the time believed that a strong middle class of farmers, artisans, and shopkeepers was necessary to counterbalance any tendency of the wellborn and wealthy to translate their status and wealth into political power and corrupt the republic. Fearing that, they supported government policies that distributed public lands cheaply to those with little or no land and supported polices to guarantee equality of opportunity in the market—all means of maintaining a strong middle class. Americans of that era opposed manipulation of the currency, high interest rates, taxation of productive labor, state-sponsored monopolies, and an established church, all means in a predominantly agrarian society of amassing great wealth and power by the few.

In the present era, the issue of the growing imbalance in wealth distribution and income has returned to the public forum. It has become clear that the norms regarding wealth distribution have undergone a sea change in the past forty years. America has become in words of two journalists a "winner take all" society. The noted political scientist Francis Fukuyama, who in 1992 famously wrote that the triumph of a capitalist economy together with liberal democracy following the Cold War had created "the end of history," has had second thoughts. In 2012, he wondered whether American democracy could survive without its middle class.[12] Other writers have taken up the concern. According to George Packer, inequality is "like an odorless gas" that "saps the strength of democracy":

> It hardens society into a class system, imprisoning people in the circumstances of their birth—a rebuke to the very idea of the American dream. Inequality divides us from one another in schools, in neighborhoods, at work, on airplanes, in hospitals, in what we eat, in the condition of our bodies, in what we think, in our children's futures, in how we die. Inequality makes it harder to imagine the lives of others . . . [and] corrodes trust among fellow citizens, making it seem as if the game is rigged. Inequality provokes a generalized anger that finds targets where it can—immigrants, foreign countries, American elites, government in all forms—and it rewards demagogues while discrediting reformers. Inequality saps the will to conceive of ambitious solutions to large collective problems, because those problems no longer seem very collective. Inequality undermines democracy.[13]

Inequality has a direct impact on the democratic process by placing greater amounts of wealth in the hands of a tiny minority who can use it to exercise undue influence on who is nominated and elected and to lobby governmental decision-making bodies, which in turn allows it to generate even more wealth for itself. The 2010 *Citizens United v. Federal Election Commission* decision by the US Supreme Court amplifies this influence by overturning a century of attempts to limit the reach of corporate money in politics.

But inequality has another dimension that is critical to democracy: inequality in civil society. The decline of union membership and collective bargaining since the start of the Reagan administration and the diminution of labor's ability to influence the governance of the workplace have greatly worsened inequality. Just as important, it has reduced the power and influence of working Americans in all phases of life. The presence of unions allows workers to have protection in the workplace against the everyday pressures, abuses, and indignities coming from employers and supervisors. It generates assertiveness, self-confidence, and collective power where otherwise there would be fear, resignation, and apathy. Without unions, participation in civil society and government suffers, and working people lose their voice in the sphere where public opinion is formed.

The decline of unions was only one part of the larger decline in civil society and the growth of civic *dis*engagement. Mass-membership associations such as the Red Cross, National Parent Teacher Association, League of Women Voters, March of Dimes, American Farm Bureau, American Legion, General Federation of Women's Clubs, and Freemasons steadily lost their community base as the developments of the 1960s and 1970s fractured their membership and pulled female activists out of the community and into the workplace. These organizations had recruited membership across class lines and combined community service and mutual aid at the local level with national-level civic engagement. They were replaced by a phenomenal growth of advocacy organizations based in Washington, managed by professionals but with hardly any members at the local level. America is no longer such a nation of joiners. It is still an open question whether the growth of social media—interactive, web-based technologies, such as social-networking sites, blogs, forums, and Twitter—will adequately replace these traditional forms of democratic mobilization.

The decline of organized labor and other civic organizations was a major loss not only to the working-class Americans but also to American democracy itself. Without regular, organized input from the grassroots, public opinion loses its representativeness. A major political science study reveals that when the opinions of poor and working-class Americans differ from that of upper-class Americans, a divergence occurs in the reaction of the state. The opinion preferences of the well-off are fairly represented in government outcomes, while those of the middling and lower ranges of income have virtually no representation at all.[14]

## The Great Recession and Emergence of a New Majority

Aside from its impact on American democracy, growing income inequality, when combined with the huge capital surpluses generated by the postindustrial economy (not only in the United States but globally) and their investment in unproductive activities, created a highly unstable, *financialized* economy. *Financialization* refers to the predominance of financial motives in corporate management, of financial institutions within the economy, and of financial assets among total assets. Almost all financial markets experienced explosive growth from the 1980s onward, especially the stock market, foreign exchange trading, futures markets, and consumer credit. But the most destabilizing development was the invention by banks and other financial institutions of exotic credit instruments, including credit-default swaps and collateralized debt obligations, which were not regulated by government. The hands-off attitude from regulators was justified to the public by the neoliberal doctrine that anything that happens as a result of voluntary market transactions is efficient, beneficent, and an expression of human freedom. But with no oversight, it became almost impossible to identify inflated asset values or bubbles.

One indicator of the importance of financial activities as the driver of growth has been that profits from manufacturing as a percentage of GDP declined continuously in the 1980s, while profits from financial institutions as a percentage of GDP rose, with the result that by the early 1990s they exceeded the manufacturing percentage and expanded their lead thereafter. In sum, the concentration of income at the top of the economic order, the financialization of the economy, and the stagnation of net investment meant that new investment went disproportionately into financial speculation.

The neoliberal economy lurched from financial bubble to financial bubble. In the 1980s, the savings and loan financial institutions, which were supposed to serve small savers, were allowed to invest in risky ventures. By the end of the decade, over 750 of these institutions went bankrupt. To avoid a run on consumer confidence, the federal government bailed them out to the tune of $160 billion. A decade later, an overseas financial bubble due to speculative investment emanating from American banks led to the East Asian crisis. In 2000, a stock market bubble burst, which had been generated by speculative investment in Internet-based enterprises—the so-called dot-com bubble. The bursting of the bubble caused a crash in artificially run-up values, which wiped out five trillion dollars within two and a half years. The dot-com bubble was immediately succeeded by the real estate bubble financed by a host of new financial institutions and instruments of debt, which drove the economy until it began to decline in 2006; as of 2012, the real estate market still had not hit bottom. Because so much consumer spending in this decade had been financed by homeowners taking out loans on their equity rather than by wage increases, the bursting of the housing bubble directly affected consumption, as well as banks, and was one of the underlying reasons for the Great Recession.

The Great Recession that started in the United States in 2008 and spread worldwide was the worst since the Great Depression of the 1930s. As financial institutions saw their assets devalued, they stopped lending. As the housing bubble burst, housing prices and housing starts fell precipitously, which in turn caused consumer spending to fall. The unemployment rate doubled to 10 percent before declining to just under 8 percent in 2012 as the economy slowly recovered. But the more accurate measure, the civilian employment to population ratio that takes into account those who have left the workforce, fell from 63.5 percent in 2007 to 58.5 percent in 2010 and has only begun to rise slowly in late 2012. A Rutgers University Heldrich Center survey in 2012 found that one-quarter of all working age Americans had lost a job in the previous four years, while another quarter had an extended family member who had lost a job.[15] As a result, most Americans rightly believe that the economy is still in recession.

A major underlying cause of the Great Recession was the sharply increased disparity in the incomes accruing to labor and capital. Labor's share in the nonfarm business sector of the economy was in a slow slide after the mid-1970s, but around 2000, that share fell much more steeply. Thus even before the crash, the wages available for consumer spending were in decline, with the difference being shifted to business and the wealthy, where it was used to fuel speculative ventures in the financial sector. Because consumer spending is by far the largest component of economic demand for goods and services, the stagnation in wages together with the rise of income inequality not only was an underlying cause of the recession but also continues to impede a robust recovery.

The long recession has created a crisis for neoliberalism. Massive bailouts using taxpayer funds to save insolvent banks and auto companies violated the neoliberal faith that markets dispensed fair rewards and punishments and that government intervention eliminated any penalty for excessive risk taking by business—the so-called moral hazard. On the other hand, newly emboldened critics of neoliberalism argued that deregulation had encouraged reckless behavior by the banks and mortgage companies and that federal oversight needed to be restored. Inequality, they now charge, is decimating the middle class. On the global level, the neoliberal Washington Consensus collapsed and with it, America's economic leadership.

The political fallout for America's political parties was also unsettling. In 2008, Americans elected Barack Obama, the country's first black president. Obama's election was the culmination of the growth within the electorate of the social and demographic groups mobilized by the third wave of democracy. These included African Americans and Latinos, who together constitute about one-quarter of the electorate; college-educated professionals, who had become a key element of the new working class brought about by postindustrialism; single women, who were influenced and empowered by feminism; and sexual minorities. When added to the older party groups—labor union members, Jews, ideological liberals, and Northerners more generally—they made up a new electoral majority, displacing the once-dominant Reagan coalition. This became clear when Obama repeated his 2008 victory in 2012, relying on the same groups. Meanwhile, the Republican Party's main voting groups, rural whites and Evangelical Protestants, were declining in their percentage within the electorate.

With majorities in both houses of Congress, Democrats implemented new policies and programs, which represented, even when necessary compromises were taken into account, a real break with old neoliberal agenda. The Patient Protection and Affordable Care Act of 2010 (PPACA) completed the agenda of the second wave of democracy by allowing almost all Americans to have access to health care. It represented a compromise with neoliberalism because it was a semiprivate program that worked by heavily subsidizing private insurance companies to extend their coverage, rather than expanding the more cost-effective public program of Medicare. On the other hand, it recognized the growing problem of economic inequality that had been exacerbated by neoliberal policies by subsidizing health care premiums for lower-income persons with revenues raised by heavily taxing the top 1 percent of income earners. It also established in principle that the insurance industry, and by implication the health care sector of the economy, was like a public utility that could be regulated for the public good.

For example, the PPACA forbade insurance companies from refusing coverage to patients with preexisting health conditions, forbade these companies from setting lifetime limits on coverage, required most employers to provide coverage for their employees, established minimum standards for health benefit plans, and required that insurance companies spend at least 80 percent of each premium dollar on health care, thus limiting profits.

The new democratic majority took other steps to distance itself from the old neoliberal consensus. It reregulated the banking industry, including the establishment of the first consumer financial protection bureau; eliminated the subsidy for the big banks in the federal student loan program, thus freeing up funds to increase grants to lower-income college students; greatly boosted auto fuel-efficiency standards to conserve energy; and heavily subsidized alternative energy sources. The new majority achieved an important cultural goal by repealing the military's "don't ask, don't tell" policy for gays. Perhaps most significantly, it broke with supply-side economics and returned to Keynesian economics in stimulating the depressed economy. Rather than use tax cuts for the rich or ballooning military spending, it expanded social and infrastructure spending instead. On the other hand, by accepting the goal of deficit reduction and making unemployment reduction secondary beginning in 2010, the Obama administration has ended up acquiescing in the neoliberal canard that the size of government is a problem. Furthermore, by incentivizing the privatization of public education, the Obama coalition kept continuity with the old neoliberal thinking.

Among Republicans, the downturn and subsequent election of President Obama rocked the party's establishment. Right-wing Populism, which had long been subordinated as the electoral muscle to sustain the power of the party's corporate wing, advanced to the forefront of the party (see the "Republican Party platform 2012" in Documents).

Unlike neoliberal Republicans, the Tea Party, as it was known, opposed increased federal spending and centralization and espoused a very much smaller federal government, greatly reduced help for the nonworking poor, a market with little or no regulation, and police action against illegal immigrants. Above all, Tea Party leaders feared a turn to socialism, which to them meant government regulation of business and handouts to the undeserving poor. In 2010, these Republicans rode to power in the House of Representatives on the strength of the reaction among segments of the public against President Obama's extension of health care coverage, which Tea Party Republicans told voters was a government takeover of the health care system.

Though grassroots Tea Party activists were not typically free-market fanatics, groups holding these views hijacked Tea Party Populism for their own interests. On the federal level, these groups took over the House of Representatives in 2010, which led to legislative gridlock. On the state level, where they faced less opposition, newly elected right-wing governors and legislators unleashed a powerful assault on labor unions, particularly teachers' unions, by curtailing or ending collective bargaining. They also slashed public employment, eliminated public funding for contraception and breast cancer screening for poor women, passed laws to greatly restrict women's legal access to abortion, and enacted voter suppression laws designed to make it harder for millions of poor people, blacks, immigrants, ex-convicts, college students, and elderly Americans to vote (see chapter six).

The Tea Party was only the cutting edge of what might be called the "Southernization" of state-level social and economic policies, a trend that had been spreading for four decades. Historically, the Southern states had been able to economically develop by attracting outside capital due to policies that promoted a cheap, nonunion labor force—"the functional equivalent of slavery," minimal government regulation, low spending on government services, including education, which in turn allowed for low taxes. Without strong federal regulation, the new Gilded Age has seen heightened competition among the states to attract corporate business investment, with more of them adopting the Southern economic development strategy. The new laws passed in Indiana, Wisconsin, and Michigan making it almost impossible to form unions are examples of this low-wage strategy.[16]

While such a strategy might work for some states in the short run, it depends on attracting businesses from the states that allow unions and have relatively high wages, high taxes, and extensive government services. Over time, declining standards in those largely Northern states eliminates the economic advantage enjoyed by the nonunion, low-wage, low-tax states. The long-run result is that the nation's economy is left with lower consumer purchasing power, lower levels of growth, lower funding levels for education and other public services, and falling living standards. That long run has now become the nation's present.

The elections of 2010 proved that once the slide into economic catastrophe had been averted, enough Americans reverted to the governing philosophy of neoliberalism to set limits on a major shift in the nation's path. That reversion empowered not only existing elites but the antidemocratic elements in public life. It also created a stalemate in the federal government that prevented experimentation along alternative paths.

Not only in the United States but also throughout the developed world political and economic elites remained under the spell of neoliberalism. Particularly in the United States, they feared a new social democratic wave funded by high government deficits. As an antidote, they endorsed fiscal austerity. Despite the fact that an increase in government debt and spending had been necessary to keep the economy from descending into a second great depression, fiscal austerity in the form of higher interest rates and cuts in government spending, particularly social spending, returned as the conventional wisdom in 2010–12. To those who had learned the lessons of history the results were all too predictable.[17] The countries of the European Union returned to recession in 2012, while the United Kingdom sank further into its economic downturn. In the United States, the refusal to enact additional stimulus and state- and local-level cutbacks in spending and employment left the economy mired in growth rates too slow to restore previous employment levels (though this was somewhat counteracted by the Federal Reserve's wise refusal to raise interest rates).

Then something astonishing happened. As politicians of both parties prioritized government spending cuts, particularly entitlements, and ignored unemployment, a mass protest of mostly young people camped out at Zucotti Park in New York City, near the Wall Street financial district. Called Occupy Wall Street (OWS), it shifted attention to rising inequality with its slogan "We are the 99 percent." The movement protested the corporate power over American politics and the unwillingness of American politicians, including President Obama, to hold bankers and other corporate titans to account in the making of the Great Recession (see "Declaration of the Occupation of New York City 2011" in Documents).

The takeover or occupation of Wall Street was in the best tradition of previous social movements that employed direct action, notably the sit-down strikes of 1936–67, which jump-started the modern labor movement, and the student sit-ins against segregation in 1961, which fueled the civil rights movement. OWS also fused the second wave of social movements that stressed class and economic issues with the third wave of new social movements that prioritized postmaterial values. Coming on the heels of the labor protests in Wisconsin earlier in the year against the high-handed tactics of a Tea Party governor and legislators in eliminating collective bargaining for most public employees, the OWS protests spread to over nine hundred other cities worldwide. It also changed American politics by challenging the conservative emphasis on deficit reduction and austerity and placing the issue of social inequality and the corporate control of politics and government on the political agenda. In the aftermath of the protests and with less than a year to his reelection campaign, President Obama unveiled a jobs plan and the media discovered the issue of inequality.

As we take stock of the developments for and against democracy during America's second Gilded Age, it is important to remember its origins. The turn against democracy began in the 1970s as a reaction against enormous advances during the 1960s and early 1970s in political, economic, and cultural democracy. The political mobilization of the corporate elite and the disuniting and demobilization of America's working people made that reaction possible and gave neoliberal policies a tenuous majority.

But working-class voters in both parties were not willing to support a wholesale dismantling of the New Deal and Great Society programs enacted in the period between the 1930s and 1970s. Despite their best efforts, neoliberals were unable to reduce Social Security benefits or privatize the system, rescind environmental legislation, or even reduce the size of the public sector in relation to the private economy. In response to the inability of the economy to create enough middle-class jobs, transfer payments as a percent of total personal income continued to grow, though at a much slower pace, from 13 percent in

1975 to 15 percent in 2005. In 2010, the US Census reported that 48.5 percent of all American families had someone receiving a federal benefit, up from 37.7 percent in 1998 and 44.5 percent in 2006.[18] In short, despite the neoliberal campaign against dependency on government, reliance on social insurance has risen for the simple but rarely recognized reason that private, for-profit investment requires less and less human labor and cannot supply an adequate number of middle-class jobs.

Neoliberals were also forced to accept the democratic advances in culture. By the 1980s, a substantial black middle class had taken root, and African Americans and Latinos were an important part of the nation's electoral system. A majority of married women had entered the workforce, and women now hold a majority of professional jobs in the United States. Abortion rights were whittled down but not taken away, and women's access to equal treatment and advancement on the job continued to expand. Gays largely defeated the backlash against them that had became a mainstay of Republican appeals to the electorate, and by 2012, a majority of all Americans approved of the legalization of gay marriage, as well as the decriminalization of marijuana. The gender norms that doomed men and women to live out predetermined roles and identities were widely challenged and began to exhibit a remarkable fluidity in the most influential circles of the culture. Sex before marriage and living together out of wedlock became new norms for most segments of the population. In daily life and in the mass media, Americans were rejecting the idea of a single monolithic culture, allowing and often appreciating difference and choice, which had emerged from the 1960s. Meanwhile, the Internet, particularly in its form of social media, has greatly intensified the participatory (user-generated) role of huge numbers of Americans in culture formation. In short, postmaterial values have spread and sunk deep roots in the culture.

On the other hand, neoliberals *were* able to weaken the links between local democratic forces and the nation-state and implement large permanent federal income tax cuts, which disproportionately benefitted the wealthy. (The top income earners pay the large majority of *income* taxes, while average Americans pay the bulk of other taxes, including state sales taxes and the federal payroll taxes that fund Social Security and Medicare.) This in turn created large budget deficits. These deficits spurred economic growth but also inhibited the creation of *new* social welfare programs. Conservatives called this "starving the beast" (the beast meant government social, not military, spending).

Neoliberals were also able to institute substantial deregulation of business, notably deregulation of financial services. Informally, they undermined laws protecting the environment, workplace safety, workers' right to organize unions, and other protections for employees through lax enforcement by the executive branch and the courts of existing laws. Thus neoliberals were effective in furthering a decline in union membership and reducing the power of labor in American political life to a minimum, similar to levels in the late nineteenth century.

## Postmaterial Democracy

Is there a new democratic path in the wake of the crash of the second Gilded Age's economy and the clear evidence that neoliberal policies have failed to sustain economic prosperity and have increased economic and political inequality? With public opinion deeply divided, the way forward is far from obvious. One thing seems inescapable in the near future. Balanced growth in the postindustrial era will require an income shift from profits back to wages and consumption both domestically and globally. It will also require investment in public goods such as education, infrastructure, and basic research. Such a shift would eventually render less necessary the ever-higher levels of debt, both public and private, that have become necessary in the past three decades to sustain economic growth. Restoring wage growth and public-goods spending does not have to rely solely on government action. In order to maintain the American commitment to the supremacy of society over the state, it can and should entail a rethinking of corporate governance policies and a revival of the presence of organized working people in the workplace and in political life.

Part of creating a more balanced economy will involve significantly increasing federal funding for programs that would expand opportunity and social mobility rather than the neoliberal agenda of cutting entitlements or the bugaboo of deficit reduction. As a result of forty years of neglect, there is a huge backlog in unaddressed public needs.

Programs to protect working people have been sorely neglected. The minimum wage in 2012 was 31 percent lower than it was in 1968, measured in inflation-adjusted dollars. The share of state funding in the financing of higher education has been steadily decreasing, which has saddled poor and middle-income students with enormous debts to pay higher tuition bills and deterred others from attending at all. Women's participation rates in the labor force badly lag other countries due to the lack of paid maternity leave and available day-care facilities. Those who do work full time face difficult dilemmas in balancing work and family. On top of this, the American Society of Civil Engineers estimates the nation faces a $2.2 trillion infrastructure backlog, including the need for a modern power grid, high-speed broadband, and waste and drinking water system upgrades. These are all unmet democratic necessities.

Another long-term way forward, suitable to a postindustrial society, would be to transition away from GDP growth as the overriding goal of national economic policy. It is not simply that with the present strain on natural resources, growth at past levels has become incompatible with a sustainable environment (see chapter seven). It is also that in an economy where American corporations derive half or more of their income from sources outside the United States, employment and the welfare of American employees are no longer closely linked to corporate growth. Just as important is the fact that in a postindustrial society with postmaterial values, raising income is less and less necessary to raising levels of personal and social happiness. People with postmaterial values aim at personal autonomy, self-expression, a supportive community, and the overall quality of life. These elements of human existence are not highly correlated with income from paid employment and consumption beyond certain levels.

Most Americans are better served with different goals than the single goal of raising GDP. For several decades now, development theorists, economists, and political thinkers have been attempting to create new measures of happiness to replace the overriding emphasis on GDP growth, measures that include things such as environmental quality, universal access to education and health care, an adequate number of middle-class jobs, and rising leisure time. In different words, the sphere of cultural democracy is diverging from and taking precedence over the economic and political spheres as the focus for human happiness. Growth in order to raise the living standards of those who are poor or low income—almost half of all Americans according to the US Census of 2010—is still necessary, but in a postindustrial society in which the fruits of production are distributed in a balanced fashion, that growth need no longer be the *sine qua non* of public policy.

# 6

# THE DEMOCRATIC CHALLENGE

*Why should there not be a patient confidence in the ultimate justice of the people? Is there any better, or equal, hope in the world?*

Abraham Lincoln, First Inaugural Address (1861)

Abraham Lincoln in the Gettysburg Address called American democracy an "unfinished work." The ideals of popular sovereignty, political equality, and majority rule promised in the Declaration of Independence and the American Constitution have inspired the struggles of generations of ordinary Americans to achieve their promise. The Civil War, the labor movement, the civil rights movement, and the second wave of feminism were attempts to realize the promise of democracy for all Americans. It took more than thirty years from the adoption of the Constitution for most states to allow white males without property to vote. Women gained that right on the national level only in 1920, and young people ages eighteen to twenty did so only in 1971. Many African Americans in the South were unable to vote in any significant numbers until after passage of the Voting Rights Act of 1965, despite the Fifteenth Amendment's guarantee.

Only since the 1960s and 1970s has the promise of inclusivity in the spheres of civil society, public opinion formation, electoral politics, and the federal government become possible. Never before have more Americans been more accepting of diversity, equality of opportunity, and openness. Yet the governing potential of this new public has only been partially realized because it has been met by a determined counterwave of opposition.

Rarely has the country faced a democratic challenge as great as today. Over the last forty years, inequality of wealth and incomes has been on the rise until all the gains made toward equality over the period from the 1930s to the 1970s have disappeared. In the past fifteen years, median incomes for Americans have begun a steady decline for the first time in history. The combined incomes of the top 400 Americans today exceed that of the bottom 150 million. The political clout in Washington of hedge fund, bank, corporate, and independent billionaire interests, amplified by the Supreme Court's *Citizens United* ruling in 2010, has discredited political equality for many Americans. The antidemocratic wave is evident in voter-suppression measures prevalent in the Republican Party (GOP)-controlled state legislatures, the federal War on Drugs with its inordinate impact on lower-income Americans and minorities, the concentration of media ownership, and the rollback in civil liberties during the War on Terror. Voters' faith in America's political leaders and established political institutions is in decline. Collective bargaining and the democratic right of employees to form associations of their own choosing at work are illusory for the vast majority of American workers and have little or no support from government. Meanwhile, the institutions of civil society are too feeble to cope with the consequences of these developments. The operation of the country's national government has been stalemated and in paralysis since the elections of 2010.

These trends have diminished democratic government at all levels. The state and federal governments have granted innumerable benefits to corporate and other moneyed interests through tax breaks, subsidies, immunities from regulatory oversight, and most recently, bailouts of large banks and industries during the Great Recession while asking for little in return. One of the two parties, the GOP, has become dominated by an extreme right wing, which brazenly obstructs bipartisan governance. The center of gravity of public discussion has been pulled so far to the right with the help of the country's economic elite, which is unwilling or unable to exercise a moderating influence, that no realistic solutions to the country's problems of unemployment, the spread of poverty among the former middle class, environmental degradation, investment in education, and discrimination against women and minorities can be contemplated, let alone acted on. This is occurring while most Americans in opinion polls favor results-based rather than narrowly construed ideologies. American political democracy today is experiencing significant challenges that point, on the one hand, to a retreat from democratic practices and, on the other, to a determined effort to counteract that trend and to make democracy more representative and inclusive.

## Democracy Stalled?

The biggest challenge in the history of American democracy has not been the tyranny of the majority but the use of undemocratic means to frustrate the rule of the majority. American democracy is rife with the resort to unscrupulous tactics to limit the political power of emerging majorities. This has usually occurred when the propertied interests and political power of a class or elite or the values of a long-dominant ethnic or racial group are threatened. In the run-up to the Civil War, the property interests of Southerners came under attack from a Northern majority. In Northern urban centers during the mid- to late nineteenth century, Evangelical Protestants felt culturally threatened by the waves of immigrant Catholics and Lutherans who would soon constitute a new electoral majority. During the early twentieth century, citizens from an Anglo-Saxon Protestant background expressed the same concerns about immigrants from Eastern Europe.

In all these instances, the threatened majority resorted to undemocratic subterfuges to keep their opponents in the minority. In the late nineteenth century, threatened Protestant majorities passed state laws making it harder for immigrant Catholics living in cities to be naturalized and registered to vote. White supremacists foreclosed the possibility of a Populist majority by literally eliminating blacks' right to vote. In the 1920s, Anglo-Saxon Protestants were able to get Congress to shut off immigration from Eastern Europe. Beginning in the late nineteenth century, gerrymandering of election districts in most states kept besieged rural Protestants from being outvoted by urban working-class ethnic voters. It was not until the 1960s that legal challenges eliminated the system of rural malapportionment of electoral districts that severely distorted the principle of "one person, one vote." Prior to the Supreme Court decision in *In re Baker v. Carr* (1962), a sparsely populated rural district in Georgia with a population of 270,000 had as much weight in House elections as an urban district with 873,000 residents.

In the present period, the appearance of a new national majority is symbolized by the consecutive elections of Barack Obama and by a popular vote that has gone Democratic in five out of six national elections. Constituted mostly of racial and ethnic minorities, younger Americans, union labor, women, and college-educated voters with postmaterial values, it has gained momentum from the Occupy Wall Street Movement that helped reshape the national dialogue on the economy, especially income and wealth inequalities, which since the days of the early republic Americans have been recognized as damaging to democracy. The new majority threatens the power wielded by the corporate and banking elites and conservative white Protestant and Catholic ethnic groups, who have responded with efforts eerily similar to those of the past to manipulate or suppress the vote of their opponents, filibuster majority rule, and use other methods to paralyze government.

A demographic pessimism has gripped the established power brokers and interests threatened by the electoral clout of the new majority. The Census Bureau estimates that white births are no longer a majority in the United States, with non-Latino whites accounting for 49.6 percent of all births in 2012. The decreasing number of older, better-off, mostly older white Americans—the base of the Republican Party—points to a turning point in American politics and society. The growing numbers of adults and minorities who vote Democratic are largely young and from lower-income backgrounds. Fully 26 percent of those in the lower class are under age thirty, while less than 10 percent are sixty-five or older. The same may be said of minorities. Some 17 percent of lower-income adults are

Latin Americans in origin compared with only 13 percent of middle-class adults and 10 percent of upper-income adults.[1]

The importance of the demographic and cultural changes energizing the new majority are brought into sharp focus when one considers that in the 1988 election, President George H.W. Bush received the identical share of the white vote that GOP nominee Mitt Romney received in 2012—59 percent. But twenty-four years ago, that share was good enough to give President Bush a popular vote margin of seven million and an Electoral College victory of 426:111. In 2012, Obama won reelection by 4.9 million votes with an Electoral College margin of 332-206.

Threats stemming from these demographic and political trends are most acutely felt among specific groups and regional interests. Lower-income white males with limited job prospects (due to a sluggish economy requiring ever higher levels of education and credentialing to succeed) feel especially vulnerable. Their insecurity is evident in distrust of affirmative action programs promulgated by President Johnson in 1965 to eliminate discrimination against women and minorities in employment and access to higher education. Polls show that overall support for affirmative action is in the 49–54 percent range. Yet 75 percent of white males disagree with affirmative action and believe that only merit should be considered in university admissions and in hiring. White men are more likely to oppose affirmative action than women, and the difference is amplified by race and ethnicity, with more white men than minority men strongly believing women already have equal job opportunities.

Changes in race, gender, and class relations and cultural norms most directly threaten economic elites and cultural interests based in the Southern states where, since the days of slavery, the "Southern way of life" has been predicated on the region's role as a low-wage, low-tax, and low-regulation region, which allows an economic oligarchy to rule an impoverished working class with few challenges. The Southern development strategy of attracting foreign and domestic investment from both the Northern parts of the United States and globally depends on having a low-wage, nonunion Southern workforce. Culturally as well, the South was most closely tied to ideals of traditional family values and gender roles rooted in Evangelical doctrines. Many in the Southern elite perceived the 1950s and 1960s mobilization of women, blacks, and other minorities into politics in terms of a besieged South on the verge of being overwhelmed by a multiracial, prolabor, secular-humanist and cosmopolitan majority.

The power base of Southern elites is most threatened by demographic changes in core red states such as Arizona, Florida, and Texas. If one or more of those states due to population changes turns from a battleground state leaning red to a blue state, it would decisively tilt the balance of power in American politics toward the new majority more heavily represented in urban areas in northeastern and western states. More recently, the Tea Party movement arose to protest the greater participation in government and society of the newly mobilized segments of the population, symbolized by the election of Barack Obama. Despite tensions between the movement's grassroots base and its national leadership, there are several common beliefs in the movement. Among these is a reverence for the Constitution interpreted to mean states' rights and minimal federal regulation of the economy. Tea Party supporters also share beliefs about the inherent goodness of unhindered markets, traditional small town values, including self-reliance and a strong work ethic, and distrust of secular values associated with demand for separation of church and state.

The Tea Party's support is drawn heavily from older, retired or semiretired white Americans living in the urban South and adamantly against the Obama administration. The Tea Party's significance is limited by its narrow social base of support, but its political importance is amplified by conservative free-market think tanks (such as the Cato Institute), and conservative media entrepreneurs (such as Glenn Beck) who characterize it as representing mainstream Americans. These free-market conservatives have sought to leverage the Tea Party's energy and electoral strength to advance policies, such as the privatization of Social Security and Medicare, which most Tea Party members oppose. The Tea Party coalition's disproportionate influence on public opinion in the 2010 elections was in large measure due to the mischaracterization of the movement by the news media as reflecting a broadly based grassroots movement.

As a result of the Tea Party majority within the GOP caucus in the House of Representatives, the party establishment and its traditional Chamber of Commerce corporate allies have lost control. The compassionate conservative position of President George W. Bush in the 2000 and 2002 elections, exemplified by the expansion of the welfare state with a prescription drug benefit to Medicare, is no longer acceptable to a Republican right-wing majority that views entitlements with disdain. The wholesale, uncompromising attack on entitlements from Social Security to Medicare makes for legislative gridlock because of the Hastert rule that requires any legislation to have the support of the majority of the party caucus before being brought up for a vote in the full House.

Since the 2010 elections, the Republican right-wing majority in the House has obstructed bipartisan compromise in the name of ideological purity. The Tea Party representatives in Congress have dominated the contentious stalemate over key budgetary issues and over financing the national debt. Conservative lobbying organizations backed by powerful donors, such as Grover Norquist's Americans for Tax Reform, have exacted pledges of "no new taxes" from Republican lawmakers, especially from Tea Party–backed representatives in largely uncontested electoral districts, binding them to nonnegotiable positions on fiscal and budgetary issues. The result has been gridlock in government, as fluid cross-party coalitions have been replaced by rigid ideological groupings that regard compromise as weakness. The gridlock is made worse by the American system of checks and balances designed to work on the basis of consensus and compromise among changing coalitions in government.

The antidemocratic bent of the new right is evident in its efforts to resuscitate some of the most reactionary political traditions in American history. Like the Southern apostle of states' rights, John C. Calhoun, Tea Party Republicans, mostly from the South, have become committed to the belief that it has the right to nullify majorities—to exercise a minority veto to preserve their way of life. Calhoun sought to defy the antislavery majority on the national level by allowing states to nullify federal law. The new Tea Party seeks to prevent a further expansion of the welfare state, regulation of business, and protections of the civil liberties of minorities and women by similarly nullifying a national majority using tactics that stymie the legislative process or manipulate and suppress the vote of those who oppose them.

The adversarial, antimajoritarian style of politics by a leading faction in the Republican Party is a recent phenomenon. Prior to the advent of intensified opposition to President Obama's administration, there existed a neoliberal consensus among Republicans and moderate to conservative Democrats on welfare reform (welfare-to-work legislation), the earned-income tax credit, and the No Child Left Behind legislation. President George W. Bush's prescription drug benefit received bipartisan support as well. Since the Great Recession, the neoliberal consensus has dissolved. The reconstituted Republican Party under the influence of the Tea Party faction in Congress has pursued an adversarial style of politics that has worked in European parliamentary democracies but does not in the American regime under the constitutional rules that guide government decision making at all levels. In a parliamentary system like Europe's, one party or a majority coalition takes control of all levers of political power—executive and legislative—enacts its agenda, and then periodically holds elections to seek the backing of the voters. The American Constitution divides power in government among different branches. Power is shared by a set of institutions with overlapping authorities in Congress, the presidency, and the courts. Politicians have to cooperate for the system to work. Ironically, the Tea Party conservatives venerate the founding fathers, but their adversarial approach to governance goes against the one thing on which both Federalists and Anti-Federalists agreed upon—that adversarial political parties were bad for the American republic.

## Majority Tyranny?

Competitive parties and fair elections are the strongest guarantees of political equality and majority rule. Yet there are concerns that the electoral system based on the single-member, simple-plurality electoral system generally used from the national to the local levels discourages participation by citizens who are dissatisfied with the choices offered by the major parties.

First, there is the issue of contested elections and real choice for voters. Meaningful elections must provide voters with a range of choices, and for much of the period after World War II, party competition at the national level has led to exceedingly close and competitive elections for Congress and the presidency. Since 1996, elections for the House of Representatives have split the vote nearly evenly, and control of the House of Representatives has been at stake in each election. The narrowness of the margin separating the two major parties takes on a new meaning when we focus on the decline in the number of competitive elections. In 2000, when the presidential election was extremely close, only 74 of the 435 House seats were won by margins of less than 55 percent. In 2002, the number of competitive districts fell to 47 out of 435 (less than 11 percent).

Graph 1 illustrates the decline in party competitiveness in American House elections during the period from 1946 to 2010. In much of the country, elections for local, state, and national legislators resemble a one-party system with over 50 percent of elections being uncontested, which limits the scope of choice for voters.

The effect of party competitiveness and voter choice on voter turnout is significant. In both the 2002 and 2006 elections, districts where the winning candidate

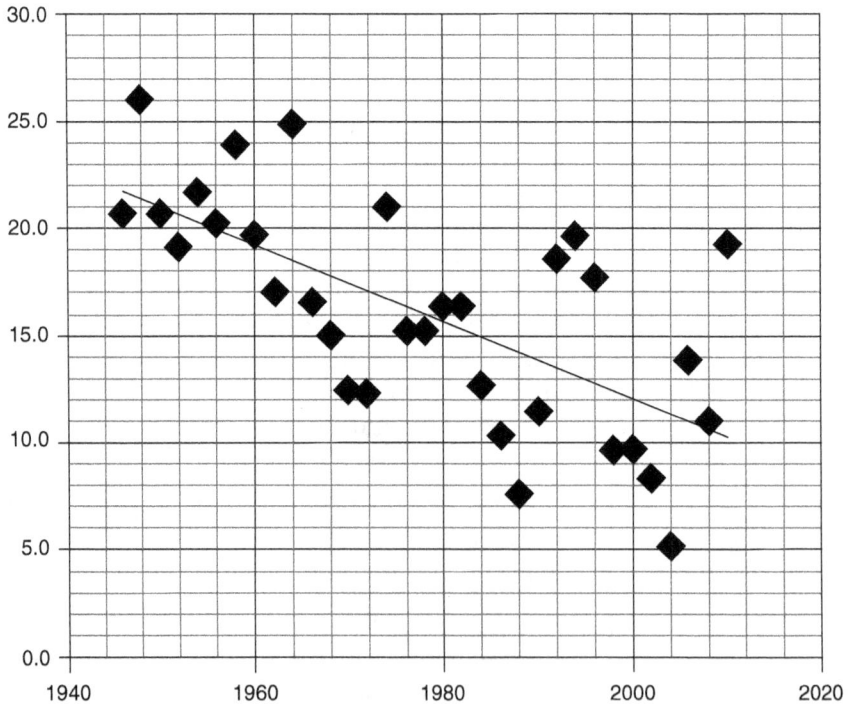

**GRAPH 1** The Percent of House of Representative Seats Won by 10 Percent or Less of the Vote, 1940–2010

This graph is based on data provided by professors Gary Jacobson, Distinguished Professor of Political Science at the University of California, San Diego, and Carl Klarner, Associate Professor of Political Science, Indiana State University.

received at least 80 percent of the vote struggled to turn out 125,000 voters. In those districts where the margin was 20 percent or less, turnout exceeded 200,000. Some estimates suggest that increased party competitiveness could expand voter turnout by more than eleven million voters.

In addition, candidates from third parties often find it impossible to get on the ballot because of strict requirements for registering third parties. This sometimes requires getting large numbers of signatures in a very short period of time. The fact that campaigns now rely heavily on television advertisements means that newcomers, unless they are independently wealthy, have difficulty raising the campaign funds to get name recognition on the ballot. Voter unfamiliarity is largely related to the prohibitive costs of political advertising.

There are also concerns about the fairness of an electoral process based on winner-take-all elections for racial and ethnic minorities and low-income individuals. Comparative studies have shown that majoritarian electoral systems are less representative, in practice, of minority interests than proportional representation systems. The former tend to have fewer minorities in office and have more limited spending on minority-friendly policies than countries with proportional representation. Those results are generally borne out in studies of how the preferences of racial minorities fare in American elections. Political scientist Zoltan Hajnal analyzed a wide range of American elections and found that African Americans are consistently more likely than other demographic groups to end up losers in elections as measured by the number of individuals from different demographic groups who voted for a candidate that lost the election. African Americans in states with a history of Jim Crow fared worse in elections independent of all other considerations (partisan leanings, the racial makeup of the electorate, and educational attainment of the population). On balance, African Americans are "15% more likely to be defeated in Senate elections. In gubernatorial elections, the gap grows to 26%."[2] Voting fairness remains fragile for African Americans and Latinos and suggests the need for remedies such as racial districts in order to obtain more equitable representation.

Recently, the use of undemocratic means to frustrate the rule of the majority has taken different forms. Earlier efforts to dilute the vote of the politically mobilized urban working class and ethnic minorities were overturned by the US Supreme Court in *Baker v. Carr* (1962) prohibiting malapportionment for its violation of "one person, one vote." Yet the Court has not prevented state legislatures and governors from using their power to draw electoral districts, putting few restrictions on the power of partisans to select their own voters. Congress requires that every decade a census must be taken of the American population and electoral districts redrawn to account for population changes. As a result, some American states such as California have gained a larger number of seats in Congress and others have lost seats, such as Indiana and New York. In most states, new districts are then drawn up by state legislators and governors to account for those changes. States with strong Tea Party–dominated legislatures, such as Virginia, have used partisan gerrymandering of congressional districts by concentrating liberal votes (the low-income, urban, African American and Latino voters) into a handful of congressional districts while spreading out conservative votes (white, rural, and better-off voters) across numerous districts that elect Republicans. The result is a large number of uncompetitive electoral districts and partisan bickering over redistricting.

There is some dispute over the extent to which strategic partisan redistricting or gerrymandering depresses party competitiveness and voter turnout. Yet there is evidence of its distorting effect on majority rule. In 2012, House Democratic candidates won over 50.5 percent of the national vote but took just 46 percent of the seats. In North Carolina, Democratic House candidates won 51 percent of the vote but only 27 percent of the House seats. In the last forty years, according to Jonathan Weisman of the *New York Times,* only once, in 1996, did the party that won the majority of votes end up with a minority of the seats. David Wasserman of the *Cook Political Report* finds that Republicans controlled redistricting in states with 40 percent of the seats in the House, while Democrats controlled redistricting in states with only 10 percent of the seats.[3]

The decreasing proportion of Democrats and Republicans representing competitive districts means that political elites have fewer incentives to cross party lines or to appeal to independents and supporters of opposing parties in their districts. The result is reduced bipartisan cooperation on major issues. Increasing polarization and declining competition also means that both parties have fewer seats at risk in elections. This explains much of the reason why the new majority has been unable to seize power through electoral means. Republicans have been able to maintain control of the House most the time since 1994 in large part because elections are seldom contested and because large campaign donors are more likely to contribute to likely winners. Few challengers are able to mount competitive campaigns. It now costs well over a million dollars to wage a competitive campaign for the House of Representatives. In the three House of Representative elections between 1998 and 2002, only thirty-three challengers in districts with some degree of incumbent vulnerability were able to raise more than $1 million, and only nine were elected. Most incumbents can easily raise that amount of money, but few challengers can.

Political democracy is based on the guarantee of political equality expressed in the right to vote. That right is under attack today. Asserting voting to be a privilege and not a right, state lawmakers across the country have enacted laws to tighten voting registration rules following the 2010 midterm elections. Since the Republican electoral landslide of 2010, states have instituted photo ID and proof of citizenship laws, ended popular measures such as Election Day voter registration, limited voter registration efforts, reduced early and absentee voting days, and reversed prior executive decisions that had made it easier for citizens with past felony convictions to restore their voting rights. Nineteen new laws and executive actions in fourteen states were passed in 2011, and over one hundred bills were introduced but did not pass. Furthermore, the Brennan Center for Justice reports that since the beginning of 2013, seven states have passed eight restrictive bills in the legislative session, and at least 82 restrictive bills were introduced in 31 states.[4] The US Department of Justice, responsible for enforcement of national voting laws such as the Voting Rights Act of 1965, is limited in its enforcement authority, since states institute the election rules that impact who is eligible to vote.

The states affected by voter restriction laws will provide over 63 percent of the electoral votes needed to win the presidency. The Brennan Center estimates that as many as five million voters have been disenfranchised by the restrictions making it harder for eligible voters to cast a vote. The CENTER calls the surge in new restrictions "the most significant cutback in voting rights in decades," adding that the impact of these measures most severely impacts youths, the elderly, and minorities who form the new majority.[5] Laws designed to make it harder to vote are often justified on the basis of preventing voter fraud and ensuring electoral fairness. But independent monitors find little evidence of voter fraud in America. The voter suppression efforts appear aimed at gaining a political edge for Republicans by limiting the vote of those most likely to vote for the Democratic Party. However, sizeable numbers of American voters seem to be unpersuaded that voter fraud represents a threat to electoral integrity and are pushing back against restrictive voting laws. In Maine and Ohio, voters have sided with the position that increasing the opportunity to vote is a fairness issue. In Maine, voters reversed a new law passed in June of 2011 that ended same-day registration. In Ohio, over three hundred thousand citizens signed petitions to temporarily suspend the state's new law curbing early voting and forced a statewide referendum. In Florida, civil society groups led by the League of Women Voters have brought lawsuits against state laws that penalize voter registration drives. It is too early to say if the outcome of the contentious disputes over election laws and regulations will reverse the long march toward expanding the voting rights of Americans or whether voter-suppression efforts will continue and grow. What is clear is that in the foreseeable future many eligible voters will find it harder to cast ballots or be deprived of their vote altogether.

One result of fewer choices and less fairness in voting and elections is that a higher percentage of eligible voters do not turn out compared to other democracies, a trend that is more pronounced among lower-income groups and racial and ethnic minorities. Voter turnout rates fluctuate, and rates have increased in presidential elections after the low-turnout 1996 election, following a prolonged decline since 1952. In presidential elections, the turnout rate has fallen from 62.8 percent of the voting-age population in the 1960 election to 52.8 percent in 1980 and only 50.3 percent in 1988. After an increase to 55.2 percent in 1992, it fell again to 50.3 percent in 2000, rising to 60 percent in 2008, the strongest turnout in nearly half a century. Turnout rates in off-year elections (when there was not a presidential election occurring at the same time) declined from around 48 percent in the 1960's to 36 percent in 2006 and 41 percent in 2010. The overall downward trend in voter turnout, with fluctuations, had a more pronounced effect on low-income Americans. The voter turnout gap, the difference between the turnout rates of Americans in the top 20 percent income bracket and Americans in the bottom 20 percent, averaged 30 percent during this period in favor of upper-income voters. Those disparities significantly influenced who counts in forming a majority.[6]

Legal measures to suppress the vote appear rooted in the fear of majority rule by a more racially and ethnically diverse population and groups espousing very different cultural beliefs from those of cultural conservatives. The strength of the reaction is no doubt made worse by job insecurity among all Americans and growing income disparities brought about by unfettered markets and globalization. These conditions help account for the intensification of class, racial, and cultural tensions that have come to characterize recent US politics.

## Civil Liberties Under Stress

Many of the civil rights gains made during the second half of the twentieth century are now in danger. Prior to the 1920s, the civil liberties proclaimed in the Bill of Rights had little bearing on the lives of most Americans. Judges generally allowed local authorities wide scope in determining which speech could be suppressed. For example, state courts during the Progressive Era regularly issued injunctions prohibiting strikers from speaking, picketing, and distributing literature during labor disputes. The investigations of the Commission on Industrial Relations established by Congress in 1912 revealed a dire state of civil liberties in many industrial communities. Labor attorney Clarence Darrow, speaking before the commission, stated, "I don't think we live in a free country or enjoy civil liberties."[7] So-called obscenity laws were used to repress speech on women's contraception. Margaret Sanger was indicted under the Comstock Act (1873) for sending birth control information through the mail. Though charges were dropped, the mere fact of prosecution had an intimidating effect on women.

Between 1900 and 1915, social movements struggled to strengthen and expand civil liberties: the fledgling motion picture industry demanded an end to local censorship, labor activists spoke out against restraints on open-air speaking; and early feminists called for an end to the broad reach of obscenity laws. More free speech cases were brought to court than had been litigated in all of the previous century. Their efforts on behalf of civil liberties were slow in bearing fruit. During the World War I, and for the first time since the Alien and Sedition Acts of 1798, the federal government enacted statutes to restrict freedom of speech. The Espionage Act of 1917 prohibited spying and interfering with the draft as well as any "false statement" that might impede conduct of the war. The Sedition Act of 1918 criminalized spoken or printed statements intended to cast "contempt, scorn, or disrepute" on the American government, as well as speech that advocated interference with the war effort. Only in the 1930s did civil liberties gain a surer footing in American politics. As discussed elsewhere in this volume, the passage of the National Labor Relations Act established the rights of employees in the private sector to discuss organizing and workplace issues with coworkers, thereby protecting a fuller freedom of association and self-organization. The Supreme Court under Justice Oliver Wendell Holmes expanded free speech rights in *Schenck v. United States* (1919) by establishing the "clear and present danger" standard for First Amendment guarantees of free speech. The ruling limited the discretion of public officials in prosecuting dissenting speech. Yet even after *Schenk,* the court provided a weak foundation for the defense of free speech in times of crisis. A week after the decision was announced, the court unanimously approved the conviction of Socialist Eugene V. Debs for sedition, despite the fact that his antiwar speech had not urged resistance to the draft or the government. It was not until 1931 that the Supreme Court strengthened the right to dissenting speech when it overturned a California statute making it a crime to display a red flag. Slowly, a judicial defense of civil liberties took hold in American democracy.

Today, the Bill of Rights guarantees of equal protection under the law and safeguards against unreasonable searches, and the right to a fair trial are under attack as a result of the War on Drugs greatly intensified under the Reagan administration and the War on Terror following 9/11. Under the umbrella of the War on Drugs, the Supreme Court has weakened protections against unreasonable searches by essentially creating a drug exception to the Bill of Rights. Michelle Alexander, a professor of law at Ohio State University, writes that "virtually all constitutionally protected civil liberties have been undermined by the war on drugs."[8] In recent years, the Supreme Court has approved mandatory drug testing of employees and students, upheld random searches and sweeps of public schools and students, permitted police to obtain search warrants based on an anonymous informant's tip, expanded the government's wiretapping authority, legitimized the use of helicopter surveillance of homes without a warrant, and allowed the forfeiture of cash, homes, and other property based on unproven allegations of illegal drug activity. Stop-and-frisk practices aimed most harshly at minorities have also increased—over 525,000 in New York City alone. In Brownsville, Brooklyn, a heavily minority area, 93 of every 100 residents have been frisked by police. In less than thirty years, the US prison population exploded from around three hundred thousand to more than three million, the highest per-capita rate of incarceration in the world, dwarfing the rates of nearly every developed industrial democracy and surpassing those of Russia, China, and Iran.

In Arizona, a bill passed by the legislature hands the state and local police broad powers to enforce immigration laws, including the power of the police to stop, investigate, and frisk anyone suspected of being in the country without documentation. The US Supreme Court recently ruled the parts of the law relating to policing constitutional, although the ruling allows for future challenges to the law on "equal protection" grounds. According to a May 2012 complaint to the US Justice Department, Latino drivers were stopped at a rate of anywhere from four to nine times more than other drivers, often leading to prolonged detentions. Arizona sheriff Joe Arpaio, the self-styled "America's toughest sheriff," whose implementation of the law has been called racist by critics, is currently being sued by various Latino groups representing individuals claiming racial profiling and the US Justice Department.

The class, age, and racial dimensions of this mass incarceration are striking. One in four federal prison inmates is a Latino. Latinos are incarcerated in state and federal prisons at a rate 2.6 times greater than whites, the vast majority convicted of relatively minor nonviolent offenses. According to the Bureau of Justice Statistics, Latinos today are the fastest growing minority group in the prison system even though they are less likely to be involved in violent crimes than any other group.

Developments such as the mandatory sentencing requirement set back democratic guarantees of due process and equal protection. Though Congress first enacted mandatory-sentencing drug laws in 1952 under the Boggs Act, the turning point in mass incarceration occurred in 1986 during the Reagan administration when Congress passed the Anti-Drug Abuse Act as part of the War on Drugs. It changed the federal supervised-release system from a rehabilitative system into a punitive system and enacted new mandatory sentences for drugs, including marijuana. Mandatory sentencing started a trend that led to the United States to imprison a larger percentage of its black and minority populations than did South Africa at the height of apartheid. One in three young African American men will serve time in prison if current trends continue. These rates cannot be explained by racial differences in rates of drug crimes. Studies show that people of all races and ethnicities use and sell illegal drugs at remarkably similar rates. While there are no significant racial differences in selling and using drugs, in some states black and Latino men have been incarcerated on drug charges at rates twenty to fifty times greater than those of white men. For the country as a whole, the incarceration rate for African Americans is six times higher than that of whites.[9] The class and racial bias inherent in the drug war is one major reason that one in every fourteen black men was behind bars in 2006 compared to one in every 106 white men. According to Alexander, the bias appears to be ingrained in federal policies that reward state and local officials with grants and other financial incentives based on mass incarceration.

The pattern of higher prosecution and conviction rates for lower-income minorities, along with their disenfranchisement, subjects minority populations to legalized discrimination for the rest of their lives, creating a growing underclass in society, a phenomenon that has been called the "new Jim Crow." Once a plea bargain labels a person as a felon, individuals are stigmatized and legally excluded from the privileges of citizenship, such as voting and serving on juries. Even if a person never served time in prison, their exclusion begins once they are branded a felon. Many whose crime was drug addiction or possession of a small amount of marijuana for recreational use are barred by law from public housing, discriminated against by private landlords, singled out in employment applications requiring self-identification as a felon, disqualified for food stamps, denied scholarships for higher education, and refused licenses for a wide range of professions. Political scientist Loc Wacquant finds that the rise of mass incarceration and its disproportionate impact on poor black communities serve as primary tools for managing disorder among low-income African Americans "in an era of deregulated, globally integrated markets."[10]

The link between class, race, and ethnicity, on the one hand, and voter suppression, on the other, is backed by considerable social science research. States with higher percentages of minorities are more likely to have stricter felon disenfranchisement laws and are less likely to have same-day voter registration. Similarly, states with larger minority populations tend to have stricter voter ID laws. Finally, there is a significant statistical connection between a state having a legal death penalty and the presence of minorities, high levels of economic inequality, and Republican strength in state legislatures.[11]

Mass incarceration practices disproportionately affect the voting rights of low-income groups and minorities. In the real world of policing and courts, many who cannot afford the price of legal counsel never meet with an attorney and face such severe penalties for many crimes that innocent people often accept plea bargains to avoid the possibility of harsh mandatory sentences. According to political scientist Richard Scher, in 2004 there were 5.2 million persons who had been convicted of a felony and were denied the right to vote in the United States.[12] Of these, 2 million had completed their sentences and 1.3 million were on probation.

According to a study of incarceration rates in ten states by the Mexican American Legal Defense and Education Fund (MALDEF), half a million Latino citizens cannot vote as a result of felony disenfranchisement. Political scientist Alan Abramowitz finds that this phenomenon accounts for about 1–2 percent of the lower voter turnout of Latinos in the United States. Combined with the institutional characteristics of our election system, such as tough voter registration requirements and strict voter ID laws, felony disenfranchisement is part of the explanation why US voter turnout is among the lowest of the world's democracies.

So-called prison gerrymandering also distorts the electoral process. Imprisoned Latino and African Americans are being counted by the census for drawing election districts in the counties where they are incarcerated rather than their home communities. They become phantom constituents because the largely white counties where they are held count them as part of the constituency for purposes of electoral apportionment and resource allocation. Since the imprisoned constituents cannot vote, they contribute to the electoral clout of mostly rural districts that benefit from mass incarceration through jobs and federal and state subsidies.

A disturbing trend in the reversal of civil liberties protections since the 1970s is that the Supreme Court has regularly shut the door of the legal system to racial and ethnic minorities wishing to challenge their unequal protection and treatment under the law. The court—the one branch that is charged with the responsibility of protecting minorities from the excesses of majoritarian democracy and guaranteeing constitutional rights for unpopular groups subject to discrimination—has so far ruled in favor of practices behind race biased mass incarceration. It has consistently upheld the right of police to use minor traffic violations as a pretext for drug searches, asserting that even if the practice disproportionately targets minorities, it does not constitute "unreasonable searches and seizures" (*Whren v. United States*, 1996).

The court has also ruled in favor of unequal sentencing for similar drug-related crimes. The courts have upheld federal laws that treated crack cocaine users and sellers (over 90 percent of those prosecuted are African Americans) one hundred times more severely in mandatory sentencing than the mostly white users of powder cocaine (*McCleskey v. Kemp,* 1987). That disparity in federal mandatory-minimum sentencing, falling most heavily on African Americans and Latinos, has been reduced as result of 2010 legislation (five grams of powder crack cocaine is now the same as 90 grams of powder cocaine). Yet the principle in *McCleskey* of unequal sentencing for similar crimes has been expanded to other areas, such as the "two strikes, you're out" rule in Georgia, which is applied at the discretion of prosecutors to 16 percent of all African American repeat offenders but to less than 1 percent of whites.

The courts have shielded the discretionary and virtually unreviewable power of prosecutors from allegations of racial bias in sentencing even when statistical evidence strongly points to unequal treatment. In *Armstrong v. United States* (1996), the Supreme Court ruled that race-based disparities of crack cocaine users by prosecutors could not be contested on grounds of racial discrimination. Prosecutors in Los Angeles regularly diverted African American crack cocaine defendants to federal courts where harsher sentencing guidelines prevailed, while white defendants were directed to state courts with more lenient guidelines. The Supreme Court set a nearly impossible standard of review, requiring defendants to identify a similarly situated white defendant who should have been charged in federal court but was not, before being entitled to discovery information from the prosecutor under the Fourteenth Amendment's equal protection clause. Defendants, thus, are required to prove beforehand the very thing they sought to prove in discovery: information regarding selective prosecution.

The civil rights of incarcerated Americans have been restricted by the widespread practice in the prison system of solitary confinement. For decades since the Geneva Conventions, governments have recognized prolonged isolation of prisoners in cruel conditions to be a dehumanizing form of punishment because it is known to drive prisoners into mental illness. Yet prolonged solitary confinement, sometimes for months or even years, has become a common form of prison management inflicting inhumane suffering on tens of thousands of prisoners. In California, nearly twelve thousand inmates are currently housed in some form of isolation, with 3,899 serving an indeterminate sentence. To prevent gang-related violence, the state of California requires three pieces of information linking an individual to gang membership before an inmate is placed in solitary confinement. But the standard is weakly enforced, and some inmates are arbitrarily confined for a variety of reasons, including mental health problems. In a recent case brought by an inmate challenging his solitary confinement, the California Appeals Court ruled that a prisoner has no constitutionally guaranteed immunity from being falsely or wrongfully accused of conduct that may result in being deprived of a protected liberty.

In 2003, the justice system employed 2.4 million people and the United States spent a record $185 billion for police protection, detention, judicial, and legal activities, representing a dramatic expansion of government at the state and local levels. Coming on the heels of the fraying of civil liberties, the advent and perpetuation of mass incarceration of poor and working class minorities have the hallmarks of a second Jim Crow.

## Democracy and the Mass Media

Political democracy requires robust guarantees of transparency in government and freedom of speech and of the press so that citizens have access to information necessary to make informed electoral choices and assess the consequences of those choices. The United States protects these two precious freedoms to a greater extent than most countries, but these freedoms are in decline.

There are many factors that contribute to an environment of self-censorship that restricts the range of public discussion. Many critical issues, including the disproportionate impact of the War on Drugs on minorities and low-income Americans, growing income inequality and poverty rates, and the hollowing out of the middle class, receive sporadic attention in discussions in the media, civil society, and government. Among the most significant factors that hinder a robust media are the power of advertising and the growing economic stress on established media newspapers from competition from internet sources of information. Recently, the *New York Times* closed its environmental desk that consistently provided high-quality reporting on environmental issues and policy.

The First Amendment to the US Constitution states that Congress shall make no law abridging the freedom of speech. One well-known federal rule supporting the First Amendment has been the fairness doctrine, requiring broadcasters to give "adequate coverage" to public issues and to ensure that "coverage accurately reflects opposing points of view." Those networks not obeying the doctrine may have their license revoked by the Federal Communications Commission, a sanction so severe that it is rarely used. The application of the doctrine is further limited by the fact that in television more than any other business time is money, and federal regulators often accept the economics of equal airtime as a justification for failure to obey the fairness doctrine. Given the economic constraints, decisions on what and how to cover the news are made by editors, owners, and sponsors without oversight.

Freedom of expression, the right to express one's opinion, is a well-established right in the United States, but that right is under attack and in retreat. In recent decades, there have also been efforts to limit expression of facts, not just opinion. Prohibiting the communication of facts flies in the face of the people's right to know in a democracy. In the case of the Pentagon Papers, the administration of President Richard Nixon attempted to restrain the publication of an unflattering factual account of the Vietnam War. The Supreme Court reversed that censorship. Under the administration of George W. Bush (2001–9), the old principle of the imperial presidency has been revived in the form of the unitary executive. Under this doctrine, the executive can suspend civil liberties, including authorizing the torture of enemy combatants and their rendition to countries known for using torture in violation of US treaty agreements. The principle has been used to limit judicial review of executive branch decisions to subject prisoners to indefinite detention without trial. In 2005, Congress passed the Detainee Act, which challenged the executive use of waterboarding and other forms of interrogation techniques on detainees. Three years later, in *Rumsfeld v. Hamdi* the Supreme Court overruled the administration's policy of classifying the detainees as enemy combatants, stating that prisoners could sue in court to change their enemy combatant designation and held that they were not to be tried in separate military tribunals but under the Geneva Convention rules. President Obama, however, has continued the argument of the unitary executive and claimed the virtually unrestricted right to kill enemy combatants (some of whom happen to be American citizens) with drones.

In the post-9/11 period, the Bush administration, under the authority of the Patriot Act, expanded the power of the FBI to collect information on private citizens but withheld the decision from the public and Congress. It was only after Congress required a mandatory audit that it was revealed that thousands of wiretaps and other intrusive information-gathering tactics were used on American citizens. More recently, the Obama administration, in response to the release by the open-source information site WikiLeaks of over 250,000 previously classified documents, has lowered the prosecutorial threshold from the "clear and present danger" standard first enunciated in 1919 by Oliver Wendell Holmes. Meanwhile, the Department of Justice is pursuing extradition charges against the WikiLeaks founder Julian Assange to prosecute him under the Espionage Act of 1917. The underlying question is whether journalists have the right to distribute information already leaked. In 2012, the government vigorously prosecuted Aaron Swartz for downloading five million academic articles from JSTOR (the online system for archiving academic journals), even though JSTOR decided not to pursue legal action. Under threat of prison time, Swartz committed suicide. While the government has aggressively pursued cases that restrict open access to information, it has brought no charges brought against any of the Wall Street bankers whose actions led to the 2008 banking crisis.

Freedom of the press and transparency in government are basic requirements for a functioning democracy. In a democracy, the media functions to provide a civic forum for public debate, a watchdog against abuse of power, and a venue for public learning and political participation. The extent to which these functions are effectively performed today is subject to considerable debate among scholars. American democracy was born and flourished in a nineteenth-century environment where major newspapers were closely aligned with political parties. By the twentieth century, journalists gained a degree of autonomy in that they were allowed to seek independent analysis, check facts, and provide readers with competing perspectives. More recently, the daily papers in many media markets have fallen under the ownership of a single media conglomerate such as Rupert Murdoch's News Corporation. With monopoly control, it is difficult for the public to hear a diversity of views. The same is true for free network television due to the prohibitive costs for space and airtime (although they may exist on cable television).

Unlike the nineteenth century when each party had its own newspaper, today only one of the major parties has a news outlet—Fox News. According to Fox and its sister radio outlets, they represent the true American public, while the rest of the media is controlled by liberals and caters to minorities. Fox provides a consistent drumbeat of inflammatory news, such as the false claim that the Obama health care plan created death panels. In this way, the right-wing media complex reinterprets the role of the media along nineteenth-century lines, replacing the function of informing and educating the public to one of mobilizing partisans. For example, Glenn Beck, then of Fox News, played a key role in the emergence of the Tea Party by amplifying their significance and using the airwaves to promote the movement. The use of these tactics gives Fox an inordinate power to shape the public agenda because more-traditional news outlets respond to these unsubstantiated allegations in the interest of fairness. These and other trends in the media have furthered a decline in serious coverage of national and world affairs by leaving much of the public ignorant and disconnected from politics. One well-known scholar of American politics, Austin Ranney, attributes the growing civic disengagement of Americans and the public's increased cynicism to the media's partisan tone.

The quality of American democracy is diminished by the media's reluctance to fully carry out its old watchdog function during elections. Thomas Mann, of the Brookings Institute, and Norman Ornstein, of the American Enterprise Institute, widely regarded as fair and balanced commentators on the Washington political scene, argue that the press missed the biggest story of the 2012 campaign and elections. Fearing a loss of advertising revenues and being portrayed as partisan, mainstream reporters ignored the extent to which the 2012 Romney campaign misrepresented facts. While both parties reinterpreted facts to gain partisan advantage, the media failed to grasp the extent to which the GOP leaders were "far more over the top" and had become "ideologically extreme, scornful of compromise; unmoved by conventional understanding of the facts, evidence, and science, and dismissive of the legitimacy of the political opposition."[13] The watchdog function of the press suffered in a misguided attempt at fairness with the result that voters were less able to hold political leaders accountable because they did not know what was actually going on. Mann and Ornstein believe the press's timid reporting rewards the continuation of such behavior.

Some analysts speculate that communication via the Internet, social media, and television talk shows supply alternative sources of the information necessary for public discourse. The proliferation of cable channels and the Internet is thought to provide much less expensive and wider access to information. The new technologies from this perspective have a democratic potential facilitating political communications, openness, and the mobilization of individuals and groups into politics. In 2008 and 2012, the Obama campaign deftly used social media to elicit donations, communicate with supporters on public concerns, and mobilize them in support of legislation. The new open-source universities are providing educational access to large numbers of citizens, even as society grapples with the many problems in maintaining the quality and integrity of the educational system. But the impact of these new technologies on the media, education, and democracy remains in doubt. Technologies that make anonymity possible often push discourse to the extreme ends of the ideological spectrum. The lack of fact checking and accountability of these new conveyors of information contribute to polarized discourses and rumor mongering that weakens an informed public discourse. The possibility for abuse raises serious questions whether these new sources can foster the genuine human interaction and civil discourse that is required in the public sphere. On the other hand, their capacity to politically mobilize new constituencies may help to revive civil society, which has been in retreat.

## Is Civil Society in Retreat?

Democracy presumes a civic culture resting on democratic beliefs and attitudes among citizens, including trust in fellow Americans, a belief that individuals can make a difference in politics, and confidence that political institutions and leaders will act in the best interest of the majority, at least most of the time. But there is much evidence that civic culture has been unraveling over the last four decades, most notably since 2008. The Southern Poverty Law Center reported in 2012 that the number of so-called patriot groups, motivated by conspiracy theories centering on fear of the United Nations and a new world order, has surged since the election of President Obama from 149 groups in 2008 to 512 in 2009 and up again in 2010 to 824. The extremist narrative skews the discussion of even very limited gun control measures, such as a national registry for gun owners, into one of gun confiscation and the machinations of a tyrannical government from whom they are preparing to defend themselves with arsenals of weapons.

The fraying of civic culture is related to the dominance of neoliberalism in politics discussed in the previous chapter. In 1964, only 29 percent of Americans agreed that "the government is pretty much run by a few big interests looking out for themselves," a prospect that Madison believed was a threat to the republic but would be self-correcting through majority rule. By 1988, fully 63 percent of voters concurred with that opinion. Americans in the 1960s, by a 75 percent majority, said they trusted government to do what is right, but only 39 percent of Americans held that opinion in 2000. Similarly, in the 1960s, 66 percent of Americans rejected the statement that "most elected officials do not care about what people like me think." By the late 1980s, 66 percent of Americans agreed with that statement.[14] This negative view of one's capacity to influence politics suggests a sizeable and growing gap between the American public and its government. A deeper explanation of these attitudes is that an emerging majority of minorities, women, and postmaterial voters have not been able to win substantial power, but to the extent that its views impede the power of the older majority, it has eroded their confidence in government as well.

Americans' lack of trust in government is also explained by the excessive power of lobbies in politics. Political scientists find that American political leaders are more likely to heed the demands of special interests and higher-income Americans while discounting those of middle- and lower-income Americans. Thus, when the top 10 percent of income earners and bottom 10 percent income earners disagree significantly on issues, the evidence shows a lack of responsiveness to the preferences of the poor. Middle-class Americans—those in the fiftieth decile of income earners—fare little better than the poor when their preferences diverge from those of the well-off (the top 10 percent of income earners). Even Americans who are more educated and more informed on political issues experience a similar fate. Their preferences have less influence over legislation than do those of the well-off, who give the largest campaign contributions and have the most influence in the community. Those findings, of course, do not mean that lower- and middle-income voters never get what they want from government policy. These voters can influence politics through volunteer activities, such as labor and religious organizations, and may exert influence on specific issues at particular moments but not overall.[15] The perception is likely to grow among average Americans that the political system works to the advantage of a few big interests rather than for the benefit of all.

Especially since the 1970s, a number of influences appear to have diminished confidence and trust that political institutions and leaders are working on behalf of the average person. In modern society, individuals face greater and more compelling requirements from their private affairs and have less time to devote to public affairs. Issues are also more varied and complex, and the time needed to understand them is consequently greater. In addition, as the bulk of government is taken over by government regulatory agencies rather than by the three traditional branches of government, democratic control requires day-to-day monitoring and lobbying, which citizens, even aided by private advocacy groups, have a hard time doing. Most citizens lack the resources to command information, influence the mass media, finance campaigns, and hire professional experts. Thus the average citizen faces many obstacles in accessing information and influencing government.

The role of money in politics today is a contributing factor. Political campaigns are more expensive than ever due to the high cost of advertising on television and radio. It is more difficult for newcomers to raise money to compete in elections unless backed by well-heeled political action committees. The role of special interest groups and political action committees (PACs) in politics is bound to grow with the Supreme Court's 5–4 decision in *Citizens United v. Federal Elections Commission* (2010) permitting wide scope for unlimited spending in advertising on behalf of special interest issues. The court affirmed the principle that special interest groups and corporations have the same First Amendment rights under the Constitution as individuals. Justice John Paul Stevens lamented the decision and called the majority "profoundly misguided." According to Justice Stevens, "The Court's ruling threatens to undermine the integrity of elected institutions around the nation." As Justice Stevens's remarks indicate, such developments amplify the perception that democracy is not working for the average American.

The impact of super PAC spending in elections is having other effects on democracy. The influx of corporate funding seems bound to shift the political balance of power further to the right, but its immediate impact was felt most severely in the GOP. The growing power and influence of wealthy donors on party caucuses and primaries is severing the link between party leaders and candidates and providing opportunities for more extreme right-wing political candidates funded by billionaire donors to gain political office and pursue their own ideological agendas. Voters do not have to be informed under *Citizens United* about the sources of funding going to individual candidates and therefore are unaware of the loyalties and obligations incurred.

The growing influence of the right wing of the GOP within the Republican Party appears related to campaign finance laws. Thomas B. Edsall of the *New York Times* writes that in the post-*Citizens United* age, the Republican Party, traditionally a more hierarchical, well-ordered, and disciplined party has experienced the greatest impact. The Republican establishment traditionally managed candidate selection at the presidential level by channeling funds to candidates emerging from a negotiated process among Republican-leaning trade associations, top corporate law firms, and bankers. Empowered by *Citizens United,* a handful of rogue billionaires, such as Sheldon Adelson, the Las Vegas and Macao casino mogul, and Harold Simmons, a Dallas-based leveraged-buyout specialist, exercise political influence in primary election through their super PAC–funded ties to right-wing populist groups. Without restrictions on participation in primary election contests, the rogue billionaires have exerted influence through their ability to fund pollsters, direct mail, and media consultants. These billionaires contributed a larger sum to the 2011–2012 election cycle than the Republican National Committee.[16]

The net effect has been to loosen the grip of Republican Party leaders and expand the voice of the more extreme wing dominated by the Tea Party. In Congress, the result has been polarization and gridlock changing the political dynamic from one in which majorities and minorities debate and modulate their positions in forming legislation to one of obstruction by a minority opposed to compromise and determined to block the power of the new majority.

American public opinion shows a marked decline in confidence in Congress, political parties, and political leaders since the 1970s. In the 1990s, only 30 percent of all Americans said they had a great deal of confidence or quite a lot of confidence in Congress, a decline of 15 percent from the 1970s. There has also been a decline in support for the major political parties. Americans today report much lower levels of attachment to political parties. Americans who reported they engaged in party work at least once in the previous year fell by 56 percent from 1973 to 1995. The proportion who reported attending a campaign rally or speech fell by 36 percent during that time period. More Americans now say that they are independent of the Democratic or Republican political parties or have no attachment to any political party. Scholars disagree over the extent and significance of these trends. However, most agree that there has been a marked change over the last four or five decades in Americans' beliefs toward their political institutions and leaders.[17]

The diminished capacity of leaders to compromise and legislate for the common good rather than narrow partisan advantage is undermining trust and confidence as shown by the low poll ratings of Congress. There are some who wonder if the American penchant for pragmatism and compromise may be in crisis. Political leaders increasingly depend on super PAC money and special interests and are elected by a small number of highly organized, ideologically partisan political activists to win their party's nomination and compete in elections. Voting records of legislators going back to Reconstruction show that both parties are more homogenously conservative and liberal and are more divided today than at any other time previously. A recent study of roll call votes by Kenneth Poole and Christopher Hare found that "in the last few Congresses, the overlap has vanished, that is, the most liberal Republican is to the right of the most conservative Democrat." The change in ideological orientation happened less because individuals changed their beliefs one way or another and more due to the replacement of officeholders. Moderate DEMOCRATS, especially in the South, have retired or been defeated by conservative Republicans, and to a lesser extent, moderate Republicans in the Northeast have been replaced by more liberal Democrats.[18]

But it would be inaccurate to assume that both political parties in Congress have been equally intransigent or that they share equal responsibility for the gridlock. Recently, Mann and Ornstein attribute the partisan style to the emergence of Newt Gingrich and Grover Norquist in the 1990s as prominent Republican leaders using a slash-and-burn style of politics that remains integral to congressional Republicans. Obama's 2008 election and the Tea Party's electoral success in 2010 have taken the partisan wars to new extremes in brinksmanship over the budget and national debt and in the use of the filibuster as a regular means to require supermajorities to govern. During the 2007–2012 period, Republicans have filibustered over 360 times, a historical record.

As with past crises in American democracy, there are countermovements to these trends toward gridlock and polarization, as well as to policies that contribute to the gaping income inequality in American society. The long-term question is whether much of America will become "Southernized"—that is, transformed into a relatively low-wage society with weak public institutions, a diminished safety net, and rule by an unaccountable oligarchy of wealth or whether democracy will be deepened and extended. The good news is that contentiousness and declining confidence in conventional politics, political leaders, and institutions has thus far not translated into a crisis of confidence in democracy itself. Ninety percent of Americans say they support democratic ideals, largely unchanged since the 1970s. Most Americans also retain trust in other Americans, and 98 percent express pride in the country. Americans who came of age in the 1960s also have relatively higher levels of trust in other citizens, with 66 percent saying that most people can be trusted, while 43 percent of those who came of age during the Depression and World War II hold those sentiments. Most Americans remain deeply committed to a democratic way of life.

These trends lead to the interpretation that Americans today are dissatisfied democrats, skeptical of current leaders and institutions but not of democratic ideals. Democracy in the United States may be undergoing a temporary democratic retreat in preparation for a deepening of the democratic process with more critical citizens who are willing to challenge traditional political authority and more likely to participate in politics and social movements. This possibility is based on the fact that these sentiments are more prevalent in the new majority that has won electoral victories in 2008 and 2012.

## The Prospects for a Democratic Surge

Revitalizing civil society and restoring civic culture require undertaking political reforms that more closely align the practice of democracy with its promise. What can be done? There are signs that grassroots support is growing for making fair and equitable representation and inclusive participation a priority. Throughout its history, American democracy has been self-correcting and, on balance, tilted toward greater political inclusivity. There is reason to hope that it will again. Civil society groups are demanding political reforms, starting with the electoral system.

Federal government reforms that would give constitutional protection to the right to vote, introduce proportional representation in federal elections, and make voting registration and procedures more democratic appear unlikely to prevail in the near future in light of the determined opposition by conservatives. Adding to this dilemma is the nature of the American electoral system that gives individual states considerable discretion in establishing the rules and procedures governing elections. Local and state officials would be expected to fiercely resist any federally imposed uniform standards.

However, the decentralized structure of the American electoral system does provide opportunities for reformers at the state level. California provides one example. Voters have passed ballot initiatives creating nonpartisan apportionment commissions to draw electoral maps based on the principle of "one person, one vote." The goal is to increase party competition. The state has adopted open primaries to make the election process more inclusive and representative and extended to independent voters a greater voice in the selection of candidates, thus diluting the influence of the more activist and partisan voters.

As a result of the new rules, party competitiveness in California is on the rise. Before 2012, it was rare for an election to be decided by a majority vote of 55 percent or less. After 2012, there were eleven such contested elections. Elections also produced a significant turnover of incumbents that aligned the balance in the congressional delegation with the size of the Democratic majority in the state. Prior to the changes, the Republicans controlled nineteen of the California delegation's House seats but only fifteen after the reforms. At the national level, Republicans nationally only lost four House seats, an outcome that was related to Republican control of various state legislatures that enabled significant partisan gerrymandering, diluting the electoral clout of newly mobilized majority.

Some states are spearheading redistricting reforms to make elections more competitive and equitable to all voters. During the 2001–02 round of redistricting, six states—Arizona, Hawaii, Montana, Idaho, New Jersey, and Washington—assigned responsibility for redrawing congressional and state legislative districts to independent redistricting commissions. Iowa has been at the forefront since 1980, when it established the nonpartisan Legislative Services Agency to redraw new legislative and congressional districts. In general, states that have delinked redistricting from partisan politics have more competitive elections than states in which legislatures control the process.

In addition, election reform advocates are calling for measures to overcome undemocratic restrictions on voting, including many voter-suppression methods prevalent in some states. Here as well, state-level reform initiatives are having an impact. In the 2000 presidential election, for example, voter turnout in the six states with Election Day registration averaged 63 percent of the voting-age population, compared to a national turnout rate of 51 percent. One recent study estimated that adoption of Election Day registration would increase voter turnout by an average of seven percent, thereby tilting the electoral system toward inclusivity rather than exclusivity.[19] Both the state and federal government have an ethical obligation to voters to provide fair and equal access to the franchise and to provide fair and transparent methods for casting, recording, and counting ballots and impartial, verifiable procedures in case of recounts and challenges to ballots.

Campaign financing reform is also integral to democratic renewal. In recent years, state and local governments have been at the forefront of reform of campaign finance practices. Seven states now have voluntary public financing systems for all statewide and legislative candidates. In Maine's first election after implementing public financing, there was a 40 percent increase in the number of contested primary elections, and 53 percent of the challengers who accepted public funds defeated their incumbent opponents.

At the level of cities, as well, there is momentum building to reform campaign finance. In New York, Governor Andrew Cuomo and a broad coalition of groups are pushing for reforms that include donor transparency, lower contribution limits, better enforcement of funding rules, and more importantly, a public financing system of elections based on New York City's municipal elections system. In the opt-in program, candidates receive six dollars in taxpayer money for every one dollar contribution from a private citizen, up to a cap. Many of these clean election laws across the country have been adopted by citizen-sponsored initiatives bypassing reluctant state legislatures. While more research is needed to evaluate the impact of these reforms, there is reason to think that disaffected voters might be less cynical if elections were perceived to be fairer and less affected by big-money donors.

Finally, a small number of local governments have replaced single-member, simple-plurality elections with cumulative voting (CV). CV is a semiproportional electoral system based on multimember districts. Under CV, voters are given as many votes as the number of seats in a district, and voters can distribute those votes in any manner they see fit, including giving all the votes to one candidate. The system makes it easier for minority groups to gain representation and encourages more of them to run for office. The evidence suggests that CV somewhat increases voter turnout when compared to similar plurality systems.

Some states are also taking steps to repudiate the War on Drugs and, by extension, its impact on felony disenfranchisement, another indicator that undemocratic practices to suppress the vote are facing pushback. Recent ballot initiatives in Colorado and Washington, which have legalized marijuana use, are likely to spread. California recently voted overwhelmingly (68 percent to 32 percent) to reform the "three strikes" law so that life sentences can only be imposed on felony convictions that are serious or violent. The enacted proposition suggests future limits on the police practice of stop and frisk that ensnared many people in the criminal justice system for nonviolent acts, such as possession of small amounts of drugs for personal use.

There are other developments that hold out hope there will be fewer opportunities to rig the system so votes of some segments of the population are diluted or ignored. There have been efforts to limit procedural maneuvers in Congress, such as the filibuster, that block the power of the majority to legislate. In the House, Republicans instituted the so-called Hastert rule, an informal rule that allows a majority in the majority caucus to block consideration of most bills requested by the White House or sent from the Senate. This anti-democratic rule forecloses the opportunity for cross-party coalitions. Recently, Speaker John Boehner broke the Hastert rule in allowing the fiscal cliff deal to be put to a full vote of the House even though it was strongly opposed by the Tea Party majority in the Republican caucus. As in the 1960s, the potential exists for electoral and political changes to bring about reforms in procedures that now make it possible for a minority to block change without the need to forge agreements for the common good.

Critical breakthroughs in American democracy have often occurred as a response to pressures from grassroots social movements. In the 1940s, largely as a result of the New Deal and World War II, a balance was struck between the power of concentrated wealth and grassroots associations, such as labor unions, to advance a more just society. In the 1950s, 1960s, and 1970s the civil rights movement, the women's movement, and the environmentalist movements changed the public discourse on the common good through their activism. Similarly, Christian evangelicals and more recently Tea Party activists have strongly influenced the public debate in the last decade. The impetus behind state and local reforms suggests that American politics may be witnessing the beginnings of a more engaged civil society and a new majority demanding greater political inclusion.

American politics today is at a turning point in a long cycle that is a product of a back-and-forth struggle over public opinion and civil society. Since 2008, the country has moved in a progressive economic direction for middle- and low-income Americans. The Patient Protection and Affordable Care Act of 2010 provides for a significant improvement in the medical and financial security for many Americans, especially those in the bottom half of the income distribution. The improvements will be paid for largely by the top 1 percent of income earners. The fiscal cliff deal of 2013 raised taxes on the affluent. According to Paul Krugman, the net effect will be that the one percenters will see their after-tax incomes fall around 6 percent; that figure will rise to 9 percent for the top tenth of 1 percent of the population. The financial reforms of the Dodd-Frank Wall Street Reform and Consumer Protection Act, while not dramatic, provide a meaningful regulatory framework for hedge funds as is evident in the lobbying by financial institutions in opposition to the bill and the strong backing of hedge fund managers for Republican Mitt Romney. With respect to cultural democracy, the strong public support for gay rights expressed by Barack Obama suggests that the definition of the American community is becoming more inclusive. The Reagan era appears to have been supplanted by a new majority that has the demographic and cultural wind at its backs and whose political clout is bound to increase unless it is disenfranchised or legally repressed by undemocratic methods.

For the new majority to gain power, it will need to cohere around a progressive political agenda that points a path forward in addressing the many issues and challenges that face the country. That agenda is discussed elsewhere in this volume, but it must map out a path to sustainable growth, decent middle-class jobs, and significant opportunities for lower-income groups and minorities to get on the ladder of success through education and job training. It must forcefully address the many challenges discussed in this chapter in order to make democracy fairer and more equitable. The primary lesson of this volume is that despite reversals, the people have persevered in advancing the American democratic spirit. Democracy is possible.

# 7

# EPILOGUE, THE ENVIRONMENT: DEMOCRACY'S FOURTH WAVE

*This land is your land; this land is my land*
*From California, to the New York Island;*
*From the redwood forest, to the gulfstream waters*
*This land was made for you and me.*

Refrain from popular folksong by Woody Guthrie (1944)

Until recently, most Americans, as other modern and modernizing peoples, have believed that nature is a separate realm from human activity, far vaster and relatively permanent. That premise, which allowed Western peoples to exploit the resources of the natural world without compunction and use the ecosphere as an enormous sewer for their waste products, is now obsolete.

Throughout its history, humankind has always changed nature, but in the past, the ability to degrade and destroy it was limited by the relatively undeveloped state of technology and the lack of population growth. As a result, there was always a boundary between developed and undeveloped areas. We could flee pollution and congestion by retreating into the vast wilderness. Now there is no wild place to flee to. As Bill McKibben argued in his 1989 book, *The End of Nature,* there is no longer a solid boundary or frontier left between man and nature. There is only an increasingly humanized nature. Many scientists, beginning in 2000 with Nobel Prize–winner Paul Crutzen, believe that humans have entered a new epoch, the *Anthropocene,* in which human activities will largely determine the earth's environment.[1]

The insight that humans, as well as other organisms, are inextricably bound to nature and that no actions can be considered without their impact on the earth's different ecosystems is now widely accepted and is the origin of the modern science of ecology. That same understanding is also the basis for what we may term the "fourth dimension of democracy."

Over the last two hundred and fifty years, humans have begun to exert conscious, democratic management over realms of human life once thought to be traditional, timeless, and outside the sphere of human control. The first was the sphere of politics and government, which premodern peoples thought was governed by God's will as manifested in the person of the monarch. The second sphere was the economy, which was originally embedded in the traditional household and later thought to be governed by the natural laws of the market. By the twentieth century, Americans began to free up personal life or culture from the unconscious dominion of the patriarchal family. Now it is time to take democracy into another realm once thought to be impervious to human control: the ecosphere. But, this time, the stakes are higher. Not taking this critical next step in the evolution of democracy may well spell something like catastrophe for modern civilization on the planet.

In 1988, the US government climate scientist James Hansen testified before the US Congress that global climate change had begun. What convinced Hansen was not the decade of above-average temperatures and droughts that battered American farmers in the 1980s but his measurement of temperatures over long periods of time. Hansen found that the rise in world temperatures was almost three times the standard deviation in temperatures—that is, the expected random variation in the range of temperatures. Hansen blamed the otherwise inexplicable rise in global temperature on the enormous increase in the emission of greenhouse gases, chiefly carbon dioxide (but also, in descending order of importance, methane, nitrous oxide, hydrofluorocarbons, and a few other exotic compounds), resulting from deforestation and the burning of fossil fuels dating from the Industrial Revolution. The next day, the *New York Times* headlined "Global Warming Has Begun, Expert Tells Senate."[2]

It is now more than two decades since Hansen made his startling claim. Since that time, tens of thousands of scientists around the world studying and testing manmade climate change have abundantly confirmed his thesis. The US National Academy of Sciences, the United Nations, and many of other conclaves of scientists have issued statements warning of the consequences of continued greenhouse gas emissions. The most comprehensive of these is the 2007 joint statement signed by the national academies of science of Australia, Belgium, Brazil, Canada, the People's Republic of China, France, Germany, India, Indonesia, Ireland, Italy, Japan, Malaysia, Mexico, New Zealand, Russia, South Africa, Sweden, the United States, and the United Kingdom.[3]

Sophisticated, computerized climate change models now predict a temperature rise of as much as five degrees by the end of the century. If that occurs, the earth's temperature would be warmer than it has been since well before the appearance of human beings on the planet—in fact, warmer than at any time since thirty million years ago. Under these conditions, much of the planet would become uninhabitable to the human species. The impact of global climate change has already been felt in the melting of the Arctic Sea ice; the unprecedented rates of melting of the northern tundra; the rise in ocean levels; the accelerating retreat of the glaciers in most places; the increasing frequency and severity of extreme meteorological events, such as droughts, floods, tornadoes, and hurricanes; and the increase by 30 percent of surface ocean acidity levels. A report compiled in 2013 by 240 scientists for the federal government finds that in the United States, average temperatures have increased about 1.5 degrees since 1895, but that 80 percent of that has occurred since 1980. Already, spring comes a week earlier in the United States. If warming continues, humans can expect in the near future the flooding of the low-lying land of countries such as Bangladesh, resulting in the displacement of perhaps 150 million people, the extinction of large numbers of species due to their inability to adapt to new climates, and greatly reduced crop yields and mass starvation due to lack of water, soil erosion, and desertification (it should be noted that because photosynthesis stops at 95 degrees Fahrenheit or 35 degrees Celsius, agriculture in many parts of the world would be rendered impossible.).

The most feared stage of global climate change would be the point at which the warming of the planet would begin to feed on itself. Scientists now note that the permafrost, which covers the region in close proximity to the poles, is melting. Once it thaws, it will release billions of tons of methane, a greenhouse gas twenty times more potent than carbon dioxide, into the atmosphere. Something similar would happen when the ice sheets of Greenland and the West Antarctic begin to melt; it would create a self-reinforcing process that would accelerate warming. Since neither the permafrost nor the ice sheets would freeze up again, the result would be irreversible climate change.

Predictions of likely catastrophic climate change are by now old news. Yet almost nothing has been done about it by the US government and by the governments of other polluting nations. The 1997 Kyoto Protocol, which was scheduled to go into effect in 2005, committed the advanced countries of the world to reducing their greenhouse gas emissions 5.2 percent below 1990 levels by 2012. However, the United States did not sign the agreement, the only large advanced economy that refused to do so. That inaction reflects the lack of consensus in the country that global climate change exists or that its consequences are dire. It also reflects the constitutional checks and balances that make it difficult for even a majority to take government action in the face of determined minority opposition. The protocol did not require greenhouse gas cuts of China, India, and other industrializing countries, even though China has now passed the United States as an emitter of greenhouse gases. An attempt at Copenhagen in 2010 to bring the United States and China into the agreement also largely failed.

The lack of action by the United States threatens globalization and American global leadership. Climate change is one of the few issues that will profoundly affect every country on the planet and cannot be addressed meaningfully only on the national level. Without concerted action, individual nations will be tempted to be free riders on the efforts of other nations. Failure to address climate change on a global level would be a powerful precedent that short-term national interests can be allowed to trump the interests of the world's community of nations.

Taking national and international action on global climate change and related issues, such as global food shortages, is also a test for the existing institutions of American democracy. The most dynamic and critical arena of modern democracies is the sphere of civil society, social movements, and public opinion formation. It is here that the struggle to respond to and shape social change is waged most fiercely, with the stakes being control of government action.

The single most important reason for the inability of the United States to seriously address climate change is that a large segment of civil society and public opinion believes the erroneous view that global climate change is not yet settled science or that it can be attributed to natural causes. There is a precedent for the denial of science's overwhelming conclusions: the debate over whether smoking causes cancer and other serious diseases. Just as the fossil fuel–based energy companies and those in the extractive industries (agriculture, mining, grazing, and forestry) have sought to distort and manipulate public opinion on environmental issues, so too did the tobacco companies seek to shape public opinion with advertising and a disinformation campaign. In 1964, the US surgeon general issued a report that definitively linked smoking to cancer and other fatal or chronic diseases, which started the process of reshaping public attitudes. Yet, because the cigarette companies and their paid scientists were able to create the impression that the link with cancer was in doubt, progress was slow. Only in 1999 did public opinion reach the tipping point when the courts forced the cigarette companies to stop their marketing targeting young people, dissolve their special groups that had manipulated public opinion, and pay the states $206 billion over twenty-five years to defray medical costs. More important, public norms turned decisively against smoking.

That tipping point has not been reached on the question of global warming. In the meantime, threatened companies have mounted a concerted, well-financed public campaign to sow doubts in the public mind about the existence of a scientific consensus on global warming. These companies and business associations lavishly fund think tanks, which support and market antienvironmental publications and pay antienvironmental science advisors to counter the conclusions accumulating from the scientific community. At the same time, these companies run elaborate media campaigns that claim they have seen the light and can be trusted by the public because they are "going green."

That campaign has been closely associated with those in America's conservative or neoliberal movement who fear and oppose all but the most minimal government regulation of big business in the belief that the market can work best for the public good if freed from state interference. Since the advent of the neoliberal era in the mid-1970s, that argument has made headway in the public sphere.

However, there are a number of problems with this faith in the beneficence of market outcomes. Previous chapters have noted that the bargaining power of workers and employers in the labor market is highly unequal, allowing the former to be taken advantage of by the latter. The inability of the market to equate production and consumption except through extreme swings in economic activity, a phenomenon known as the business cycle, has led all governments in advanced economies to intervene in markets to moderate these cycles.

With regard to the environment, faith in the market assumes that market prices take *all* costs into account. But many costs, such as those associated with responding to environmental degradation, caring for the chronic diseases caused by pollution, disposing of waste, cleaning up toxic spills, and other costs picked up or suffered by the public, are *external* to the transactions of the firm—that is, left off its books. Insofar as this is the case, market outcomes cannot take these costs into account, and businesses will continue their antisocial activities. It would take action emanating from outside the market—for example, a carbon tax, government subsidies to cheapen the cost of alternative energy sources, or a comprehensive change in public norms—for markets to enforce conservation on business.

The intense opposition to acting on global climate change exemplifies the enormous obstacles environmentalists have faced whenever they attempt to regulate the industrial sources of pollution and environmental breakdown. It is easy for those who care deeply about the environment to become frustrated and pessimistic about its prospects. However, the broad base and potential for change should not be underestimated. The strength of environmentalism goes well beyond its manifestation as a social movement composed of dedicated activists working in a variety of advocacy groups of relatively recent vintage. Environmentalism, in fact, is a culture—a set of values, attitudes, and practices—deeply rooted in modern life, both in America and other advanced nations. Beginning in the late nineteenth and early twentieth century, environmental consciousness emerged in American public opinion among the urban middle classes as they confronted the unprecedented ability of industrial capitalism to degrade the natural environment.

The concern for environmental quality was a key component of the urban middle class's new focus on their standard of living. Unlike a commodity, which was purchased and possessed before it was consumed, environmental quality was a collective good or commons, something that made life more healthy, pleasant, and beautiful. One of the first indications of environmental consciousness was the trend that began in the late nineteenth century of middle-class families moving out of the city to the surrounding new suburbs. The goal was to be free of the city's congestion, disease-causing pollution, and ugliness. Having ready access to open space for leisure activities, clean air and water, and aesthetically pleasing, natural surroundings allowed families to raise healthy children and improve their quality of life. By the twentieth century, the United States became the world's first country to have the majority of its citizens living in suburbs rather than in cities or rural areas. Those remaining in the cities demanded health and other city ordinances that reduced pollution, noise, congestion, and the disposal of industrial waste in their neighborhoods.

Another feature of emerging environmentalism was the desire to preserve uniquely beautiful areas so that they could be appreciated aesthetically and spiritually by present and future generations. America's most influential advocate for preservation was John Muir. Living and working in the mountain West, Muir helped convince Americans of the spiritual value of contact with wild nature. In his writings, he extolled deep human contact with nature because it inspired and healed the soul. Nature was not dead matter but alive with spirit. As he once observed, "A few minutes ago every tree was excited, bowing to the roaring storm, waving, swirling, tossing their branches in glorious enthusiasm like worship. But though to the outer ear these trees are now silent, their songs never cease."[4]

Muir and the Sierra Club, which he founded in 1892, helped found the American national park system. Muir took America's first environmentalist president, Theodore Roosevelt, camping in the magnificent Yosemite Valley in California and convinced him that it needed national protection. With Roosevelt's support, Congress mandated the US National Park System in 1899, starting with the Yosemite and Sequoia national parks. Roosevelt went on to create sixteen national monuments, fifty-one wildlife refuges, and doubled the number of national parks. But in 1906, Roosevelt clashed with Muir over the damming of the beautiful Hetch Hetchy Valley in Yosemite. The conservationist Roosevelt supported the use of its river for water and electricity to benefit the people of San Francisco. The dispute, which ended badly for Muir and the Sierra Club, highlighted the differences between conservation and environmentalism. Conservation was about the efficient use of resources for production, while environmentalism gained its popularity as a consumer ethic.

The flowering of American environmentalism occurred in the three decades after World War II, when it became a mass movement. The unprecedented rise in Americans' standard of living created a much larger constituency for environmental values, culture, and programs. Between 1948 and 1973, the median inflation-adjusted wage of the typical American worker almost doubled. The home ownership rate rose from 43.6 percent in 1940 to 62.9 percent in 1970.[5] By then, virtually every family owned an automobile. Unprecedented affluence and growing leisure time allowed millions of workers to join the middle class, escape city life to the suburbs, and take weekend and summer excursions into the countryside in the family car. Government pensions and welfare for the disabled and dependent children, called Social Security; strong unions negotiating high wages and benefits, such as health care and vacations; and lifetime employment in large corporations minimized economic insecurity and the overwhelming focus on making a living that went along with it.

As a result of these changes, survival came to be taken for granted and postmaterial values began to rival material values, a shift that has occurred in all highly developed countries and is closely correlated with level of income. The new values were ones of personal autonomy, self-expression, self-fulfillment, tolerance of cultural diversity, gender equality, and overall quality of life, including environmentalism. These values—closely associated with the "expressive individualism" discussed in chapter two—began to eclipse the older survival values, including adherence to traditional religion, respect for authority and male dominance, identification with one's social class, and sacrifice of one's individuality for the common good. The first generation that felt this value shift was the baby boom generation that matured in the 1960s and 1970s, when the environmental movement also came of age.

If John Muir could be said to be the founding father of environmentalism, its founding mother was Rachel Carson. As both a naturalist and editor-in-chief of the publications of the US Fish and Wildlife Service, Carson had developed a deep love of nature. Out of that love, she became alarmed at the destructive impact of chemical pesticides on the environment. Recognizing the powerful alliance of the US Department of Agriculture, state and county agencies, large agribusinesses, and chemical companies that lay behind this assault on natural ecosystems, she grew determined to expose its dangers. In 1962, she published a bombshell of a book, *Silent Spring*. The book argued, using the latest scientific evidence, that pesticides such as DDT were killing off songbirds and other wildlife, including the bald eagle, America's national bird. Carson predicted that dangerous pests would soon develop resistance to chemical pesticides and weakened ecosystems would become susceptible to invasive species. Four of the book's chapters depicted the way pesticides caused cancers and other human illnesses.

The chemical companies fought back using their paid scientists. They accused her of wanting to return to the dark ages and of being a fanatic. The attacks backfired. Under the influence of postmaterial values, Americans were already beginning to become disenchanted with the commitment to technological progress at any cost, as they observed the health impact of radioactive fallout from above-ground nuclear testing and the discovery of a cancer-causing herbicide on cranberries sold in the supermarkets that year. *Silent Spring* touched a nerve in the public. Within the year, President Kennedy's Science Advisory Committee backed Carson's claims.

Environmentalism quickly became a mass movement. Membership in the Sierra Club grew fivefold in the 1960s and today has risen to 1.3 million. Environmentalists founded new organizations, such as the National Environmental Defense Fund, while older ones, such as Wilderness Society and National Audubon Society, grew apace. Altogether, such groups had approximately five hundred thousand members by the end of the decade. Critical in the evolution of environmental consciousness was the fact that tens of millions of Americans watched popular television shows depicting wildlife; bought photography books conveying the beauty and reverence evoked by natural wonders, such as the Grand Canyon, Yellowstone Park, and the Great Smoky Mountains; took trips to the newly expanded national parks; and read reports on the latest environmental science.

A major sign that environmentalism had become a popular national movement came with the establishment by the Congress in 1970 of Earth Day, which is also celebrated by 175 countries around the world, every April 22.

Under pressure from environmental groups, scientists, and a newly sensitive public opinion, Congress sprang into action. During the 1960s, President Lyndon Johnson signed into law over three hundred new environmental laws. The most important were the 1964 Wilderness Act and the 1968 Wild and Scenic Rivers Acts. The 1964 law protected 9.1 million acres from development and preserved uniquely beautiful landscapes; today 106 million acres are protected as wilderness areas. During that decade, Congress also legislated clean air and water acts and updated them in the following decades in response to new problems and as new evidence became available.

The surge in environmental legislation continued under President Richard Nixon. Although most environmentalists were Democrats, Nixon sought to lure them into the Republican Party by supporting their proposals. In 1969, he signed the National Environmental Policy Act, perhaps the most far-reaching environmental act in the nation's history. It required federal agencies to consider the environmental impact of all their policies. The act's preamble created new national policy:

> to encourage productive and enjoyable harmony between man and his environment; to promote efforts which will prevent or eliminate damage to the environment and biosphere and stimulate the health and welfare of man; [and] to enrich the understanding of the ecological systems and natural resources important to the Nation . . .[6]

The following year, Congress established the Environmental Protection Agency (EPA) to set and enforce national standards mandated under various federal environmental laws. Today, the EPA employs seventeen thousand people and has ten regional offices and twenty-seven laboratories. In 1973, Congress passed and Nixon signed the Endangered Species Act. The act created a list of species in danger of extinction and, most importantly, sought to protect or restore the habitat necessary for the perpetuation of that species. The environmental accomplishments of the Nixon administration exemplify how two-party competition can facilitate the agenda of groups—in this case environmentalists—whose votes are perceived to be in play.

During these years, Americans began to understand the principles of ecology: the scientific study of how organisms, including humans, interact with their environments. Under its influence, many Americans increasingly appreciated the necessity of preserving biodiversity, the predator-prey balance, essential biological cycles, and critical habitats. Forests and wetlands, which in the nineteenth century had been seen as dark and forbidding places, were now esteemed. Wolves, bears, and mountain lions, which were once feared and relentlessly hunted, now came to be seen as precious resources.

New pollution problems also furthered an ecological understanding. As industrialism spread across the planet, the relationship between humans and their environment became more impersonal, complicated, and less easily perceived. Two major examples of this galvanized the environmental movement in the 1970s and 1980s.

In the post-World War II period, farmers relied more heavily on synthetic nitrogen fertilizer. In addition, Americans released the phosphorous from detergents and human waste into the environment. The resulting pollution flowed into lakes and rivers, fed blooms of phytoplankton, starved the water of oxygen (eutrophy), and killed fish and other animal populations. An enormous dead zone of 8,500 square miles (22,000 square kilometers) appeared in the Gulf of Mexico where the Mississippi River emptied into it. The problem is worldwide. A recent survey showed that 54 percent of lakes in Asia, 53 percent in Europe, 48 percent in North America, 41 percent in South America, and 28 percent in Africa are eutrophic.[7]

Acid rain was another example of a problem in which the source of the pollutant and its destination was widely separated. Though acid rain has one major natural source (volcanoes), it became a stubborn problem only with the extensive burning of coal by electricity-generating plants. To relieve the pollution in the immediate environment, the power companies built tall smokestacks, dispersing ammonium, carbon, nitrogen, and sulfur into far-reaching upper winds. These compounds reacted with water vapor in clouds to produce acid, which fell to earth and killed off or damaged aquatic life in lakes, rivers, and high-altitude forests. To remediate these far-flung problems required federal legislation and a difficult process of interstate cooperation. The results were decidedly mixed.

The major reason was that those industries whose profits were threatened by pollution control continually resisted environmental progress. There were four major groups that opposed environmental objectives: the extractive industries, mainly agriculture and mining; the expanding segment of manufacturing, mainly the chemical industry; power-generating utility firms, especially those that relied on the burning of coal; and land developers, who stood to profit from suburban sprawl and the development of natural spaces. Political opposition was particularly strong in regions such as the South and mountain West where the cultural values associated with these industries were still widespread. These values included sacrifice of one's individuality for the sake of the survival of the group, obedience to authority, hard physical labor, conservative religion, and a utilitarian approach toward nature. The central public argument of the opposition was that environmentalism was a drag on the economy and cost jobs, which the environmentalists tried to answer with their own studies and by crafting legislation that aided industries and localities that could not afford pollution control equipment.

The 1980s began an era of close-quarters political combat between environmentalists and industry opponents in which the terrain of struggle shifted back and forth. Because environmentalists were strongest in Congress, the opposition often relied on lobbying the executive branch to limit the financial impact of the new legislation. When that occurred, environmentalists turned to the courts to compel the president to enforce the law. If they were entirely defeated on the federal level, the opposition lobbied to have the states enforce environmental laws, a terrain where they usually wielded greater political power. The American system of federalism and divided government provides many arenas in which governmental action can be delayed, stymied, or defeated, and both sides took advantage of it.

The most important arena of battle became the rule-making process undertaken by regulatory commissions, most notably the federal EPA. Environmentalists had broad public support, but industry opponents had more resources at their command. They could counter environmentalists with their cadre of lawyers, paid scientific experts, and media consultants. Thus, when regulatory commissions turned to their advisory panels of experts, the opponents had an advantage. They also had the financial resources to fund expensive media campaigns against environmentalism and convince segments of the public that they were actually environmentalists themselves and could be trusted. Over time, it became clear that only in cases where a broad public consensus existed could a regulatory agency rigorously enforce the spirit and the letter of environmental laws.

A major turning point in the political conflict that has marked environmental issues came in 1994 when the Republican Party took over Congress, and the right wing took over the Republican Party. Republican moderates, who had often supported environmental legislation, lost their positions of power or their seats in Congress. The bipartisan consensus that existed in the country over environmental protection dissolved. Because environmentalism as an issue was not powerful enough by itself to determine voting behavior, this meant that a vote for Republicans on an issue such as foreign policy or tax cuts was also a vote against environmentalism. Under these circumstances, government initiatives on environmental issues almost ground to a halt.

The lack of progress since the 1990s on environmental action, despite overwhelming public support, has led environmentalists to emphasize voluntary action in the sphere of lifestyle. The emerging idea has been to take personal responsibility for lightening the human load on the planet through adopting a green consumption ethic more in harmony with the planet. For example, the unwillingness of the auto companies to produce fuel-efficient cars and their reliance on gas-guzzling sport-utility vehicles, which worsened global warming, has led green consumers to turn ownership of fuel-efficient hybrid or electric cars into status symbols. Because it has become difficult to legislate the elimination of pesticide residues or genetic engineering from the cultivation of fruits and vegetables, environmentally conscious consumers often eat organic, an emerging industry that today tops twenty-five billion dollars in sales. If it was impossible to get manufacturers to limit the use of nonbiodegradable materials, such as plastics, it was now possible to conscientiously recycle those items.

Some consumers have attempted to minimize the consumption of commodities per se. Like Henry David Thoreau, the nineteenth-century American exemplar of simple living, they try to avoid the accumulation of "stuff," believing that "a man is rich in proportion to the number of things he can afford to let alone." In these and other ways, environmentalism has become a way of life, a culture embraced by millions.

The growing power of the green consumption ethic has made itself felt in the expanding array of products and services offered by companies. This has obviously been the case in the consumption of natural or organic foods now sold in supermarkets and cars that exceed current federal standards for fuel efficiency. But it has also led companies to produce goods such as clothes made of organic cotton, solar-powered electronic equipment, and eco-friendly dwellings made of recycled and fuel-conserving materials. The retail behemoth Walmart advertises itself as earth friendly because it now encourages its suppliers to use more environmentally friendly practices and has increased substantially the fuel efficiency of its truck fleet.

The growing power of earth-friendly consumption patterns is part of an emerging environmental economy that enables environmentalists to counter the argument of opponents that its goals would be a drag on economic growth. In addition to the food industry and other eco-friendly goods, the environmental economy includes the consumption of goods for outdoor recreation, such as camping, hiking, and boating equipment, which in turn requires the preservation of open spaces and healthy forests, lakes, and rivers. Tourism to the national parks and other wilderness areas boosts local economies. Closely related to this is the higher value of real estate in more natural, forested areas. The green economy also includes the production of capital goods such as wind turbines, solar cells, and pollution-abatement equipment. The environmental economy is increasingly a distinct interest, which in many parts of the country rivals the rest of the economy. For example, the US Forest Service estimated recently that its income from outdoor recreation was expected to be thirty times greater than that from resource extraction.[8]

Though the green economic interest is increasingly powerful and undercuts the argument that environmental legislation is a drag on the economy, environmentalists face a more intractable problem. The pace of development fueled by population growth and the spread of high consumption patterns to less developed regions of the world has outflanked and outrun the successes of environmentalists. There is the paradox that as people flee the central city to the suburbs to escape congestion and pollution, the pleasantness of the environment attracts many others. Then comes the inevitable complement of highways, shopping centers, asphalt parking lots, and congestion, with the result that the suburbs come to resemble the cities. The same problem afflicts fast-developing countries, whose populations have traded environmental degradation for jobs and higher consumption. Still another example comes from attempts in the United States to reduce pollution and the use of oil by compelling the redesign of automobiles. Despite great advances, the number of miles driven by autos has more than tripled since 1970, thus worsening the overall problem. The problem seems to be growth and development itself.

Environmentalists have rarely attempted to limit growth. When they have, their only successes have come by creating a firm boundary between development and relatively natural spaces through public preserves and private land trusts (notably, the Nature Conservancy).

Is it possible to have both development and a sustainable environment? For how long can finite ecosystems coexist with a world economy growing at 3 percent or more a year? The attempt to reconcile the two has led to the 1987 United Nations' goal of sustainable development. But the world's leaders have never confronted the possibility that a no-growth or minimal-growth economy, at least among the most advanced nations, might be necessary to preserve the earth's environment. They have assumed that development goals can be reconciled with the environment without rethinking the basis of human society and the large-scale restructuring it might require.

Environmentalist leaders are not so sure. They often refer to the need for a sustainable *environment* in which human activities are limited to those that do not create a breakdown in the natural systems necessary to conserve the environment. According to environmentalist Lester R. Brown, the world economy in the last half-century has been a "global Ponzi scheme" in which growth and profits are funded by consuming the earth's "asset base." (A Ponzi scheme is a fraudulent investment operation that pays returns to the investor out of his or her own funds or the funds of subsequent investors.) If the economy grows by depleting the world's major aquifers, fisheries, topsoil, and atmosphere, at some point in the foreseeable future further growth will become impossible. Brown's *Plan B 4.0: Mobilizing to Save Civilization* is one comprehensive attempt to reform the world's commitment to development to avoid this outcome.

Looked at in historical perspective, environmentalism has been a major addition to democracy viewed as a way of life. It has added a new sphere—nature itself—to the human sphere, which it seeks to govern for the common good. In doing so, it has relied on coordinated action in the other three dimensions of democracy: politics and government, the economy, and culture. In the sphere of civil society, social movements, and public-opinion formation, environmentalists have sought to influence public opinion to check pollution, preserve beautiful spaces, and protect the environment. They have also relied on private action through the growth of an environmental economy, primarily in the form of a new consumption ethic, to redirect industrial growth. Finally, environmentalists have created a new and at times alternative culture—green living—to act as an alternative to the culture of environmentally destructive consumption.

Can environmentalists succeed? As a powerful, growing, and deeply rooted democratic movement across the modern world, fueled by human experience of the earth's deteriorating ecosphere, it is likely to become more powerful. But in light of the determined opposition it has provoked from the representatives of developmental capitalism, it is unlikely in the near future to come close to achieving its objectives.

The sobering question that looms is this one: will it take catastrophic deterioration of the earth's environment for an environmentalist ethic to be fully accepted, or will the success of environmentalist reform forestall that catastrophe?

# DOCUMENTS

## Creative Democracy—the Task before Us (1939)

### John Dewey

*This essay was written in 1939 during the rise of the Nazis as the world slid toward World War II. In it, America's great philosopher of democracy emphasized democracy as a working ideal and faith— "the task before us"—rather than as an existing set of institutions, procedures, or legal framework. Dewey's ideal of the sovereignty of the people and his faith in the people's capacity to rule was neither naive nor utopian. It was based on the existence of conditions in everyday life that would allow for the largest degree of participation and the production of democratic values and ways of thinking. Dewey talked about local community involvement as one such condition. The reader of today may ask what other public associations can supply the means necessary to revitalize our democracy. Where is the soil out of which our own demo-cratic idealism may sprout?*

Under present circumstances I cannot hope to conceal the fact that I have managed to exist eighty years. Mention of the fact may suggest to you a more important fact—namely, that events of the utmost significance for the destiny of this country have taken place during the past four-fifths of a century, a period that covers more than half of its national life in its present form. For obvious reasons I shall not attempt a summary of even the more important of these events. I refer here to them because of their bearing upon the issue to which this country committed itself when the nation took shape—the creation of democracy, an issue which is now as urgent as it was a hundred and fifty years ago when the most experienced and wisest men of the country gathered to take stock of conditions and to create the political structure of a self-governing society.

For the net import of the changes that have taken place in these later years is that ways of life and institutions which were once the natural, almost the inevitable, product of fortunate conditions have now to be won by conscious and resolute effort. Not all the country was in a pioneer state eighty years ago. But it was still, save perhaps in a few large cities, so close to the pioneer stage of American life that the traditions of the pioneer, indeed of the frontier, were active agencies in forming the thoughts and shaping the beliefs of those who were born into its life. In imagination at least the country was still having an open frontier, one of unused and unappropriated resources. It was a country of physical opportunity and invitation. Even so, there was more than a marvelous conjunction of physical circumstances involved in bringing to birth this new nation. There was in existence a group of men who were capable of readapting older institutions and ideas to meet the situations provided by new physical conditions—a group of men extraordinarily gifted in political inventiveness.

At the present time, the frontier is moral, not physical. The period of free lands that seemed boundless in extent has vanished. Unused resources are now human rather than material. They are found in the waste of grown men and women who are without the chance to work, and in the young men and young women who find doors closed where there was once opportunity. The crisis that one hundred and fifty years ago called out social and political inventiveness is with us in a form which puts a heavier demand on human creativeness.

At all events this is what I mean when I say that we now have to re-create by deliberate and determined endeavor the kind of democracy which in its origin one hundred and fifty years ago was largely the product of a fortunate combination of men and circumstances. We have lived for a long time upon the heritage that came to us from the happy conjunction of men and events in an earlier day. The present state of the world is more than a reminder that we have now to put forth every energy of our own to prove worthy of our heritage. It is a challenge to do for the critical and complex conditions of today what the men of an earlier day did for simpler conditions.

If I emphasize that the task can be accomplished only by inventive effort and creative activity, it is in part because the depth of the present crisis is due in considerable part to the fact that for a long period we acted as if our democracy were something that perpetuated itself automatically; as if our ancestors had succeeded in setting up a machine that solved the problem of perpetual motion in politics. We acted as if democracy were something that took place mainly at Washington and Albany—or some other state capital—under the impetus of what happened when men and women went to the polls once a year or so—which is a somewhat extreme way of saying that we have had the habit of thinking of democracy as a kind of political mechanism that will work as long as citizens were reasonably faithful in performing political duties.

Of late years we have heard more and more frequently that this is not enough; that democracy is a way of life. This saying gets down to hardpan. But I am not sure that something of the externality of the old idea does not cling to the new and better statement. In any case we can escape from this external way of thinking only as we realize in thought and act that democracy is a personal way of individual life; that it signifies the possession and continual use of certain attitudes, forming personal character and determining desire and purpose in all the relations of life. Instead of thinking of our own dispositions and habits as accommodated to certain institutions we have to learn to think of the latter as expressions, projections and extensions of habitually dominant personal attitudes.

Democracy as a personal, an individual, way of life involves nothing fundamentally new. But when applied it puts a new practical meaning in old ideas. Put into effect it signifies that powerful present enemies of democracy can be successfully met only by the creation of personal attitudes in individual human beings; that we must get over our tendency to think that its defense can be found in any external means whatever, whether military or civil, if they are separated from individual attitudes so deep-seated as to constitute personal character.

Democracy is a way of life controlled by a working faith in the possibilities of human nature. Belief in the Common Man is a familiar article in the democratic creed. That belief is without basis and significance save as it means faith in the potentialities of human nature as that nature is exhibited in every human being irrespective of race, color, sex, birth and family, of material or cultural wealth. This faith may be enacted in statutes, but it is only on paper unless it is put in force in the attitudes which human beings display to one another in all the incidents and relations of daily life. To denounce Nazism for intolerance, cruelty and stimulation of hatred amounts to fostering insincerity if, in our personal relations to other persons, if, in our daily walk and conversation, we are moved by racial, color or other class prejudice; indeed, by anything save a generous belief in their possibilities as human beings, a belief which brings with it the need for providing conditions which will enable these capacities to reach fulfillment. The democratic faith in human equality is belief that every human being, independent of the quantity or range of his personal endowment, has the right to equal opportunity with every other person for development of whatever gifts he has. The democratic belief in the principle of leadership is a generous one. It is universal. It is belief in the capacity of every person to lead his own life free from coercion and imposition by others provided right conditions are supplied.

Democracy is a way of personal life controlled not merely by faith in human nature in general but by faith in the capacity of human beings for intelligent judgment and action if proper conditions are furnished. I have been accused more than once and from opposed quarters of an undue, a utopian, faith in the possibilities of intelligence and in education as a correlate of intelligence. At all events, I did not invent this faith. I acquired it from my surroundings as far as those surroundings were animated by the democratic spirit. For what is the faith of democracy in the role of consultation, of conference, of persuasion, of discussion, in formation of public opinion, which in the long run is self-corrective, except faith in the capacity of the intelligence of the common man to respond with commonsense to the free play of facts and ideas which are secured by effective guarantees of free inquiry, free assembly and free communication? I am willing to leave to upholders of totalitarian states of the right and the left the view that faith in the capacities of intelligence is utopia. For the faith is so deeply embedded in the methods which are intrinsic to democracy that when a professed democrat denies the faith he convicts himself of treachery to his profession.

When I think of the conditions under which men and women are living in many foreign countries today, fear of espionage, with danger hanging over the meeting of friends for friendly conversation in private gatherings, I am inclined to believe that the heart and final guarantee of democracy is in free gatherings of neighbors on the street corner to discuss back and forth what is read in uncensored news of the day, and in gatherings of friends in the living rooms of houses and apartments to converse freely with one another. Intolerance, abuse, calling of names because of differences of opinion about religion or politics or business, as well as because of differences of race, color, wealth or degree of culture are treason to the democratic way of life. For everything which bars freedom and fullness of communication sets up barriers that divide human beings into sets and cliques, into antagonistic sects and factions, and thereby undermines the democratic way of life. Merely legal guarantees of the civil liberties of free belief, free expression, free assembly are of little avail if in daily life freedom of communication, the give and take of ideas, facts, experiences, is choked by mutual suspicion, by abuse, by fear and hatred. These things destroy the essential condition of the democratic way of living even more effectually than open coercion which—as the example of totalitarian states proves—is effective only when it succeeds in breeding hate, suspicion, intolerance in the minds of individual human beings.

Finally, given the two conditions just mentioned, democracy as a way of life is controlled by personal faith in personal day-by-day working together with others. Democracy is the belief that even when needs and ends or consequences are different for each individual, the habit of amicable cooperation—which may include, as in sport, rivalry and competition—is itself a priceless addition to life. To take as far as possible every conflict which arises—and they are bound to arise—out of the atmosphere and medium of force, of violence as a means of settlement into that of discussion and of intelligence is to treat those who disagree—even profoundly—with us as those from whom we may learn, and in so far, as friends. A genuinely democratic faith in peace is faith in the possibility of conducting disputes, controversies and conflicts as cooperative undertakings in which both parties learn by giving the other a chance to express itself, instead of having one party conquer by forceful suppression of the other—a suppression which is none the less one of violence when it takes place by psychological means of ridicule, abuse, intimidation, instead of by overt imprisonment or in concentration camps. To cooperate by giving differences a chance to show themselves because of the belief that the expression of difference is not only a right of the other persons but is a means of enriching one's own life-experience, is inherent in the democratic personal way of life.

If what has been said is charged with being a set of moral commonplaces, my only reply is that that is just the point in saying them. For to get rid of the habit of thinking of democracy as something institutional and external and to acquire the habit of treating it as a way of personal life is to realize that democracy is a moral ideal and so far as it becomes a fact is a moral fact. It is to realize that democracy is a reality only as it is indeed a commonplace of living.

Since my adult years have been given to the pursuit of philosophy, I shall ask your indulgence if in concluding I state briefly the democratic faith in the formal terms of a philosophic position. So stated, democracy is belief in the ability of human experience to generate the aims and methods by which further experience will grow in ordered richness. Every other form of moral and social faith rests upon the idea that experience must be subjected at some point or other to some form of external control; to some "authority" alleged to exist outside the processes of experience. Democracy is the faith that the process of experience is more important than any special result attained, so that special results achieved are of ultimate value only as they are used to enrich and order the ongoing process. Since the process of experience is capable of being educative, faith in democracy is all one with faith in experience and education. All ends and values that are cut off from the ongoing process become arrests, fixations. They strive to fixate what has been gained instead of using it to open the road and point the way to new and better experiences.

If one asks what is meant by experience in this connection my reply is that it is that free interaction of individual human beings with surrounding conditions, especially the human surroundings, which develops and satisfies need and desire by increasing knowledge of things as they are. Knowledge of conditions as they are is the only solid ground for communication and sharing; all other communication means the subjection of some persons to the personal opinion of other persons. Need and desire—out of which grow purpose and direction of energy—go beyond what exists, and hence beyond knowledge, beyond science. They continually open the way into the unexplored and unattained future.

Democracy as compared with other ways of life is the sole way of living which believes wholeheartedly in the process of experience as end and as means; as that which is capable of generating the science which is the sole dependable authority for the direction of further experience and which releases emotions, needs and desires so as to call into being the things that have not existed in the past. For every way of life that fails in its democracy limits the contacts, the exchanges, the communications, the interactions by which experience is steadied while it is also enlarged and enriched. The task of this release and enrichment is one that has to be carried on day by day. Since it is one that can have no end till experience itself comes to an end, the task of democracy is forever that of creation of a freer and more humane experience in which all share and to which all contribute.

### Preamble to the US Declaration of Independence (July 4, 1776)

*In two paragraphs, America's revolutionaries sketched out the principles of democratic government: that governments derive their powers and their legitimacy from the people; that government's purpose is to protect and serve the rights of the people to life, liberty, and the pursuit of happiness; and that the people have a right to alter or abolish the government at their will. The phrase "all men are created equal" has served as a standard for future generations of Americans. In Lincoln's words, the founders "meant to set up a standard maxim for free society, which should be familiar to all, and revered by all; constantly looked to, constantly labored for, and even though never perfectly attained, constantly approximated, and thereby constantly spreading and deepening its influence, and augmenting the happiness and value of life to all people of all colors everywhere."*

IN CONGRESS, July 4, 1776.

### The Unanimous Declaration of the Thirteen United States of America,

When in the Course of human events, it becomes necessary for one people to dissolve the political bands which have connected them with another, and to assume among the powers of the earth, the separate and equal station to which the Laws of Nature and of Nature's God entitle them, a decent respect to the opinions of mankind requires that they should declare the causes which impel them to the separation.

We hold these truths to be self-evident, that all men are created equal, that they are endowed by their Creator with certain unalienable Rights, that among these are Life, Liberty and the pursuit of Happiness.—That to secure these rights, Governments are instituted among Men, deriving their just powers from the consent of the governed,—That whenever any Form of Government becomes destructive of these ends, it is the Right of the People to alter or to abolish it, and to institute new Government, laying its foundation on such principles and organizing its powers in such form, as to them shall seem most likely to effect their Safety and Happiness. Prudence, indeed, will dictate that Governments long established should not be changed for light and transient causes; and accordingly all experience hath shewn, that mankind are more disposed to suffer, while evils are sufferable, than to right themselves by abolishing the forms to which they are accustomed. But when a long train of abuses and usurpations, pursuing invariably the same Object evinces a design to reduce them under absolute Despotism, it is their right, it is their duty, to throw off such Government, and to provide new Guards for their future security.—Such has been the patient sufferance of these Colonies; and such is now the necessity which constrains them to alter their former Systems of Government. The history of the present King of Great Britain is a history of repeated injuries and usurpations, all having in direct object the establishment of an absolute Tyranny over these States. To prove this, let Facts be submitted to a candid world.

## Women's Rights Convention, Seneca Falls, New York
## Declaration of Sentiments (1848)

*Written mainly by Elizabeth Cady Stanton and modeled after the Declaration of Independence, this document was the founding statement of first-wave feminism, the women's rights movement. The document was widely rejected and ridiculed by the press all over the country. Women did not receive suffrage or "the elective franchise" until the ratification in 1920 of the Nineteenth Amendment to the Constitution, seventy-two years later.*

When, in the course of human events, it becomes necessary for one portion of the family of man to assume among the people of the earth a position different from that which they have hitherto occupied, but one to which the laws of nature and of nature's God entitle them, a decent respect to the opinions of mankind requires that they should declare the causes that impel them to such a course.

We hold these truths to be self-evident: that all men and women are created equal; that they are endowed by their Creator with certain inalienable rights; that among these are life, liberty, and the pursuit of happiness; that to secure these rights governments are instituted, deriving their just powers from the consent of the governed. Whenever any form of government becomes destructive of these ends, it is the right of those who suffer from it to refuse allegiance to it, and to insist upon the institution of a new government, laying its foundation on such principles, and organizing its powers in such form, as to them shall seem most likely to effect their safety and happiness. Prudence, indeed, will dictate that governments long established should not be changed for light and transient causes; and accordingly all experience hath shown that mankind are more disposed to suffer, while evils are sufferable, than to right themselves by abolishing the forms to which they were accustomed. But when a long train of abuses and usurpations, pursuing invariably the same object evinces a design to reduce them under absolute despotism, it is their duty to throw off such government, and to provide new guards for their future security. Such has been the patient sufferance of the women under this government, and such is now the necessity which constrains them to demand the equal station to which they are entitled.

The history of mankind is a history of repeated injuries and usurpations on the part of man toward woman, having in direct object the establishment of an absolute tyranny over her. To prove this, let facts be submitted to a candid world.

He has never permitted her to exercise her inalienable right to the elective franchise.

He has compelled her to submit to laws, in the formation of which she had no voice.

He has withheld from her rights which are given to the most ignorant and degraded men—both natives and foreigners.

Having deprived her of this first right of a citizen, the elective franchise, thereby leaving her without representation in the halls of legislation, he has oppressed her on all sides.

He has made her, if married, in the eye of the law, civilly dead.

He has taken from her all right in property, even to the wages she earns.

He has made her, morally, an irresponsible being, as she can commit many crimes with impunity, provided they be done in the presence of her husband. In the covenant of marriage, she is compelled to promise obedience to her husband, he becoming, to all intents and purposes, her master—the law giving him power to deprive her of her liberty, and to administer chastisement.

He has so framed the laws of divorce, as to what shall be the proper causes, and in case of separation, to whom the guardianship of the children shall be given, as to be wholly regardless of the happiness of women—the law, in all cases, going upon a false supposition of the supremacy of man, and giving all power into his hands.

After depriving her of all rights as a married woman, if single, and the owner of property, he has taxed her to support a government which recognizes her only when her property can be made profitable to it.

He has monopolized nearly all the profitable employments, and from those she is permitted to follow, she receives but a scanty remuneration. He closes against her all the avenues to wealth and distinction which he considers most honorable to himself. As a teacher of theology, medicine, or law, she is not known.

He has denied her the facilities for obtaining a thorough education, all colleges being closed against her.

He allows her in Church, as well as State, but a subordinate position, claiming Apostolic authority for her exclusion from the ministry, and, with some exceptions, from any public participation in the affairs of the Church.

He has created a false public sentiment by giving to the world a different code of morals for men and women, by which moral delinquencies which exclude women from society, are not only tolerated, but deemed of little account in man.

He has usurped the prerogative of Jehovah himself, claiming it as his right to assign for her a sphere of action, when that belongs to her conscience and to her God.

He has endeavored, in every way that he could, to destroy her confidence in her own powers, to lessen her self-respect, and to make her willing to lead a dependent and abject life.

Now, in view of this entire disfranchisement of one-half the people of this country, their social and religious degradation—in view of the unjust laws above mentioned, and because women do feel themselves aggrieved, oppressed, and fraudulently deprived of their most sacred rights, we insist that they have immediate admission to all the rights and privileges which belong to them as citizens of the United States.

In entering upon the great work before us, we anticipate no small amount of misconception, misrepresentation, and ridicule; but we shall use every instrumentality within our power to effect our object. We shall employ agents, circulate tracts, petition the State and National legislatures, and endeavor to enlist the pulpit and the press in our behalf. We hope this Convention will be followed by a series of Conventions embracing every part of the country.

## Gettysburg Address (1863)

## Abraham Lincoln

> *In the greatest public speech delivered by an American, President Abraham Lincoln memorialized the soldiers of the Union Army who had sacrificed their lives at the Battle of Gettysburg to save the nation. It is significant that Lincoln referred to America as a "nation" rather than as a "union" of states. Lincoln also defined American democracy as one not simply of procedures and laws but also of participatory democracy: a "government of the people, by the people, for the people." Contrary to those who believe that saving the union and emancipating slaves were distinct and competing goals of the war, Lincoln argued they were one and the same. Thus he referred to emancipation in the phrase "a new birth of freedom." Finally, Lincoln's call "for us the living" to "take increased devotion to that cause" remaining before us echoes through the ages and beckons Americans today to take up the cause of giving democracy a new birth of freedom.*

Four score and seven years ago our fathers brought forth on this continent, a new nation, conceived in Liberty, and dedicated to the proposition that all men are created equal.

Now we are engaged in a great civil war, testing whether that nation, or any nation so conceived and so dedicated, can long endure. We are met on a great battlefield of that war. We have come to dedicate a portion of that field, as a final resting place for those who here gave their lives that that nation might live. It is altogether fitting and proper that we should do this.

But, in a larger sense, we can not dedicate—we can not consecrate—we can not hallow—this ground. The brave men, living and dead, who struggled here, have consecrated it, far above our poor power to add or detract. The world will little note, nor long remember what we say here, but it can never forget what they did here. It is for us the living, rather, to be dedicated here to the unfinished work which they who fought here have thus far so nobly advanced. It is rather for us to be here dedicated to the great task remaining before us—that from these honored dead we take increased devotion to that cause for which they gave the last full measure of devotion—that we here highly resolve that these dead shall not have died in vain—that this nation, under God, shall have a new birth of freedom—and that government of the people, by the people, for the people, shall not perish from the earth.

## The President's Strike Commission Report (1894)

### by US Commissioner of Labor Carroll D. Wright

*The 1894 Pullman Strike was the largest strike in American history. Though it was crushed by the combined forces of the nation's railroad corporations and the federal government, it represented a turning point in the transition between an older and a newer form of democratic thinking. Nineteenth-century thinking was premised on the idea that the distribution of property in society was sufficiently equal and that only government could bring about a dangerous inequality. Thus government should be strictly limited. Twentieth-century democratic thinking recognized that large combinations—notably consolidated business, unions, and professional associations—had replaced individual enterprise and that the competitive market was being reshaped by these associations. To assure that this new market situation adequately served the public good, the new thinking argued that government needed to supervise, regulate, limit, and, in general, act as a watchdog in the conduct of market activity. The following excerpt is from the 1894 Report on the Pullman Strike by the United States Strike Commission created by President Grover Cleveland.*

The rapid concentration of power and wealth, under stimulating legislative conditions, in persons, corporations, and monopolies has greatly changed the business and industrial situation. Our railroads were chartered upon the theory that their competition would amply protect shippers as to rates, etc., and employees as to wages and other conditions. Combination has largely destroyed this theory, and has seriously disturbed the natural working of the laws of supply and demand, which in theory, are based upon competition for labor between those who "demand" it as well as among those who supply it. The interstate commerce act and railroad-commission legislation in over thirty states are simply efforts of the people to free themselves from the results of this destruction of competition by combination. Labor is likewise affected by this progressive combination. While competition among railroad employers of labor is gradually disappearing, competition among those who supply labor goes on with increasing severity. For instance, as we have shown, there is no longer a competitive demand among the 24 railroads at Chicago for switchmen. They have ceased competing with each other; they are no longer 24 separate and competing employers; they are virtually one. To be sure, this combination has not covered the whole field of labor supply as yet, but it is constantly advancing in that direction. . . . In view of this progressive perversion of the laws of supply and demand by capital and changed conditions, no man can well deny the right nor dispute the wisdom of unity for legislative and protective purposes among those who supply labor.

However men may differ about the propriety and legality of labor unions, we must all recognize the fact that we have them with us to stay and to grow more numerous and powerful. Is it not wise to fully recognize them by law; to admit their necessity as labor guides and protectors, to conserve their usefulness, increase their responsibility, and to prevent their follies and aggressions by conferring upon them the privileges enjoyed by corporations, with like proper restrictions and regulations? The growth of corporate power and wealth has been the marvel of the past fifty years. Corporations have undoubtedly benefited the country and brought its resources to our doors. It will not be surprising if the marvel of the next fifty years be the advancement of labor to a position of like power and responsibility. We have heretofore encouraged the one and comparatively neglected the other. Does not wisdom demand that each be encouraged to prosper legitimately and to grow into harmonious relations of equal standing and responsibility before the law? This involves nothing hostile to the true interests and rights of either.

## State of the Union Message to Congress (January 11, 1944)

### Franklin Delano Roosevelt

> *This speech, often called "The Second Bill of Rights," enumerated economic rights to supplement America's more familiar political rights. In this excerpt Roosevelt argued that for all to have equal opportunity in the "pursuit of happiness," citizens should be guaranteed certain minimum standards of life, including the right to a job. "Necessitous men are not free men," Roosevelt said, explaining that men who were hungry and out of a job were the raw material for dictatorships. Providing jobs to all those willing and able to work meant that government would use its fiscal and monetary policies to promote a full-employment economy. Though still controversial, most Americans support the idea of using the federal government to stimulate economic expansion.*

This Republic had its beginning, and grew to its present strength, under the protection of certain inalienable political rights—among them the right of free speech, free press, free worship, trial by jury, freedom from unreasonable searches and seizures. They were our rights to life and liberty.

As our Nation has grown in size and stature, however—as our industrial economy expanded—these political rights proved inadequate to assure us equality in the pursuit of happiness.

We have come to a clear realization of the fact that true individual freedom cannot exist without economic security and independence. "Necessitous men are not free men." People who are hungry and out of a job are the stuff of which dictatorships are made.

In our day these economic truths have become accepted as self-evident. We have accepted, so to speak, a second Bill of Rights under which a new basis of security and prosperity can be established for all regardless of station, race, or creed.

Among these are:

> The right to a useful and remunerative job in the industries or shops or farms or mines of the Nation;
>
> The right to earn enough to provide adequate food and clothing and recreation;
>
> The right of every farmer to raise and sell his products at a return which will give him and his family a decent living;
>
> The right of every businessman, large and small, to trade in an atmosphere of freedom from unfair competition and domination by monopolies at home or abroad;
>
> The right of every family to a decent home;
>
> The right to adequate medical care and the opportunity to achieve and enjoy good health;
>
> The right to adequate protection from the economic fears of old age, sickness, accident, and unemployment;
>
> The right to a good education.

All of these rights spell security. And after this war is won we must be prepared to move forward, in the implementation of these rights, to new goals of human happiness and well-being.

America's own rightful place in the world depends in large part upon how fully these and similar rights have been carried into practice for our citizens. For unless there is security here at home there cannot be lasting peace in the world.

## Remarks at the Howard University Commencement (June 4, 1965)

### Lyndon Baines Johnson

> *President Lyndon Johnson's speech at Howard University, excerpted here, marked the high-water mark of the wave of economic democracy starting in the mid-nineteenth century. Johnson returned to Franklin Delano Roosevelt's "Second Bill of Rights" in defining citizenship as the right of all Americans to share fully in American life. Negative freedom as espoused in the first Bill of Rights was only part of the solution to robust democracy: "It is not enough just to open the gates of opportunity. All our citizens must have the ability to walk through those gates," Johnson said. "We seek . . . not just equality as a right and a theory but equality as a fact and equality as a result." The speech argued for the abolition of poverty and for affirmative action policies for African Americans. Not long after this speech, a powerful white backlash ended the War on Poverty. Many whites viewed government policies to end poverty and affirmative action as a giveaway to unworthy people.*

Dr. Nabrit, my fellow Americans:

In far too many ways American Negroes have been another nation: deprived of freedom, crippled by hatred, the doors of opportunity closed to hope.

In our time change has come to this Nation, too. The American Negro, acting with impressive restraint, has peacefully protested and marched, entered the courtrooms and the seats of government, demanding a justice that has long been denied. The voice of the Negro was the call to action. But it is a tribute to America that, once aroused, the courts and the Congress, the President and most of the people, have been the allies of progress.

Thus we have seen the high court of the country declare that discrimination based on race was repugnant to the Constitution, and therefore void. We have seen in 1957, and 1960, and again in 1964, the first civil rights legislation in this Nation in almost an entire century.

The voting rights bill will be the latest, and among the most important, in a long series of victories. But this victory—as Winston Churchill said of another triumph for freedom—"is not the end. It is not even the beginning of the end. But it is, perhaps, the end of the beginning."

That beginning is freedom; and the barriers to that freedom are tumbling down. Freedom is the right to share, share fully and equally, in American society—to vote, to hold a job, to enter a public place, to go to school. It is the right to be treated in every part of our national life as a person equal in dignity and promise to all others.

But freedom is not enough. You do not wipe away the scars of centuries by saying: Now you are free to go where you want, and do as you desire, and choose the leaders you please.

You do not take a person who, for years, has been hobbled by chains and liberate him, bring him up to the starting line of a race and then say, "you are free to compete with all the others," and still justly believe that you have been completely fair.

Thus it is not enough just to open the gates of opportunity. All our citizens must have the ability to walk through those gates.

This is the next and the more profound stage of the battle for civil rights. We seek not just freedom but opportunity. We seek not just legal equity but human ability, not just equality as a right and a theory but equality as a fact and equality as a result.

For the task is to give 20 million Negroes the same chance as every other American to learn and grow, to work and share in society, to develop their abilities—physical, mental and spiritual, and to pursue their individual happiness.

To this end equal opportunity is essential, but not enough, not enough. Men and women of all races are born with the same range of abilities. But ability is not just the product of birth. Ability is stretched or stunted by the family that you live with, and the neighborhood you live in—by the school you go to and the poverty or the richness of your surroundings. It is the product of a hundred unseen forces playing upon the little infant, the child, and finally the man.

This graduating class at Howard University is witness to the indomitable determination of the Negro American to win his way in American life.

But for the great majority of Negro Americans—the poor, the unemployed, the uprooted, and the dispossessed—there is a much grimmer story. They still, as we meet here tonight, are another nation. Despite the court orders and the laws, despite the legislative victories and the speeches, for them the walls are rising and the gulf is widening.

Of course Negro Americans as well as white Americans have shared in our rising national abundance. But the harsh fact of the matter is that in the battle for true equality too many—far too many—are losing ground every day.

We are not completely sure why this is. We know the causes are complex and subtle. But we do know the two broad basic reasons. And we do know that we have to act.

First, Negroes are trapped—as many whites are trapped—in inherited, gate-less poverty. They lack training and skills. They are shut in, in slums, without decent medical care. Private and public poverty combine to cripple their capacities.

We are trying to attack these evils through our poverty program, through our education program, through our medical care and our other health programs, and a dozen more of the Great Society programs that are aimed at the root causes of this poverty.

We will increase, and we will accelerate, and we will broaden this attack in years to come until this most enduring of foes finally yields to our unyielding will.

But there is a second cause—much more difficult to explain, more deeply grounded, more desperate in its force. It is the devastating heritage of long years of slavery; and a century of oppression, hatred, and injustice.

For Negro poverty is not white poverty. Many of its causes and many of its cures are the same. But there are differences—deep, corrosive, obstinate differences—radiating painful roots into the community, and into the family, and the nature of the individual.

These differences are not racial differences. They are solely and simply the consequence of ancient brutality, past injustice, and present prejudice. They are anguishing to observe. For the Negro they are a constant reminder of oppression. For the white they are a constant reminder of guilt. But they must be faced and they must be dealt with and they must be overcome, if we are ever to reach the time when the only difference between Negroes and whites is the color of their skin.

Nor can we find a complete answer in the experience of other American minorities. They made a valiant and a largely successful effort to emerge from poverty and prejudice.

The Negro, like these others, will have to rely mostly upon his own efforts. But he just can not do it alone. For they did not have the heritage of centuries to overcome, and they did not have a cultural tradition which had been twisted and battered by endless years of hatred and hopelessness, nor were they excluded—these others—because of race or color—a feeling whose dark intensity is matched by no other prejudice in our society.

Nor can these differences be understood as isolated infirmities. They are a seamless web. They cause each other. They result from each other. They reinforce each other.

Much of the Negro community is buried under a blanket of history and circumstance. It is not a lasting solution to lift just one corner of that blanket. We must stand on all sides and we must raise the entire cover if we are to liberate our fellow citizens.

One of the differences is the increased concentration of Negroes in our cities. More than 73 percent of all Negroes live in urban areas compared with less than 70 percent of the whites. Most of these Negroes live in slums. Most of these Negroes live together—a separated people.

Men are shaped by their world. When it is a world of decay, ringed by an invisible wall, when escape is arduous and uncertain, and the saving pressures of a more hopeful society are unknown, it can cripple the youth and it can desolate the men.

There is also the burden that a dark skin can add to the search for a productive place in our society. Unemployment strikes most swiftly and broadly at the Negro, and this burden erodes hope. Blighted hope breeds despair. Despair brings indifferences to the learning which offers a way out. And despair, coupled with indifferences, is often the source of destructive rebellion against the fabric of society.

There is also the lacerating hurt of early collision with white hatred or prejudice, distaste or condescension. Other groups have felt similar intolerance. But success and achievement could wipe it away. They do not change the color of a man's skin. I have seen this uncomprehending pain in the eyes of the little, young Mexican-American schoolchildren that I taught many years ago. But it can be overcome. But, for many, the wounds are always open.

Perhaps most important—its influence radiating to every part of life—is the breakdown of the Negro family structure. For this, most of all, white America must accept responsibility. It flows from centuries of oppression and persecution of the Negro man. It flows from the long years of degradation and discrimination, which have attacked his dignity and assaulted his ability to produce for his family.

This, too, is not pleasant to look upon. But it must be faced by those whose serious intent is to improve the life of all Americans.

There is no single easy answer to all of these problems.

Jobs are part of the answer. They bring the income which permits a man to provide for his family.

Decent homes in decent surroundings and a chance to learn—an equal chance to learn—are part of the answer.

Welfare and social programs better designed to hold families together are part of the answer.

Care for the sick is part of the answer.

An understanding heart by all Americans is another big part of the answer.

And to all of these fronts—and a dozen more—I will dedicate the expanding efforts of the Johnson administration.

But there are other answers that are still to be found. Nor do we fully understand even all of the problems. Therefore, I want to announce tonight that this fall I intend to call a White House conference of scholars, and experts, and outstanding Negro leaders—men of both races—and officials of Government at every level.

This White House conference's theme and title will be "To Fulfill These Rights."

Its object will be to help the American Negro fulfill the rights which, after the long time of injustice, he is finally about to secure.

To move beyond opportunity to achievement.

To shatter forever not only the barriers of law and public practice, but the walls which bound the condition of many by the color of his skin.

To dissolve, as best we can, the antique enmities of the heart which diminish the holder, divide the great democracy, and do wrong—great wrong—to the children of God.

And I pledge you tonight that this will be a chief goal of my administration, and of my program next year, and in the years to come. And I hope, and I pray, and I believe, it will be a part of the program of all America.

For what is justice?

It is to fulfill the fair expectations of man.

Thus, American justice is a very special thing. For, from the first, this has been a land of towering expectations. It was to be a nation where each man could be ruled by the common consent of all—enshrined in law, given life by institutions, guided by men themselves subject to its rule. And all—all of every station and origin—would be touched equally in obligation and in liberty.

Beyond the law lay the land. It was a rich land, glowing with more abundant promise than man had ever seen. Here, unlike any place yet known, all were to share the harvest.

And beyond this was the dignity of man. Each could become whatever his qualities of mind and spirit would permit—to strive, to seek, and, if he could, to find his happiness.

This is American justice. We have pursued it faithfully to the edge of our imperfections, and we have failed to find it for the American Negro.

So, it is the glorious opportunity of this generation to end the one huge wrong of the American Nation and, in so doing, to find America for ourselves, with the same immense thrill of discovery which gripped those who first began to realize that here, at last, was a home for freedom.

## Student Nonviolent Coordinating Committee Position Paper
## The Basis of Black Power

### Stokely Carmichael

*This excerpt of a position paper was written by Stokely Carmichael, president of the student civil rights activist group, the Student Nonviolent Coordinating Committee (SNCC). It heralded the shift from civil rights to Black Power. In particular, it justified asking white volunteers within the SNCC to leave. It was also one of the first influential statements criticizing the way the dominant American culture, including white paternalism, marginalized African Americans and limited their initiative.*

The myth that the Negro is somehow incapable of liberating himself, is lazy, etc., came out of the American experience. In the books that children read, whites are always "good" (good symbols are white), blacks are "evil" or seen as savages in movies, their language is referred to as a "dialect," and black people in this country are supposedly descended from savages.

Any white person who comes into the movement has the concepts in his mind about black people, if only subconsciously. He cannot escape them because the whole society has geared his subconscious in that direction.

Miss America coming from Mississippi has a chance to represent all of America, but a black person from either Mississippi or New York will never represent America. Thus the white people coming into the movement cannot relate to the black experience, cannot relate to the word "black," cannot relate to the "nitty gritty," cannot relate to the experience that brought such a word into existence, cannot relate to chitterlings, hog's head cheese, pig feet, ham-hocks, and cannot relate to slavery, because these things are not a part of their experience. They also cannot relate to the black religious experience, nor to the black church, unless, of course, this church has taken on white manifestations.

## White Power

Negroes in this country have never been allowed to organize themselves because of white interference. As a result of this, the stereotype has been reinforced that blacks cannot organize themselves. The white psychology that blacks have to be watched, also reinforces this stereotype. Blacks, in fact, feel intimidated by the presence of whites, because of their knowledge of the power that whites have over their lives. One white person can come into a meeting of black people and change the complexion of that meeting, whereas one black person would not change the complexion of that meeting unless he was an obvious Uncle Tom. People would immediately start talking about "brotherhood," "love," etc.; race would not be discussed.

If people must express themselves freely, there has to be a climate in which they can do this. If blacks feel intimidated by whites, then they are not liable to vent the rage that they feel about whites in the presence of whites—especially not the black people whom we are trying to organize, i.e., the broad masses of black people. A climate has to be created whereby blacks can express themselves. The reasons that whites must be excluded is [sic] not that one is anti-white, but because the effects that one is trying to achieve cannot succeed because whites have an intimidating effect. Oft-times the intimidating effect is in direct proportion to the amount of degradation that black people have suffered at the hands of white people.

These things which revolve around the right to organize have been accomplished mainly because of the entrance of white people into Mississippi, in the summer of 1964. Since these goals have now been accomplished, whites' role in the movement has now ended. What does it mean if black people, once having the right to organize, are not allowed to organize themselves? It means that blacks' ideas about inferiority are being reinforced. Shouldn't people be able to organize themselves? Blacks should be given this right. Further, white participation means in the eyes of the black community that whites are the "brains" behind the movement, and that blacks cannot function without whites. This only serves to perpetuate existing attitudes within the existing society, i.e., blacks are "dumb," "unable to take care of business," etc. Whites are "smart," the "brains" behind the whole thing.

Thus an all-black project is needed in order for the people to free themselves. This has to exist from the beginning. This relates to what can be called "coalition politics." There is no doubt in our minds that some whites are just as disgusted with this system as we are. But it is meaningless to talk about coalition if there is no one to align ourselves with, because of the lack of organization in the white communities. There can be no talk of "hooking up" unless black people organize blacks and white people organize whites. If these conditions are met, then perhaps at some later date—and if we are going in the same direction—talks about exchange of personnel, coalition, and other meaningful alliances can be discussed.

## Black Self-Determination

The charge may be made that we are "racists," but whites who are sensitive to our problems will realize that we must determine our own destiny. In an attempt to find a solution to our dilemma, we propose that our organization (SNCC) should be black-staffed, black-controlled, and black-financed. We do not want to fall into a similar dilemma that other civil rights organizations have fallen into. If we continue to rely upon white financial support we will find ourselves entwined in the tentacles of the white power complex that controls this country. It is also important that a black organization (devoid of cultism) be projected to our people so that it can be demonstrated that such organizations are viable.

More and more we see black people in this country being used as a tool of the white liberal establishment. Liberal whites have not begun to address themselves to the real problem of black people in this country—witness their bewilderment, fear, and anxiety when nationalism is mentioned concerning black people. An analysis of the white liberal's reaction to the word "nationalism" alone reveals a very meaningful attitude of whites of any ideological persuasion toward blacks in this country. It means previous solutions to black problems in this country have been made in the interests of those whites dealing with these problems and not in the best interests of black people in this country. Whites can only subvert our true search and struggle for self-determination, self-identification, and liberation in this country. Reevaluation of the white and black roles must NOW take place so that whites no longer designate roles that black people play but rather black people define white people's roles.

Too long have we allowed white people to interpret the importance and meaning of the cultural aspects of our society. We have allowed them to tell us what was good about our Afro-American music, art, and literature. How many black critics do we have on the "jazz" scene? How can a white person who is not part of the black psyche (except in the oppressor's role) interpret the meaning of the blues to us who are manifestations of the songs themselves?

It must be pointed out that on whatever level of contact blacks and whites come together, that meeting or confrontation is not on the level of the blacks but always on the level of the whites. This only means that our everyday contact with whites is a reinforcement of the myth of white supremacy. Whites are the ones who must try to raise themselves to our humanistic level. We are not, after all, the ones who are responsible for a genocidal war in Vietnam; we are not the ones who are responsible for neocolonialism in Africa and Latin America; we are not the ones who held a people in animalistic bondage over 400 years. We reject the American dream as defined by white people and must work to construct an American reality defined by Afro-Americans.

## White Radicals

It is very ironic and curious that aware whites in this country can champion anti-colonialism in other countries in Africa, Asia, and Latin America, but when black people move toward similar goals of self-determination in this country they are viewed as racists and anti-white by these same progressive whites. In proceeding further, it can be said that this attitude derives from the overall point of view of the white psyche as it concerns the black people. This attitude stems from the era of the slave revolts when every white man was a potential deputy or sheriff or guardian of the state. Because when black people got together among themselves to work out their problems, it becomes [sic] a threat to white people, because such meetings were potential slave revolts.

It can be maintained that this attitude or way of thinking has perpetuated itself to this current period and that it is part of the psyche of white people in this country whatever their political persuasion might be. It is part of the white fear-guilt complex resulting from the slave revolts. There have been examples of whites who stated that they can deal with black fellows on an individual basis but become threatened or menaced by the presence of groups of blacks. It can be maintained that this attitude is held by the majority of progressive whites in this country.

## Black Identity

A thorough re-examination must be made by black people concerning the contributions that we have made in shaping this country. If this re-examination and re-evaluation is not made, and black people are not given their proper due and respect, then the antagonisms and contradictions are going to become more and more glaring, more and more intense, until a national explosion may result.

When people attempt to move from these conclusions it would be faulty reasoning to say they are ordered by racism, because, in this country and in the West, racism has functioned as a type of white nationalism when dealing with black people. We all know the habit that this has created throughout the world and particularly among nonwhite people in this country.

Therefore any re-evaluation that we must make will, for the most part, deal with identification. Who are black people, what are black people, what is their relationship to America and the world? It must be repeated that the whole myth of "Negro citizenship," perpetuated by the white elite, has confused the thinking of radical and progressive blacks and whites in this country. The broad masses of black people react to American society in the same manner as colonial peoples react to the West in Africa, and Latin America, and had the same relationship—that of the colonized toward the colonizer.

## Postmaterialism

### Ronald Franklin Inglehart

> *In this summary of his influential thesis, the political scientist Ronald Inglehart argues that the 1960s represented a major turning point in the development of modern societies. Widespread affluence generated by the advance of productivity-enhancing technology had enabled citizens in advanced democracies to shift from material values stressing economic security to postmaterial values stressing quality of life. Though at first held by only a minority of Americans, these values, according to Inglehart, are now dominant in American society and culture. The shift to postmaterial values helps explain the third wave of democracy discussed in this book.*

Postmaterialism [is a] value orientation that emphasizes self-expression and quality of life over economic and physical security. The term *postmaterialism* was first coined by American social scientist Ronald Inglehart in *The Silent Revolution: Changing Values and Political Styles Among Western Publics* (1977).

Until the 1970s, it was nearly universal for individuals to prioritize so-called materialist values such as economic growth and maintaining order; on the other hand, postmaterialists give top priority to such goals as environmental protection, freedom of speech, and gender equality. The shift, particularly among citizens living in Western countries, reflected a change from an environment in which one was aware that survival was precarious to a post-World War II world where most felt that survival could be taken for granted. Age cohorts born after World War II in advanced industrial societies spent their formative years under levels of prosperity that were unprecedented in human history, and the welfare state reinforced the feeling that survival was secure, producing an intergenerational value change that has gradually transformed the political and cultural norms of these societies. Survey evidenced [sic] gathered in the United States, western Europe, and Japan since the 1970s has demonstrated that an intergenerational shift has made central new political issues and provided the impetus for new political movements.

This theory of intergenerational value change has two key hypotheses: (1) that an individual's priorities reflect the socioeconomic environment, with individuals placing the greatest subjective value on those things that are in relatively short supply, and (2) that the relationship between socioeconomic environment and value priorities involves a substantial time lag because one's basic values reflect the conditions that prevailed during one's preadult years.

Consequently, after a period of sharply rising economic and physical security, one would expect to find substantial differences between the value priorities of older and younger groups, as they would have been shaped by different experiences in their formative years. Researchers have found that more recently born age cohorts tend to emphasize postmaterialist goals to a far greater extent than older cohorts, seemingly reflecting generational change rather than simple aging effects. In the early 1970s materialists held an overwhelming numerical preponderance over postmaterialists in Western countries, outnumbering them nearly four to one. By the turn of the 21st century, however, materialists and postmaterialists had become equally numerous in many Western countries. The ratio varies considerably according to the given country's level of existential security, with impoverished and strife-torn countries having a preponderance of materialists and prosperous and secure ones having a preponderance of postmaterialists. For example, at the turn of the 21st century, materialists outnumbered postmaterialists in Pakistan by more than 50 to 1 and in Russia by nearly 30 to 1. But, in prosperous and stable countries such as the United States and Sweden, postmaterialists outnumbered materialists by 2 to 1 and 5 to 1, respectively.

Postmaterialism itself is only one aspect of a still broader process of cultural change that has reshaped the political outlook, religious orientations, gender roles, and sexual mores of advanced industrial society. Postmodern orientations place less emphasis on traditional cultural norms, especially those that limit individual self-expression. A major component of the postmodern shift is a move away from both religious and bureaucratic authority bringing declining emphasis on all kinds of authority. Deference to authority has high costs, as individuals must subordinate their personal goals to those of a broader entity; under conditions of insecurity, however, people are more than willing to do so. Under threat of invasion, internal disorder, or economic collapse, people eagerly seek strong authority figures who can protect them.

Conversely, conditions of prosperity and security are conducive to tolerance of diversity in general and democracy in particular. This helps explain a long-established finding: rich societies are much likelier to be democratic than poor ones. One contributing factor is that the authoritarian reaction is strongest under conditions of insecurity.

The postmodern shift involves an intergenerational change in a wide variety of basic social norms, from cultural norms linked with ensuring survival of the species to norms linked with the pursuit of individual well-being. For example, postmaterialists and the young are markedly more tolerant of homosexuality than are materialists and the elderly, and they are far more permissive than materialists in their attitudes toward abortion, divorce, extramarital affairs, prostitution, and euthanasia. There is also a gradual shift in job motivations, from maximizing one's income and job security toward a growing insistence on interesting and meaningful work. Economic accumulation for the sake of economic security was the central goal of industrial society. Ironically, their attainment set in motion a process of gradual cultural change that has made these goals less central, bringing about a rejection of the hierarchical institutions that helped attain them.

## 2012 Republican Platform

*The 2012 Republican Party platform is notable for the influence of the right-wing Tea Party. The platform, excerpts of which are presented here, rejected the guarantee of health care for all Americans and offered only the free market as an alternative. In the name of freedom it completely rejected the right of American workers to have unions or a voice in the workplace through collective bargaining. It rejected the right of non-heterosexuals to have marriage rights. It called for a constitutional amendment that would ban the use of deficit spending to expand the economy. It called for a human life amendment that would ban abortions in all circumstances. It also called for the dispersal of government lands to private hands. Finally, the platform defended state laws that suppressed the vote of poor people, minorities, and senior citizens.*

## Repealing Obamacare

The Patient Protection and Affordable Care Act—Obamacare—was never really about healthcare, though its impact upon the nation's health is disastrous. From its start, it was about power, the expansion of government control over one sixth of our economy, and resulted in an attack on our Constitution, by requiring that U.S. citizens purchase health insurance. We agree with the four dissenting justices of the Supreme Court: "In our view the entire Act before us is invalid in its entirety." It was the high-water mark of an outdated liberalism, the latest attempt to impose upon Americans a euro-style bureaucracy to manage all aspects of their lives. Obamacare has been struck down in the court of public opinion and is falling by the weight of its own confusing, unworkable, budget-busting, and conflicting provisions.... Congressional Republicans are committed to its repeal; and a Republican President, on the first day in office, will use his legitimate waiver authority under that law to halt its progress and then will sign its repeal. Then the American people, through the free market, can advance affordable and responsible healthcare reform that meets the needs and concerns of patients and providers.

## Freedom in the Workplace

We support the right of States to enact Right-to-Work laws and encourage them to do so to promote greater economic liberty. Ultimately, we support the enactment of a National Right-to-Work law to promote worker freedom and to promote greater economic liberty. We will aggressively enforce the recent decision by the Supreme Court barring the use of union dues for political purposes without the consent of the worker.

We salute the Republican Governors and State legislators who have saved their States from fiscal disaster by reforming their laws governing public employee unions. We urge elected officials across the country to follow their lead in order to avoid State and local defaults on their obligations and the collapse of services to the public. To safeguard the free choice of public employees, no government at any level should act as the dues collector for unions. A Republican President will protect the rights of conscience of public employees by proposing legislation to bar mandatory dues for political purposes.

## Balancing the Budget

Republican Members of Congress have repeatedly tried to reform the budget process to make it more transparent and accountable, in particular by voting for a Balanced Budget Amendment to the Constitution, following the lead of 33 States which have put that restraint into their own constitutions. We call for a Constitutional amendment requiring a super-majority for any tax increase with exceptions for only war and national emergencies, and imposing a cap limiting spending to the historical average percentage of GDP so that future Congresses cannot balance the budget by raising taxes.

## A Sacred Contract: Defense of Marriage

A serious threat to our country's constitutional order, perhaps even more dangerous than presidential malfeasance, is an activist judiciary, in which some judges usurp the powers reserved to other branches of government. A blatant example has been the court-ordered redefinition of marriage in several States. This is more than a matter of warring legal concepts and ideals. It is an assault on the foundations of our society, challenging the institution which, for thousands of years in virtually every civilization, has been entrusted with the rearing of children and the transmission of cultural values.

That is why Congressional Republicans took the lead in enacting the Defense of Marriage Act, affirming the right of States and the federal government not to recognize same-sex relationships licensed in other jurisdictions. . . . We reaffirm our support for a Constitutional amendment defining marriage as the union of one man and one woman. We applaud the citizens of the majority of States which have enshrined in their constitutions the traditional concept of marriage, and we support the campaigns underway in several other States to do so.

## Voter Integrity to Ensure Honest Elections

We applaud legislation to require photo identification for voting and to prevent election fraud, particularly with regard to registration and absentee ballots. We support State laws that require proof of citizenship at the time of voter registration to protect our electoral system against a significant and growing form of voter fraud. Every time that a fraudulent vote is cast, it effectively cancels out a vote of a legitimate voter. With every right comes a responsibility. . . . In the event those conditions worsen, the federal government must not assume the State governments' or their political subdivisions' financial responsibility or require the nation's taxpayers to pay for the misrule of a few State governments.

## The Second Amendment: Our Right to Keep and Bear Arms

We acknowledge, support, and defend the law-abiding citizen's God-given right of self-defense. We call for the protection of such fundamental individual rights recognized in the Supreme Court's decisions in *District of Columbia v. Heller* and *McDonald v. Chicago* affirming that right, and we recognize the individual responsibility to safely use and store firearms. This also includes the right to obtain and store ammunition without registration. . . . We condemn frivolous lawsuits against gun manufacturers and oppose federal licensing or registration of law-abiding gun owners. We oppose legislation that is intended to restrict our Second Amendment rights by limiting the capacity of clips or magazines or otherwise restoring the ill-considered Clinton gun ban.

## The Ninth Amendment: Affirming the People's Rights

Faithful to the "self-evident" truths enshrined in the Declaration of Independence, we assert the sanctity of human life and affirm that the unborn child has a fundamental individual right to life, which cannot be infringed. We support a human life amendment to the Constitution and endorse legislation to make clear that the Fourteenth Amendment's protections apply to unborn children. We oppose using public revenues to promote or perform abortion or fund organizations, which perform or advocate it and will not fund or subsidize health care which includes abortion coverage. We support the appointment of judges who respect traditional family values and the sanctity of innocent human life. We oppose the non-consensual withholding or withdrawal of care or treatment, including food and water, from people with disabilities, including newborns, as well as the elderly and infirm, just as we oppose active and passive euthanasia and assisted suicide.

## Respect for Our Flag: Symbol of the Constitution

The symbol of our constitutional unity, to which we all pledge allegiance, is the flag of the United States of America. By whatever legislative method is most feasible, Old Glory should be given legal protection against desecration. We condemn decisions by activist judges to deny children the opportunity to say the Pledge of Allegiance in its entirety, including "Under God," in public schools and encourage States to promote the pledge. We condemn the actions of those who deny our children the means by which to show respect for our great country and the constitutional principles represented by our flag.

## Private Stewardship of the Environment

Experience has shown that, in caring for the land and water, private ownership has been our best guarantee of conscientious stewardship, while the worst instances of environmental degradation have occurred under government control.... Congress should reconsider whether parts of the federal government's enormous landholdings and control of water in the West could be better used for ranching, mining, or forestry through private ownership. Timber is a renewable natural resource, which provides jobs to thousands of Americans. All efforts should be made to make federal lands managed by the U.S. Forest Service available for harvesting. It makes sense that those closest to a situation are best able to determine its remedy. That is why a site- and situation-specific approach to an environmental problem is more likely to solve it, instead of a national rule based on the ideological concerns of politicized central planning. We therefore endorse legislation to require congressional approval before any rule projected to cost in excess of $100 million to American consumers can go into effect.

## Declaration of the Occupation of New York City (2011)
### Occupy Wall Street, New York City General Assembly

*The occupation—a form of sit-in—of Zucotti Park, adjoining the Wall Street financial district of New York City, was part of a worldwide movement protesting the reckless behavior of the banks in causing the Great Recession of 2008, which the world still faces. Even more, Occupy Wall Street (OWS) focused attention on the way multinational corporations had undermined American jobs, standards of living, environmental and food standards, and democratic governance. One of its hallmarks was that it committed itself to democratic decision making based on consensus. Observers called it an alternative to the Tea Party, but OWS refused to make programmatic suggestions for change or to create an ongoing organization, though it influenced the political agenda by raising the issue of rising inequality.*

As we gather together in solidarity to express a feeling of mass injustice, we must not lose sight of what brought us together. We write so that all people who feel wronged by the corporate forces of the world can know that we are your allies.

As one people, united, we acknowledge the reality: that the future of the human race requires the cooperation of its members; that our system must protect our rights, and upon corruption of that system, it is up to the individuals to protect their own rights, and those of their neighbors; that a democratic government derives its just power from the people, but corporations do not seek consent to extract wealth from the people and the Earth; and that no true democracy is attainable when the process is determined by economic power. We come to you at a time when corporations, which place profit over people, self-interest over justice, and oppression over equality, run our governments. We have peaceably assembled here, as is our right, to let these facts be known.

- They have taken our houses through an illegal foreclosure process, despite not having the original mortgage.
- They have taken bailouts from taxpayers with impunity, and continue to give Executives exorbitant bonuses.
- They have perpetuated inequality and discrimination in the workplace based on age, the color of one's skin, sex, gender identity and sexual orientation.
- They have poisoned the food supply through negligence, and undermined the farming system through monopolization.
- They have profited off of the torture, confinement, and cruel treatment of countless animals, and actively hide these practices.
- They have continuously sought to strip employees of the right to negotiate for better pay and safer working conditions.
- They have held students hostage with tens of thousands of dollars of debt on education, which is itself a human right.
- They have consistently outsourced labor and used that outsourcing as leverage to cut workers' healthcare and pay.
- They have influenced the courts to achieve the same rights as people, with none of the culpability or responsibility.
- They have spent millions of dollars on legal teams that look for ways to get them out of contracts in regards to health insurance.
- They have sold our privacy as a commodity.
- They have used the military and police force to prevent freedom of the press.
- They have deliberately declined to recall faulty products endangering lives in pursuit of profit.
- They determine economic policy, despite the catastrophic failures their policies have produced and continue to produce.
- They have donated large sums of money to politicians, who are responsible for regulating them.
- They continue to block alternate forms of energy to keep us dependent on oil.
- They continue to block generic forms of medicine that could save people's lives or provide relief in order to protect investments that have already turned a substantial profit.
- They have purposely covered up oil spills, accidents, faulty bookkeeping, and inactive ingredients in pursuit of profit.

- They purposefully keep people misinformed and fearful through their control of the media.
- They have accepted private contracts to murder prisoners even when presented with serious doubts about their guilt.
- They have perpetuated colonialism at home and abroad.
- They have participated in the torture and murder of innocent civilians overseas.
- They continue to create weapons of mass destruction in order to receive government contracts.★

To the people of the world,

We, the New York City General Assembly occupying Wall Street in Liberty Square, urge you to assert your power. Exercise your right to peaceably assemble; occupy public space; create a process to address the problems we face, and generate solutions accessible to everyone. To all communities that take action and form groups in the spirit of direct democracy, we offer support, documentation, and all of the resources at our disposal.

Join us and make your voices heard!

★*These grievances are not all-inclusive.*

# NOTES

## Introduction

1. John Dewey, "Creative Democracy—The Task Before Us," in J. A. Boydston ed., John Dewey: The Later Works, 1925–1953, vol. 14 (Carbondale: Southern Illinois University Press, 1988), 224–30. Originally published 1939.
2. This definition is adapted from John Dewey in *The Public and its Problems* (1927; repr., Chicago: Swallow Press, 1954), 147.
3. Political scientists often distinguish between thick and thin definitions of democracy. However, the definition of thick democracy used in this book is unique. For a typical example of use of the term see Larry Diamond, *The Spirit of Democracy: The Struggle to Build Free Societies Throughout the World* (New York: Holt Paperback, 2008), 21–23.

## Chapter 1

1. George Kateb, "The Moral Distinctiveness of Representative Democracy," in *The Inner Ocean: Individualism and Democratic Culture* (Ithaca, N.Y.: Cornell University Press, 1992), 40.
2. John Adams to Hezekiah Niles, 1818, quoted in Bernard Bailyn, *The Ideological Origins of the American Revolution* (Cambridge, Mass.: Harvard University Press, 1992), 160.
3. Roy P. Basler, ed., *Abraham Lincoln, His Speeches and Writings* (Cleveland, Ohio: De Capo Press, 2001), 361.
4. Barrington Moore, Jr., *Social Origins of Dictatorship and Democracy: Lord and Peasant in the Making of the Modern World* (Boston: Beacon Press, 1966).
5. Abraham Lincoln, "Message to Congress," July 4, 1861, History Tools, http://www.historytools.org/sources/lincoln-messages.html (accessed Feb. 19, 2013).
6. James M. McPherson, "A New Birth of Freedom," in *Drawn with the Sword: Reflections on the American Civil War* (New York: Oxford University Press, 1990), 177–91.
7. Eric Foner, *The Story of American Freedom* (New York: W.W. Norton, 1999), 112–13.
8. Eric Foner, *Reconstruction: America's Unfinished Revolution, 1863–1877* (New York: Harper & Row, 1988).
9. Quoted in Drew R. McCoy, *The Elusive Republic: Political Economy in Jeffersonian America* (Chapel Hill: University of North Carolina Press, 1980), 255.

10. Herbert Croly, *The Promise of American Life* (1909; repr., Boston: Northeastern University Press, 1989).
11. "Census of Housing," US Census Bureau, http://www.census.gov/hhes/www/housing/census/historic/owner.html (accessed February 17, 2013).
12. Ron Inglehart, *Culture Shift in Advanced Society* (Princeton, N.J.: Princeton University Press, 1990); unlike Inglehart, we do not include the values of social conservatives in the term *postmaterialism* because they subordinate individual self-expression and self-fulfillment to the needs of the group, whether that be family or community.
13. Thomas Hauser, *Muhammad Ali: His Life and Times* (New York: Simon and Schuster, 1991), 187.
14. Samuel P. Huntington, "The United States," in *The Crisis of Democracy: Report on the Governability of Democracies to the Trilateral Commission,* ed. Michel Crozier, Samuel P. Huntington, and Joji Watanuki (New York: New York University Press, 1975), 75–6.
15. "A History of the Chicago Women's Liberation Union," CWLU Herstory Project, http://www.cwluherstory.org/no-more-miss-america.html (accessed February 15, 2013).
16. Van Gosse, "Postmodern America: A New Democratic Order in the Second Gilded Age," in *The World the 60s Made,* ed. Van Gosse and Richard Moser (Philadelphia: Temple University Press, 2003), 1–36; Jeffrey M. Berry, *The New Liberalism: The Rising Power of Citizen Groups* (Washington, D.C.: Brookings Institution Press, 1999).

## Chapter 2

1. Alexis de Tocqueville, *Democracy in America,* abridged ed., trans. Elizabeth Trapnell Rawlings (Boston: Bedford/St. Martins, 2009), 132.
2. Abraham Lincoln, "Address before the Wisconsin State Agricultural Society," Sept. 30, 1859, Abraham Lincoln Online, Speeches and Writings, http://www.abrahamlincolnonline.org/lincoln/speeches/fair.htm (accessed May 27, 2013).
3. "Summary of Stephen R. Covey's The 7 Habits of Highly Effective People," QuickMBA, http://www.quickmba.com/mgmt/7hab/ (accessed May 27, 2013).
4. "Jack Welch," *Wikipedia,* http://en.wikipedia.org/wiki/Jack_Welch (accessed February 22, 2013).
5. "Henrik Ibsen, The New Woman," Lilia Melani home page, http://academic.brooklyn.cuny.edu/english/melani/cs6/newwoman.html (accessed February 17, 2013).
6. Walter Lippmann, *Public Opinion* (1922; repr., New York: Penguin, 1946).
7. C. Wright Mills, "Culture and Politics," in *Power, Politics and People: The Collected Essays of C. Wright Mills* (New York: Ballantine Books, 1963), 241.
8. Ronald Inglehart, "Postmodernization Erodes Respect for Authority, but Increases Support for Democracy," in Pippa Norris, ed., *Critical Citizens: Support for Democratic Government* (New York: Oxford University Press, 1999), 236–56.
9. Stephanie Coontz, *Marriage, A History: From Obedience to Intimacy or How Love Conquered Marriage* (New York: Viking, 2005), 247–80, quote on p. 276.

## Chapter 3

1. Thomas Jefferson to James Madison, October 28, 1785, in *The Papers of Thomas Jefferson,* ed. Julian Parks Boyd, Lyman Henry Butterfield, Charles T. Cullen, and John Catanzariti, vol. 1, chap. 15 (Princeton, N.J.: Princeton University Press, 1950), doc. 32.
2. Quoted in *America's History,* ed. James A. Henretta, Rebecca Edwards, Robert O. Self, 7th ed. vol. 1: To 1877 (Boston and New York: Bedford/St. Martins, 2008), 243.
3. Stanley Lebergott, "The Pattern of Employment since 1800," in *American Economic History,* ed. Seymour E. Harris (New York: McGraw Hill, 1961), 161.

4. Pete Seeger, "Talking Union," Metrolyrics, http://www.metrolyrics.com/talking-union-lyrics-pete-seeger.html (accessed February 17, 2013).

5. Annelise Orleck, *Common Sense and a Little Fire: Women and Working-Class Politics in the United States, 1900–1965* (Chapel Hill: University of North Carolina Press, 1995).

6. Henry Carter Adams, *Relation of the State to Industrial Action* (Baltimore, Md.: American Economic Association, 1887).

7. Upton Sinclair, *The Jungle* (New York: Doubleday, 1906), 112-13.

8. Gunnar Myrdal, *An American Dilemma,* vol. 1 of *The Negro Problem and Modern Democracy* (New York: Harper & Row, 1944), 13.

9. Quoted in James Livingston, *The World Turned Inside Out: American Thought and Culture at the End of the Twentieth Century* (Lanham, Md.: Rowman & Littlefield, 2010), 8.

10. Michael Lind, "The Fiscal Cliff Is a Lie," *Salon,* November 27, 2012, http://www.salon.com/2012/11/27/the_fiscal_cliff_is_a_lie/ (accessed May 27, 2013).

11. Bruce Bartlett, "A Conservative Case for the Welfare State," *New York Times,* December 25, 2012, http://economix.blogs.nytimes.com/2012/12/25/a-conservative-case-for-the-welfare-state/ (accessed February 20, 2013).

## Chapter 4

1. Charles Arthur Conant, "The Economic Basis of Imperialism," in *The United States in the Orient: The Nature of the Economic Problem* (1900; repr., Port Washington, N.Y.: Kennikat Press, 1971), 1–33.

2. Carl P. Parrini, "Theories of Imperialism," in *Redefining the Past: Essays in Diplomatic History in Honor of William Appleman Williams,* ed. Lloyd C. Gardner (Corvallis: Oregon State University, 1986), 65–83.

3. Martin Luther King Jr., "Beyond Vietnam: A Time to Break Silence," Information Clearing House, http://www.informationclearinghouse.info/article2564.htm. (accessed February 18, 2013).

4. Amartya Sen, "Democracy as a Universal Value," *Journal of Democracy* 10:3 (1999), 5.

5. Dave Hill and Ravi Kumar, *Global Neoliberalism and Education and Its Consequences* (New York: Routledge, 2009), 13.

## Chapter 5

1. Samuel P. Huntington, "The United States," in *The Crisis of Democracy: Report on the Governability of Democracies to the Trilateral Commission,* ed. Michel Crozier, Samuel P. Huntington, and Joji Watanuki (New York: New York University Press, 1975), 102–13.

2. Quoted in James Livingston, *The World Turned Inside Out: American Thought and Culture at the End of the Twentieth Century* (Lanham, Md.: Rowman & Littlefield, 2010), 8.

3. "Supreme Court History, Law, Power, and Personality," PBS, http://www.pbs.org/wnet/supremecourt/personality/sources_document13.html (accessed February 15, 2013).

4. Jefferson Cowie, *Stayin' Alive: The 1970s and the Last Days of the Working Class* (New York: The New Press, 2010), 229.

5. Ibid., 323.

6. James Livingston, *Against Thrift: Why Consumer Culture Is Good for the Economy, the Environment, and Your Soul* (New York: Basic Books, 2011), 155–6, 211–29.

7. Rex Nutting, "Obama Spending Binge Never Happened," Market Watch, *Wall Street Journal,* May 22, 2012, http://articles.marketwatch.com/2012–05–22/commentary/31802270_1_spending-federal-budget-drunken-sailor (accessed February 17, 2013).

8. "Temporary Assistance to Needy Families," Wikipedia, http://en.wikipedia.org/wiki/Temporary_Assistance_for_Needy_Families (accessed May 30, 2013).

9. Congressional Budget Office, *Trends in the Distribution of Household Income between 1979 and 2007* (Washington, D.C.: Congressional Budget Office, 2011).

10. "Gini Coefficient," *Wikipedia,* http://en.wikipedia.org/wiki/Gini_coefficient (accessed February 15, 2013).

11. David Leonhardt. "A Closer Look at Income Mobility," *New York Times,* May 14, 2005, http://www.nytimes.com/2005/05/14/national/class/15MOBILITY-WEB.html (accessed June 1, 2013); Bhashkar Mazumder, "Is Intergenerational Economic Mobility Lower Now Than in the Past?" *Chicago Fed Letter* 297 (April 2012), 1–4; Jason DeParle, "Harder for Americans to Rise from Lower Rungs," *New York Times,* January 4, 2012, A1.

12. Francis Fukuyama, "The Future of History," *Foreign Affairs* 91, no. 1 (2012): 53–61.

13. George Packer, "The Broken Social Contract," *Foreign Affairs* 90, no. 6 (2011): 220–31.

14. Martin Gilens, "Inequality and Democratic Responsiveness," *Public Opinion Quarterly* 69 (2005): 778–96.

15. Mark Szeltner, Carl Van Horn, and Cliff Zukin, *Diminished Lives and Futures: A Portrait of America in the Great-Recession Era* (Rutgers, N.J.: John J. Heldrich Center for Workforce Development, 2013).

16. Michael Lind, "The Red State Model Is (Also) Broken," *Salon,* November 22, 2011, http://www.salon.com/2011/11/22/the_red_state_model_is_also_broken/ (accessed February 20, 2013); "How to End the New War between the States," *Salon,* August 16, 2011, http://www.salon.com/2011/08/16/lind_red_blue_states/ (accessed February 20, 2013).

17. The evidence is overwhelming that increased government spending during economic downturns brings increased economic growth. See Paul Krugman, *End This Depression Now!* (New York: W.W. Norton, 2012), 231–8.

18. Binyamin Appelbaum and Robert Gebeloff, "Even Critics of Safety Net Increasingly Depend on It," *New York Times,* February 11, 2012, A1.

## Chapter 6

1. Kim Parker, "Yes, the Rich Are Different," Pew Research on Social and Demographic Trends, August 27, 2012, http://www.pewsocialtrends.org/2012/08/27/yes-the-rich-are-different/ (accessed February 22, 2013).

2. Zoltan Hajnal, "Who Loses in American Democracy?: A Count of Votes Demonstrates the Limited Representation of African-Americans," *American Political Science Review* 103 (2009): 37–57. Hajnal argues that minorities can still exercise influence when the majority is divided and by shifting the equilibrium in the median position of the electorate even when the majority is cohesive.

3. Griff Palmer, "How Maps Help Republicans Keep Edge in the House," *New York Times,* December 14, 2012, A10; Jonathan Weisman, "In Talks House Majority Weighs Loyalty to Voters," *New York Times,* December 10, 2012, A-20.

4. Brennan Center for Justice, New York University School of Law, http://www.brennancenter.org/analysis/election-2013-voting-laws-roundup (accessed June 1, 2013).

5. Michael Cooper, "New State Rules Raising Hurdles at Voting Booth," New York Times, October 2, 2011, http://www.nytimes.com/2011/10/03/us/new-state-laws-are-limiting-access-for-voters.html?pagewanted=all (accessed June 1, 2013).

6. Marcus Ethridge and Howard Handelman, *Politics in a Changing World* (Boston: Wadsworth, 2010), 116.

7. Eric Foner, *The Story of American Freedom* (New York: W.W. Norton, 1999), 164.

8. Michelle Alexander, *The New Jim Crow: Mass Incarceration in the Age of Colorblindness* (New York: The New Press, 2012), 62.

9. Ibid.

10. Loc Wacquant, "Four Strategies to Curb Carceral Costs: On Managing Mass Imprisonment in the United States," *Studies in Political Economy* 69 (2002): 401–12.

11. Jason T. Carmichael and David Jacobs, "The Political Sociology of the Death Penalty: A Pooled Time-Series Analysis," *American Sociological Review* 67 (2002): 109–31.
12. Richard K. Scher, *The Politics of Disenfranchisement: Why Is It So Hard to Vote in America?* (Armonk, N.Y.: M.E. Sharpe, 2011), 52.
13. Thomas Mann and Norman Ornstein, "Let's Just Say It: The Republicans Are the Problem," *Washington Post*, April 27, 2012, http://articles.washingtonpost.com/2012 -04-27/opinions/35453898_1_republican-party-party-moves-democratic-party (accessed June 1, 2013).
14. David Kamens and Charles Cappell, "Confidence and Cynicism in American Institutions: Consequences for Political Participation" (paper presented at the Cultural Turn IV Conference, University of California, Santa Barbara, March 7–8, 2003).
15. Martin Gilens, "Inequality and Democratic Responsiveness," *Public Opinion Quarterly* 69 (2005): 778–96.
16. Thomas B. Edsall, "Billionaires Going Rogue," *New York Times*, October 28, 2012, http:// campaignstops.blogs.nytimes.com/2012/10/28/billionaires-going-rogue/ (accessed June 1, 2013).
17. Robert Putnam, "Bowling Alone: America's Declining Social Capital," *Journal of Democracy* 6 (1995): 65–78.
18. Julian Zelizer, "Gridlock in Congress: Blame the GOP," CNN Opinion, May 21, 2012, http://www.cnn.com/2012/05/21/opinion/zelizer-congress-polarization (accessed February 21, 2013).
19. Alan Abramowitz, *Voice of the People: Elections and Voting in the United States* (New York: McGraw Hill, 2004), 249.

## Chapter 7

1. Paul J. Crutzen and Christian Schwägerl, "Living in the Anthropocene: Toward a New Global Ethos," Environment360, http://e360.yale.edu/feature/living_in_the _anthropocene_toward_a_new_global_ethos/2363/ (accessed February 17, 2013).
2. Philip Shabecoff, "Global Warming Has Begun, Expert Tells Senate," *New York Times*, June 24, 1988, http://www.nytimes.com/1988/06/24/us/global-warming-has -begun-expert-tells-senate.html (accessed February 17, 2013).
3. Union of Concerned Scientists, "Scientific Consensus on Global Warming," http:// www.ucsusa.org/ssi/climate-change/scientific-consensus-on.html (accessed June 1, 2013); Richard A. Muller, "The Conversion of a Climate Change Skeptic," *New York Times*, July 28, 2012, http://www.nytimes.com/2012/07/30/opinion/the-conversion -of-a-climate-change-skeptic.html?pagewanted=all (accessed February 17, 2013).
4. John Muir, *The Eight Wilderness-Discovery Books* (1918; repr., London: Diadem Books, 1991), 243.
5. Lawrence Mischel, "The Wedges between Productivity and Median Compensation Growth," Economic Policy Institute, April 26, 2012, http://www.epi.org/publication /ib330-productivity-vs-compensation/ (accessed February 17, 2013); "Census of Housing," US Census Bureau, http://www.census.gov/hhes/www/housing/census /historic/owner.html (accessed February 17, 2013).
6. "Director's Order 12, Intent of NEPA and NPS Mission," National Park Service, http://www.nature.nps.gov/protectingrestoring/do12site/01_intro/012_intent.htm (accessed February 17, 2013).
7. "Eutrophication," *Wikipedia*, http://www.newworldencyclopedia.org/entry /Eutrophication (accessed February 17, 2013).
8. Samuel P. Hays, *A History of Environmental Politics since 1945* (Pittsburgh: University of Pittsburgh Press, 2000), 156.

# BIBLIOGRAPHICAL ESSAY

## Introduction: Democracy as a Way of Life

A number of books have attempted to periodize democratic history in America, among
them Eric Foner, *The Story of American Freedom* (New York: W.W. Norton, 1999); Mor-
ton Keller, *America's Three Regimes: A New Political History* (New York: Oxford University Press, 2007); Michael Schudson, *The Good Citizen: A History of American Civic Life*
(New York: The Free Press, 1998); and Robert H. Wiebe, *Self-Rule: A Cultural History of
American Democracy* (Chicago: University of Chicago Press, 1995). The idea of "waves of
democracy" has been discussed on the global level by Samuel P. Huntington, *The Third
Wave: Democratization in the Late Twentieth Century* (Norman: University of Oklahoma,
1991); and by John Markoff, *Waves of Democracy: Social Movements and Political Change*
(Thousand Oaks, Calif.: Pine Forge Press, 1996). While these studies explore democracy
in government and politics, our book goes beyond government and shows how civil
society, the economy and workplace, and culture become subject in successive waves to
the spirit of democracy.

Joseph A. Schumpeter, *Capitalism, Socialism, and Democracy* (New York: Harper & Row,
1942), chaps. 21 and 22 begins the modern political science view that democracy must
be defined realistically; in short, democracy is that which exists. For alternatives to that
view and the idea that democracy is a way of life and a regulative ideal, see John Dewey,
*The Public and Its Problems* (1927; repr., Chicago: Swallow Press, 1954); and Carole Pate-
man, *Participation and Democratic Theory* (Cambridge, UK: Cambridge University Press,
1970). We have also been influenced by Richard Krouse, "Polyarchy and Participation:
The Changing Democratic Theory of Robert Dahl," *Polity* 14 (1982): 441–63; Melvin
L. Rogers, "Dewey and His Vision of Democracy," *Contemporary Pragmatism* 7 (2010):
69–91; and John J. Stuhr, "Democracy as a Way of Life," in *Philosophy and the Reconstruction of Culture: Pragmatic Essays after Dewey,* ed. John J. Stuhr (Albany: State University
of New York Press, 1993), 37–57. To these relatively contemporary works should be
added Alexis de Tocqueville, *Democracy in America,* vols. I and II (New York: Bantam,
2000) translated by Henry Reeve. We have also relied on the commentary by Larry
Siedentrop in *Tocqueville* (New York: Oxford, 1994).

The idea that modernity and democratic possibility emerged on the heels of the breakdown of older family, kinship group, and dynastic forms of social organization has been inspired by and adapted from Linda Nicholson, *Gender and Theory: The Limits of Social Theory in the Age of the Family* (New York: Columbia University Press, 1986); Karl Polanyi, *The Great Transformation: The Political and Economic Origins of Our Time* (Boston: Beacon Press, 1944); and Eli Zaretsky, *Capitalism, the Family, & Personal Life* (New York: Harper & Row, 1973). The breakdown of feudal and other authority structures by the rise of capitalism and how that paved the way for political and economic democracy is the central thesis of Barrington Moore Jr., *Social Origins of Dictatorship and Democracy: Lord and Peasant in the Making of the Modern World* (Boston: Beacon Press, 1966) and a host of other historical works, including many of those cited in the bibliographical essay for chapter one.

That the American prodemocratic left is the dominant trend in American history is argued in Martin J. Sklar, "Thoughts on Capitalism and Socialism: Utopian and Realistic," *Journal of the Gilded Age and Progressive Era* 2 (2003): 361–76. For the opposite view see Eli Zaretsky, *Why America Needs a Left: A Historical Argument* (Malden, Mass.: Polity Press, 2012).

## Chapter 1: The Three Waves of Democracy

An excellent survey of the role of the common people in the American Revolution can be found in Edward Countryman, *The American Revolution*, rev. ed. (New York: Hill and Wang, 2003). The democratic nature of the revolution and how it dissolved the semifeudal class relations in the American colonies is argued by Gordon S. Wood, *The Radicalism of the American Revolution* (New York: Alfred A. Knopf, 1992). On the making of the Constitution, see Gordon S. Wood, *Creation of the American Republic, 1776–1787* (New York: Oxford University Press, 1969). On Madison, the literature is voluminous, but we have been influenced especially by Douglass Adair, " 'That Politics May Be Reduced to a Science': David Hume, James Madison, and the Tenth *Federalist*," *Huntington Library Quarterly* 20 (1957): 343–60; and more recently, Colleen A. Sheehan, *James Madison and the Spirit of Republican Self-Government* (New York: Cambridge University Press, 2009). Good introductions to the democratic meanings of the revolution and the Constitution are available in the early chapters of Michael Schudson, *The Good Citizen: A History of American Civic Life* (New York: The Free Press, 1998); and Eric Foner, *The Story of American Freedom* (New York: W.W. Norton, 1999).

On the rise of civil society, we have relied on Johann N. Neem, *Creating a Nation of Joiners: Democracy and Civil Society in Early National Massachusetts* (Cambridge, Mass.: Harvard University Press, 2008); and Theda Skocpol, *Diminished Democracy: From Membership to Management in America Civic Life* (Norman: University of Oklahoma Press, 2003). A good survey of American social movements is contained in the *Encyclopedia of American Social Movements,* ed. Immanuel Ness, 3 vols. (New York: M.E. Sharpe, 2004). The rise of political parties is discussed in Richard Hofstadter, *The Idea of a Party System: The Rise of Legitimate Opposition in the United States, 1780–1840* (Berkeley: University of California Press, 1969); and Ronald P. Formisano, "Deferential-Participant Politics: The Early Republic's Political Culture, 1789–1840," *American Political Science Review* 68 (1974): 473–87.

For a survey of the democratization of early American politics, see Sean Wilentz, *The Rise of American Democracy: Jefferson to Lincoln* (New York: W.W. Norton, 2005). Introductions to the significance of the Civil War and Lincoln's leadership are available in the essays by James M. McPherson, collected in *Abraham Lincoln and the Second American Revolution*

(New York: Oxford University Press, 1990); *Drawn with the Sword* (New York: Oxford University Press, 1996); and *Is Blood Thicker Than Water?: Crises of Nationalism in the Modern World* (New York: Random House, 1998). For a recent biography of Lincoln, see Eric Foner, *The Fiery Trial: Abraham Lincoln and American Slavery* (New York: W.W. Norton, 2010). On the Civil War as a democratic alternative to the authoritarian German path to modernity, see Barrington Moore Jr.'s chapter "The American Civil War: The Last Capitalist Revolution," in *Social Origins of Dictatorship and Democracy: Lord and Peasant in the Making of the Modern World* (Boston: Beacon Press, 1966), 111–55; and David M. Potter, "The Civil War in the History of the Modern World: A Comparative View," in *The South and the Sectional Conflict* (Baton Rouge: Louisiana State University Press, 1968). On Calhoun we have consulted Lacy K. Ford Jr., "Inventing the Concurrent Majority: Madison, Calhoun, and the Problem of Majoritarianism in American Political Thought," *The Journal of Southern History* 60 (1994): 19–58.

A good introduction to the shift in late nineteenth-century America on the relationship of state and society is James L. Huston, "The American Revolutionaries, the Political Economy of Aristocracy, and the American Concept of the Distribution of Wealth, 1765–1900," *American Historical Review* 98 (1993): 1079–105. For a readable survey of the American labor movement, see Melvyn Dubofsky and Foster Rhea Dulles, *Labor in America, A History* (Arlington Heights, Ill.: Harlan Davidson, 1984). A discussion of industrial democracy in the early twentieth century can be found in Joseph McCartin, *Labor's Great War: The Struggle for Industrial Democracy and the Origins of Modern American Labor Relations, 1912–21* (Chapel Hill: University of North Carolina Press, 1997). A good survey of law relating to capitalism is Herbert Hovenkamp, *Enterprise and American Law 1836–1937* (Cambridge, Mass.: Harvard University Press, 1991). On the mix of capitalism and socialism, the reader should start with Martin J. Sklar, "Capitalism and Socialism in the Emergence of Modern America: The Formative Era, 1890–1916," in *Reconstructing History,* ed. Elizabeth Fox-Genovese and Elisabeth Lasch-Quinn (New York: Routledge, 1999), 304–21.

On the democratization of culture in the late twentieth century, our starting point is Van Gosse's "Postmodern America: A New Democratic Order in the Second Gilded Age," in *The World the 60s Made,* ed. Van Gosse and Richard Moser (Philadelphia: Temple University Press, 2003), 1–36; and Van Gosse, *Rethinking the New Left: An Interpretive History* (New York: Palgrave Macmillan, 2005). Postindustrialism is explored in Martin J. Sklar, "Some Political and Cultural Consequences of the Disaccumulation of Capital: Origins of Postindustrial Development in the 1920s," in *The United States as a Developing Country: Studies in U.S. History in the Progressive Era and the 1920s* (Cambridge, UK: Cambridge University Press, 1992), 143–96; Daniel Bell, "The Cultural Contradictions of Capitalism," in *The Cultural Contradictions of Capitalism* (1976; repr., New York: Basic Books, 1996), 33–85; and James Livingston, *Pragmatism and the Political Economy of Cultural Revolution, 1850–1940* (Chapel Hill: University of North Carolina Press, 1994). The transformation of marriage and family and its significance is surveyed by Stephanie Coontz in *The Way We Never Were: American Families and Nostalgia Trap* (New York: Basic Books, 1992); and *Marriage, A History: From Obedience to Intimacy or How Love Conquered Marriage* (New York: Viking, 2005); and by John D'Emilio and Estelle B. Freedman in *Intimate Matters: A History of Sexuality in America* (Chicago: University of Chicago Press, 1988). Anthony Giddens discusses the democratization of intimacy in *The Transformation of Intimacy: Sexuality, Love and Eroticism in Modern Societies* (Stanford, Calif.: Stanford University Press, 1992). Terry H. Anderson's *The Movement and the Sixties* (New York: Oxford University Press, 1995) gives a thorough narrative history of the 1960s' social movements. For an introduction to the rights revolution, see chapter 6 of Schudson's *The Good Citizen.* Also see Frank Dobbin and John R. Sutton, "The Strength of a Weak State: The Rights Revolution and the Rise of Human Resources management Divisions," *American Journal of Sociology* 104 (1988): 441–76. Sociologists' approaches to new social movements are discussed in Steven M. Buechler, "New Social Movement Theories," *Sociological Quarterly* 36 (1995): 441–64.

## Chapter 2: Democracy in Culture: American Individualisms

Discussion of individualism these days has been dominated by its critics, such as Robert N. Bellah, *Habits of the Heart: Individualism and Commitment in American Life* (Berkeley: University of California Press, 1985); and Michael J. Sandel, *Democracy's Discontent: America in Search of a Public Philosophy* (Cambridge, Mass.: Harvard University Press, 1998). On the other hand, see George Kateb, *The Inner Ocean: Individualism and Democratic Culture* (Ithaca, N.Y.: Cornell University Press, 1992). Alexis de Tocqueville's two-volume *Democracy in America,* trans. Henry Reeve (New York: Bantam, 2000) is a meditation on the dangers of and solutions to the privatizing tendencies in individualism.

For an excellent discussion of the rise of the self-made man in social-historical context, see E. Anthony Rotundo, *American Manhood: Transformation in Masculinity from the Revolution to the Modern Era* (New York: Basic Books, 1993). Also important is Daniel T. Rodgers, *The Work Ethic in Industrial America, 1850–1920* (Chicago: University of Chicago Press, 1974). For examples, see Benjamin Franklin, *Autobiography of Benjamin Franklin* (1791; repr., New York: Soho Books, 2010); and John William Ward's *Andrew Jackson: Symbol for an Age* (New York: Oxford University Press, 1953). On free labor ideology, see Eric Foner, *Free Soil, Free Labor, Free Men: The Ideology of the Republican Party before the Civil War* (New York: Oxford University Press, 1970). On the rags-to-riches ideal, see the biography of Andrew Carnegie by Harold Livesey, *Andrew Carnegie and the Rise of Big Business* (Boston: Little Brown, 1975). Nancy Cott's *The Bonds of Womanhood: "Woman's Sphere" in New England, 1780–1835* (New Haven, Conn.: Yale University Press, 1977) discusses the female shadow side of male individualism. For John Dewey's incisive criticisms of self-made-man individualism, see *Individualism: Old and New* (1929; repr., New York: Capricorn Books, 1962); and *Liberalism and Social Action* (New York: Capricorn Books, 1935).

On the social individual and criticism of that type, one should start with David Riesman, *The Lonely Crowd: A Study of the Changing American Character* (New Haven, Conn.: Yale University Press, 1950); and Vance Packard, *The Hidden Persuaders* (1957; repr., New York: Penguin, 1991). Expressive individualism is developed in Bellah's *Habits of the Heart,* while William G. McLoughlin's *Revivals, Awakenings, and Reform* (Chicago: University of Chicago Press, 1978) sees it as emerging from a new awakening. David Brooks, *Bobos in Paradise: The New Upper Class and How They Got There* (New York: Simon & Schuster, 2001) is a humorous critique. On postmaterial values, see Ronald Inglehart, *Culture Shift in Advanced Industrial Society* (Princeton, N.J.: Princeton University Press, 1990).

## Chapter 3: American Democracy in the Economy and Workplace

On the political origins of government regulation, see Daniel T. Rodgers, *Atlantic Crossings: Social Politics in a Progressive Age* (Cambridge, Mass.: Harvard University Press, 1999). A look at various regulatory initiatives shows that business leaders played a critical role; regulation was not forced on them. On the federal reserve system, see James Livingston, *Origins of Federal Reserve System: Money, Class and Corporate Capitalism, 1890–1913*

(Ithaca, N.Y.: Cornell University Press, 1986); on health and safety regulation, see Donald W. Rogers, *Making Capitalism Safe: Workplace Safety and Health Regulation in America, 1880–1940* (Urbana: University of Illinois Press, 2009); and for meat-packing and other regulation, see Gabriel Kolko, *Triumph of Conservatism, A Reinterpretation of American History, 1900–1916* (New York: Free Press, 1963). More generally, one should look at Martin J. Sklar's *The Corporate Reconstruction of American Capitalism, 1890–1916: The Market, the Law, and Politics* (Cambridge, UK: Cambridge University Press, 1988). For a philosophical argument against government planning and regulation, look at Friedrich A. Hayek, *The Road to Serfdom* (1944; repr., Chicago: University of Chicago Press, 2007). An answer to that argument, written the same year, is Karl Polanyi's *The Great Transformation: The Political and Economic Origins of Our Time* (Boston: Beacon Press, 1944). The overwhelming evidence for the long-standing cooperation of government and business in nation building is discussed in Michael Lind's *Land of Promise: An Economic History of the United States* (New York: HarperCollins, 2012).

On the New Deal, see William E. Leuchtenberg's classic *Franklin D. Roosevelt and the New Deal, 1932–1940* (New York: Harper & Row, 1963). See also Eric Foner's "The New Deal and the Redefinition of Freedom," in his *The Story of American Freedom* (New York: W.W. Norton, 1999), 195–218. On consumer consciousness as a democratic force, see Meg Jacobs, *Pocketbook Politics: Economic Citizenship in Twentieth-Century America* (Princeton, N.J.: Princeton University Press, 2007); and James Livingston, *Against Thrift: Why Consumer Culture Is Good for the Economy, the Environment, and Your Soul* (New York: Basic Books, 2011). For an introduction to recent work on the relation of democracy to the economy, see Meg Jacobs, William J. Novak, and Julian E. Zelizer, *The Democratic Experiment: New Directions in American Political History* (Princeton, N.J.: Princeton University Press, 2003).

Beginners in Keynesian economics may start with Lawrence R. Klein, *The Keynesian Revolution* (New York: Macmillan, 1947). One should also read the indispensable short essay on the limits of Keynesian intervention by the Keynesian Michal Kalecki, "Political Aspects of Full Employment," *Political Science Quarterly* 14 (1943): 322–31.

The mix of capitalism and socialism is developed in Martin J. Sklar, "Capitalism and Socialism in the Emergence of Modern America: The Formative Era, 1890–1916," in *Reconstructing History,* ed. Elizabeth Fox-Genovese and Elisabeth Lasch-Quinn (New York: Routledge, 1999), 304–21. The American emphasis on private social benefits is discussed in Jacob S. Hacker, *The Divided Welfare State: The Battle over Public and Private Social Benefits in the United States* (Cambridge, UK: Cambridge University Press, 2002); and Suzanne Mettler, *The Submerged State: How Invisible Government Policies Undermine American Democracy* (Chicago: University of Chicago Press, 2011). On the workplace rule of law developed by collective bargaining, see the indispensable essay by David Brody, "The Uses of Political Power I: Industrial Battleground," in *Workers in Industrial America: Essays on the 20th Century Struggle* (New York: Oxford University Press, 1980), 173–214. Nelson Lichtenstein traces the decline of workplace rights in *State of the Union: A Century of American Labor* (Princeton, N.J.: Princeton University Press, 2002).

## Chapter 4: Democracy and US Foreign Policy

The argument that America has always been an expansionist country, whether on land or in markets (the open door), is made by William Appleman Williams, *The Tragedy of American Diplomacy* (Cleveland, Ohio: World, 1959). The open-door origins of US World War II policy are discussed in John Costello, *The Pacific War, 1941–1945* (New York: Quill, 1982). Carl Parrini and Martin J. Sklar make the argument for surplus capital as the underlying origin of the new American foreign policy in "New Thinking about the Market, 1896–1904: Some Economists on Investment and the Theory of Surplus Capital," *Journal of Economic History* 43 (1983): 559–78. For a survey of American foreign policy based on the idea that it is an empire, see Lloyd C. Gardner, Walter F. LaFeber, and Thomas J. McCormick, *Creation of the American Empire,* 2 vols. (New York: Rand McNally, 1973). The postimperialist revision of the imperialist analysis is developed in Richard L. Sklar, "Postimperialism: A Class Analysis of Multinational Corporate Expansion," *Comparative Politics* 9 (1976): 75–92; and *Postimperialism and World Politics,* ed. David G. Becker and Richard L. Sklar (Westport, Conn.: Praeger, 1999). In the same vein, see the symposium "Imperialism: A Useful Category of Historical Analysis?" in *Radical History Review* 57 (1993): 4–84, which includes articles by Carl Parrini and Keith Haynes and responses by Marilyn Young, Linda Carty, Bruce Cummings, Prasenjit Duara, Michael Geyer, Eric Hobsbawm, Harry Magdoff, and Emily Rosenberg. A useful interpretation is Frank Ninkovich, *The Wilsonian Century: US Foreign Policy since 1900* (Chicago: University of Chicago Press, 1999).

The democratization of nation-states in the 1970s–90s period is the theme of Samuel P. Huntington, *The Third Wave: Democratization in the Late Twentieth Century* (Norman: University of Oklahoma, 1991); an update can be found in Larry Diamond, *The Spirit of Democracy: The Struggle to Build Free Societies throughout the World* (New York: Henry Holt, 2008). On democracy as a new international norm, see Amartya Sen, "Democracy as a Universal Value," *Journal of Democracy* 10 (1999): 3–17.

For a primer on international neoliberalism, see David Harvey, *A Brief History of Neoliberalism* (New York: Oxford University Press, 2006). The origins of the Great Recession is discussed by Ben Bernanke in "The Global Saving Glut and the U.S. Current Account Deficit," March 10, 2005, http://www.federalreserve.gov/boarddocs/speeches/2005/200503102/ (accessed on February 15, 2013). The international impact of neoliberal international economic policy is argued in Joseph E. Stiglitz, *Globalization and its Discontents* (New York: W.W. Norton, 2002).

# Chapter 5: The Neoliberal Era: Postindustrial Society in a New Gilded Age

On the second Gilded Age and the problem of inequality, see Paul Krugman, *Conscience of a Liberal* (New York: W.W. Norton, 2007); Larry M. Bartells, *Unequal Democracy: The Political Economy of the New Gilded Age* (Princeton, N.J.: Princeton University Press, 2008); Joseph E. Stiglitz, *The Price of Inequality: How Today's Divided Society Endangers Our Future* (New York: W.W. Norton, 2012); and the seminal article by Thomas Piketty and Emmanuel Saez, "The Evolution of Top Incomes: A Historical and International Perspective," *American Economic Review: Papers and Proceedings 96* (2006): 200–5

Postindustrialism is discussed in Daniel Bell, "The Cultural Contradictions of Capitalism," in *The Cultural Contradictions of Capitalism* (1976; repr., New York: Basic Books, 1996), 33–85; and James Livingston, *Against Thrift: Why Consumer Culture Is Good for the Economy, the Environment, and Your Soul* (New York: Basic Books, 2011). On the rise of neoliberalism, see Samuel Huntington, "The United States," in *The Crisis of Democracy: Report on the Governability of Democracies to the Trilateral Commission,* ed. Michel Crozier, Samuel P. Huntington, and Joji Watanuki (New York: New York University Press, 1975); and George Gilder, *Wealth and Poverty* (New York: Basic Books, 1981). Discussions of the 1970s as a turning point can be found in Jefferson Cowie, *Stayin' Alive: The 1970s and the Last Days of the Working Class* (New York: The New Press, 2010);

Bruce Schulman and Julian E. Zelizer, *Rightward Bound: Making America Conservative in the 1970s* (Cambridge, Mass.: Harvard University Press, 2008); and Judith Stein, *Pivotal Decade: How the United States Traded Factories for Finance in the Seventies* (New Haven, Conn.: Yale University Press, 2010).

For a persuasive argument that the second Gilded Age has not vanquished the democratic trends of the 1960s, see Van Gosse, "Postmodern America: A New Democratic Order in the Second Gilded Age," in *The World the 60s Made,* ed. Van Gosse and Richard Moser (Philadelphia: Temple University Press, 2003), 1–36; and Jeffrey M. Berry, *The New Liberalism: The Rising Power of Citizen Groups* (Washington, D.C.: Brookings Institution Press, 1999). John B. Judis and Ruy Teixeira predicted the rise of the Obama majority in *The Emerging Democratic Majority* (New York: Scribner, 2002). Important insights as to the nature of party changes can be found in the Salon.com columns of Michael Lind. The origins of the Great Recession are discussed in Joseph E. Stiglitz, *Freefall: America, Free Markets, and the Sinking of the World Economy* (New York: W.W. Norton, 2010); and John Bellamy Foster and Fred Magdoff, *The Great Financial Crisis: Causes and Consequences* (New York: Monthly Review Press, 2009). On the makeup of government spending see Nate Silver, "What is Driving Growth in Government Spending?" *New York Times,* January 16, 2013, A16.

# Chapter 6: The Democratic Challenge

The analysis of the social composition and political influence of the Tea Party draws on Theda Skopkol and Venessa Williamson, *The Tea Party and the Remaking of Republican Conservatism* (New York: Oxford University Press, 2012); and David Campbell and Robert Putnam, "Crashing the Tea Party," *New York Times,* August 16, 2011, A23. On civil liberties, see Eric Foner, *The Story of American Freedom* (New York: W.W. Norton, 1998), 163–93. The analysis of the War on Drugs and civil liberties is based on Michelle Alexander, *The New Jim Crow: Mass Incarceration in the Age of Colorblindness* (New York: The New Press, 2012), and Jose Luiz Morin's "Latinas/os and US Prisons: Trends and Challenges," *Latino Studies* 6 (2008): 11–34. On the topic of felony disenfranchisement, the chapter draws on Jeff Manza and Christopher Uggen, *Locked Out: Felon Disenfranchisement and American Democracy* (New York: Oxford University Press, 2006); and Jeff Yates and Richard Fording, "Politics and State Punitiveness in Black and White," *Journal of Politics* 67 (2005): 1099–121.

Sources on how mass incarceration perpetuates race and class inequality include Sanford Schram, "Contextualizing Racial Disparities in American Welfare Reform," *Perspectives on Politics* 3 (2005): 253–68; and Jason T. Carmichael and David Jacobs, "The Political Sociology of the Death Penalty: A Pooled Time-Series Analysis," *American Sociological Review* 67 (2002): 109–31.

The discussion of civil society, civic culture, and disaffected citizens relies on the research of Gabriel Almond and Sydney Verba, *The Civic Culture: Political Attitudes and Democracy in Five Nations* (Boston: Little Brown, 1965); Pippa Norris, *Critical Citizens: Global Support for Democratic Governance* (New York: Oxford, 1999), and *Democratic Deficit: Critical Citizens Revisited* (New York: Cambridge University Press, 2011); and Robert Putnam's *Bowling Alone: The Collapse and Revival of American Community* (New York: Simon and Schuster, 2000). The research of Morris Fiorina, Samuel Abrams, and Jeremy Pope, *The Culture Wars?: The Myth of a Polarized America* (New York: Pearson College Division, 2005), informs the discussion of public opinion in the context of the ideological polarization of political elites.

Analysis of how majoritarian electoral systems disproportionately disadvantage minorities is based on research by Zoltan Hajnal, "Who Loses in American Democracy?: A Count of Votes Demonstrates the Limited Representation of African-Americans," *American Political Science Review* 103 (2009): 37–57; and Alan Abramowitz, *Voice of the People: Elections and Voting in the United States* (New York: McGraw Hill, 2004). The analysis of partisan gerrymandering, voter identification, and other voter restrictions is based on the studies of the Brennan Center for Justice, "The Case for Voter Registration Modernization," http://www.brennancenter.org/ (accessed February 17, 2013); and Richard K. Schram, *The Politics of Disenfranchisement: Why Is It So Hard to Vote in America?* (New York: M.E. Sharpe, 2011).

The shift to the right of the Republican Party and the procedural stalemate in Congress is based on Norman Ornstein and Thomas Mann, *It's Even Worse Than It Looks: How the Constitutional System Collided with the Politics of Extremism* (New York: Basic Books, 2012); and Fareed Zakaria's "Why Polarization Has Gone Wild in America (and What to Do about It)," CNN World, July 24, 2011, http://globalpublicsquare.blogs.cnn.com/2011/07/24/why-political-polarization-has-gone-wild/ (accessed February 20, 2013).

The influence of the Southern Republicans on the Republican Party's uncompromising political stance is based on George Packer, "Southern Discomfort," *New Yorker,* January 21, 2012 http://www.newyorker.com/talk/comment/2013/01/21/130121taco_talk_packer (accessed June 2, 2013). On the surge of extremist groups following President Obama's election, see Charles Blow, "Revolutionary Language," *New York Times,* January 11, 2013, A19.

The analysis of the underrepresentation of minorities and low-income Americans is based on Martin Gilens, "Inequality and Democratic Responsiveness," *Public Opinion Quarterly* 69 (2005): 778–96; and Tavis Smiley and Cornel West, *The Rich and the Rest of Us: A Poverty Manifesto* (New York: SmileyBooks, 2012). On special-interest lobbying and money in elections, see Robert Reich, *Super Capitalism: The Transformation of Business, Democracy and Everyday Life* (New York: Vintage Books, 2008). On the leveling impact of the health care act, see Paul Krugman, "The Big Deal," *New York Times,* January 20, 2013, A21.

## Chapter 7: Epilogue, the Environment: Democracy's Fourth Wave

The argument for manmade global warming is based on overwhelming scientific evidence. See, for example, Arnold J. Bloom, *Global Climate Change: Convergence of Disciplines* (Sunderland, Mass.: Sinauer Associates, 2009). Rachel Carson's *Silent Spring* (New York: Houghton Mifflin, 1962) launched the postwar environmental movement. More recent popular environmental texts that have influenced the writing of this chapter include Barry Commoner, *Making Peace with the Planet* (New York: Pantheon, 1990); Bill McKibben, *The End of Nature* (New York: Random House, 1989); and Jared Diamond, *Collapse: How Societies Choose to Fail or Succeed,* rev. ed. (New York: Penguin, 2011). On environmental politics and recent trends, we have relied on two books by Samuel P. Hays, *A History of Environmental Politics since 1945* (Pittsburgh: University of Pittsburgh Press, 2000), and *Beauty, Health, and Permanence: Environmental Politics in the United States, 1955–1985* (Cambridge, UK: Cambridge University Press, 1987). Lester R. Brown argues that sustainable development is possible in *Plan B, 4.0: Mobilizing to Save Civilization* (New York: W.W. Norton, 2009). The argument that capitalism and environmental protection are incompatible is made by John Bellamy Foster in *Ecology against Capitalism* (New York: Monthly Review Press, 2002).

# INDEX

# www.routledge.com/history

# Critical Moments in American History

## Series Editor: William Thomas Allison,
Georgia Southern University

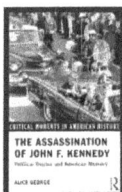

The Battle of the Greasy Grass/Little Bighorn:
Custer's Last Stand in Memory, History, and Popular Culture
By Debra Buchholtz
ISBN 13: 978-0-415-89559-0 (pbk)

The Assassination of John F. Kennedy:
Political Trauma and American Memory
By Alice L. George
ISBN 13: 978-0-415-89557-6 (pbk)

Freedom to Serve:
Truman, Civil Rights, and Executive Order 9981
By Jon E. Taylor
ISBN 13: 978-0-415-89448-7 (pbk)

The Battles of Kings Mountain and Cowpens:
The American Revolution in the Southern Backcountry
By Melissa Walker
ISBN 13: 978-0-415-89561-3 (pbk)

The Nativist Movement in America:
Religious Conflict in the 19th Century
By Katie Oxx
ISBN 13: 978-0-415-80748-7 (pbk)

The Cuban Missile Crisis:
The Threshold of Nuclear War
By Alice L. George
ISBN 13: 978-0-415-89972-7 (pbk)

The 1980 Presidential Election:
Ronald Reagan and the Shaping of the American
Conservative Movement
By Jeffrey D. Howison
ISBN 13: 978-0-415-52193-2 (pbk)

For additional resources visit the series website at:
www.routledge.com/cw/criticalmoments

Available from all good bookshops

www.routledge.com/history

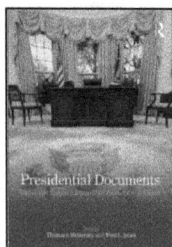

# Presidential Documents

## Words that Shaped a Nation from Washington to Obama, 2nd Edition

Edited by
**Thomas J. McInerney**
and **Fred L. Israel**

"State papers are instruments of power, and Presidential Documents illustrates the diverse ways American presidents have striven to mold the nation's destiny. This collection, well-selected and ably annotated, is a fine introduction to the perennial mysteries of the American presidency."
– Arthur Schlesinger, Jr

In this lively, authoritative collection, Thomas J. McInerney presents famous and lesser-known speeches, letters, and other important documents from every U.S. president from George Washington to Barack Obama.

Whether printed in full or excerpted, these history-making documents are an invaluable resource as well as a fascinating browse. Including familiar documents such as the Emancipation Proclamation, to personal correspondence such as a letter from George H.W. Bush to his children, this collection brings together the famous statements that came to represent each administration with intimate glimpses into the thought processes of various presidential leaders.

Now in its second edition, *Presidential Documents* has been re-designed to increase its usefulness in the classroom. Part openers introduce each era of the American presidency with a concise political and historical overview, highlighting the challenges each leader faced, and placing the documents in context. Whether used as a complement to an American history survey text or as a collection of primary documents for courses on the American Presidency, *Presidential Documents* provides an engrossing look at the work of the leaders of the United States, in all their complexity.

978-0-415-89575-0 (pbk)
978-0-415-89574-3 (hbk)
September 2012

For more information and to order a copy visit
www.routledge.com/9780415895750

Available from all good bookshops

For Product Safety Concerns and Information please contact our EU
representative  GPSR@taylorandfrancis.com
Taylor & Francis Verlag GmbH, Kaufingerstraße 24, 80331 München, Germany